THE EVERYTHING

Bible Study Book with CD

Dear Reader,

Apart from personal prayer there is nothing more important in the Christian life than reading and studying the Bible. It is through reading God's written Word that we find out what God Himself is all about, how He wants to relate to us, and what He desires from us in return.

But when it comes to making the Bible a part of your daily experience in the faith, the question that often arises is this: How do I read and study the Bible in a personally meaningful and accurate way? It's the key question that we have attempted to answer.

This book is not an in-depth study or comprehensive overview of the entire Bible. Our purpose is to give you the reader some effective guidelines and methods when it comes to reading and studying the Bible, whether alone or in a group. The bulk of the book gives you examples of interactive Bible studies as we take you through it book by book: by important events, themes, and by characters. We hope the questions in the exercises will give you a richer understanding of the text and application of its truth as you grow to know and love God better.

James Stuart Bell

Tracy Sumner

The EVERYTHING® Series

Editorial

Innovation Director	Paula Munier
Editorial Director	Laura M. Daly
Executive Editor, Series Books	Brielle K. Matson
Associate Copy Chief	Sheila Zwiebel
Acquisitions Editor	Lisa Laing
Development Editor	Katrina Schroeder
Production Editor	Casey Ebert

Production

Director of Manufacturing	Susan Beale
Production Project Manager	Michelle Roy Kelly
Prepress	Erick DaCosta
	Matt LeBlanc
Interior Layout	Heather Barrett
	Brewster Brownville
	Colleen Cunningham
	Jennifer Oliveira
Cover Design	Erin Alexander
	Stephanie Chrusz
	Frank Rivera

Visit the entire Everything® Series at *www.everything.com*

THE EVERYTHING®
BIBLE STUDY BOOK

All you need to understand the Bible—
on your own or in a group

James Stuart Bell and Tracy Sumner

Adams Media
Avon, Massachusetts

To my daughter, Caitlin Joy Bell, make it your lifetime goal to study God's Word.
—JB
To my father, Mac Sumner, for giving me life and for being a source
of encouragement in my writing and authoring career.
—TS

Published by Adams Media, an F+W Publications Company
57 Littlefield Street, Avon, MA 02322 U.S.A.
www.adamsmedia.com

ISBN-10: 1-59869-398-0

ISBN-13: 978-1-59869-398-0

Printed in the United States of America.

J   I   H   G   F   E   D   C   B   A

Library of Congress Cataloging-in-Publication Data

Bell, James Stuart.
The everything Bible study book with CD / James Stuart Bell and Tracy Sumner.
p. cm. – (The everything series)
ISBN-13: 978-1-59869-398-0 (pbk.)
ISBN-10: 1-59869-398-0 (pbk.)
1. Bible–Study and teaching. I. Sumner, Tracy. II. Title.

BS600.3.B45 2007
220.071–dc22
2007018993

This book is available at quantity discounts for bulk purchases.
For information, please call 1-800-289-0963.

Contents

Acknowledgments

Special thinks for the leadership of Lisa Laing, who believed in the vision for this book and introduced me to the *Everything*® series, and for Tracy Sumner, who has been part of my team at Whitestone Communications for the last five years and has done excellent work.

—JB

It didn't take me long in the publishing business to see that a book doesn't just happen. It takes the combined efforts of many different people with many different skills and talents to make it happen. I'd like to thank those people here. Thanks to the good people at Adams Media for investing their time and energies in this project. Thanks to Jim Bell, my partner and co-author on this project, for his direction and patience with me during some stressful and busy times during the writing phase. And thanks most of all to my heavenly Father, first for sending my Lord and Savior Jesus Christ to give me eternal life and also for giving me the gifts and talents he has given me for his own use.

—TS

Top Ten Greatest Things about Studying the Bible

1. The Bible is not just God's way of speaking to you, but also His way of blessing you with every gift He wants you to have.

2. You learn what the Christian life is all about, what it looks like, and how you can practically live it out in every day and in every way.

3. When you read the Bible, you are reading the words and messages of God Himself.

4. It is something God encourages—even commands—His people to do.

5. It enables you to tell others about your faith because now you have a better idea of what you're talking about.

6. You hear and interact with God as you read His words.

7. You get all the things you're really seeking from God—love, comfort, forgiveness, wisdom, hope, security, and so on.

8. You learn the details of stories you may know the basics about now—for example, Noah and the ark, Jonah and the whale.

9. You can fully understand the Good News of the salvation message—that Jesus died for your sins and will give you eternal life.

10. There are hundreds of promises from God to you that you can count on if you believe and obey His Word.

Introduction

▶ ONE OF THE MOST DOMINANT THEMES in the Bible—Old Testament and New Testament alike—is the importance of reading, studying, memorizing, knowing, and meditating upon God's written Word. For example, God told Joshua, the man charged with the responsibility of leading the Jewish people into the Promised Land, "Be careful to obey all the instructions Moses gave you. Do not deviate from them, turning either to the right or to the left. Then you will be successful in everything you do. Study this Book of Instruction continually. Meditate on it day and night so you will be sure to obey everything written in it. Only then will you prosper and succeed in all you do" (Joshua 1:7–8).

There is a theme running throughout the Bible, and it's this: A huge part of being a believer is spending time reading, studying, meditating, and personally applying God's written Word. Still, the problem for many Christians is that they don't know how to approach reading and studying the Bible. Do they just start at Genesis and work their way through to the end of Revelation? Do they just start with a book whose name sounds good to them that day? Or do they just concentrate on the New Testament?

Answering these questions by providing ways you can easily follow to read and study the Bible is the reason for this book. As you read through it, you will learn some of the methods of reading and studying the Bible, some of the benefits of Bible study, some of the uses for Scripture, and, of course, some actual Bible studies.

As you learn to study the Bible for yourself, you will find that just making the effort can be quite challenging. But as you figure out what method works best for you, you will realize that reading the Bible is not just challenging (you should always feel challenged and even provoked when you read God's Word) but also enjoyable and enlightening.

One final thing we want you to understand about the Bible before you launch into your own personal study: When it comes to the big picture of the Bible, the following anonymous quotation sums up what the Bible is all about: "In the Old Testament we have Jesus predicted. In the Gospels we have Jesus revealed. In Acts we have Jesus preached. In the Epistles we have Jesus explained. In the Revelation we have Jesus expected."

From "In the beginning…" on, every word in the Bible points to the fulfillment of God's promise and plan to bring salvation to all humankind through His Son, Jesus Christ. So as you learn to study the Bible for yourself, keep in mind that every word you read—every promise, challenge, and story—between its covers is about Jesus and what he means to you.

The first four chapters provide a background to the Bible and how to study it. The bulk of this book, Chapters 5–21, presents what we consider to be among the most important sections of the entire Bible. If you want to study the Bible comprehensively you won't want to neglect these. We try to provide the background, meaning, and potential application to life that you will need to truly profit from what is important in Scripture.

So as you read this book, allow yourself to learn to read and study the Bible! As you do, you'll find out that it is in every way a great book—the *greatest*!

Special Note about the CD

The accompanying CD contains sheets that you can print out for use in a Bible study group. You'll find an informational form for participants to fill out stating what they would like to get out of the study group, a handout for each chapter including additional resources and study questions, an outline of the book, and a final survey form for participants. Feel free to use these forms in any way that best suits your particular study group.

Chapter 1

A Bible Study How-to

Like just about anything else, if you want to effectively read and study the Bible and apply it's principles to your own life, you're going to have to have a plan. In this chapter, you'll find some techniques for Bible reading and study—all of which are tried and true over the centuries— that will help make it easier for you to become better acquainted with what God's Word has to say to you personally.

The Importance of Studying the Bible Effectively

There once was a story of a man who needed to buy a new family car. Since he was a man of prayer who often went to the Bible when it was time to make big decisions, he opened his King James Bible at random and pointed to one verse on the page, hoping to find some kind of direction for his decision. That verse was Acts 1:14, which reads:

"These all continued with one *accord*..."

The very next day the man went to the local Honda dealership, where he purchased a brand new Honda Accord. Never mind the fact that he and his wife had four children—three of them teenagers—and that this particular car was much too small to meet their needs. As far as he was concerned, the Word of God had spoken to him very clearly.

While most believers know that God can certainly give direction by guiding people to specific passages of Scripture—and by other means—more often than not, the "open-and-point" method of Bible study isn't going to yield the kind of results, knowledge, or direction needed to make sound decisions. Taking that a step further, God wants each of us to be ready and willing to make a commitment when it comes to studying our Bibles.

The topic of this chapter is how the individual believer/reader can more effectively study the Bible. If you've been wondering about that in your own life, then it shows you are ready—or getting ready—to make the kind of commitment it takes to make Bible reading and study a regular, everyday part of your Christian life.

This chapter includes a list of things you'll need as well as some ways to use those things in order to learn and apply not just what the Bible has to say but also what it has to say to *you*. And you can bet that it's well worth the time and effort it will certainly take!

What You'll Need or at Least Find Useful

There are several items—all of which are readily available for purchase or download—that can help make Bible study both easier and more beneficial to the one who wishes to take the time to make studying the Bible a life priority. While some of these items are essential for good Bible study—for example, you can't very well study the Bible unless you have one—some of them aren't absolutely necessary but can be very helpful.

Here are the things you will need or will find helpful:

Study Bible

You can't very well study the Bible without your very own copy. Fortunately, there are hundreds of Bibles in dozens of translations available today. Some of them, those we refer to as "study Bibles," include mini concordances (lists of words) and dictionaries, and some include cross references so that you can better understand a verse or passage and put it in context with the entirety of the Bible.

QUESTION?

What is the best time of day to study the Bible?
There is no bad time of day to study the Bible, but the Bible itself implies that we should begin each day in God's Word. The practical element of starting the day that way is that it makes it easier to commit time to Bible study.

There are study Bibles for different age groups, different ministries, and different life stations, so if you take the time you can find a study Bible that best meets your needs.

If you can afford it, purchase more than one translation of the Bible. It would be useful to have a copy of the King James Version and a copy of a version that uses more modern English, such as the New American Standard, the New Living Translation, or the New International Version, just to name a few. The Scripture you'll find quoted in this book is from the New Living Translation.

Bible Concordance

Most of us aren't experts in the original Biblical languages—Hebrew, Greek, and Aramaic—so a good concordance is a great help to those of us who want to study the Bible in depth. A Biblical concordance is a published list of keywords in the Bible text, and it includes thumbnail definitions and the context in which all those words are used. A concordance is especially useful when it comes to finding keywords and phrases in the Bible.

There are several concordances in both printed and electronic form—some you can even use for free online. The best known are *Strong's Exhaustive Concordance* and *Young's Analytical Concordance to the Bible.*

ESSENTIAL

When you go to purchase a concordance, it is helpful to buy one that is compatible with the version of the Bible you are using. For example, *Strong's Exhaustive Concordance* is regarded as a companion to the King James Version of the Bible. A few minutes of research or shopping will help you to buy the right concordance.

Bible Dictionary

Like concordances, there are many quality Bible dictionaries in both printed and electronic form, and most of them are readily available at your local bookstore or as downloads from the Internet. You can use some of them for free by simply going online. Try the Holman Bible Dictionary at *www.studylight.org/dic/hbd/* or the Smith Bible Dictionary at *www.study light.org/dic/sbdl.*

Bible dictionaries are different from concordances in that they cover topics, events, places, and people rather than keywords. For example, if you wanted to study personal salvation, the Bible dictionary would give you the scriptural basics on that subject, while the concordance would direct you to passages in the Bible where that word (or variations of it) is used.

Bible dictionaries are also important in that they give the reader easier access to the different contexts of what they are reading. For example, any Bible dictionary will tell the reader the time and historic context of the writings of the Old Testament prophets as well as the target audiences of the New Testament writings of the apostle Paul.

ALERT!

There are several Bible commentaries available today that are considered classics in Christian literature. While these commentaries offer excellent insights to the Bible, some of them are, because of the outdated English used, difficult to understand for the modern reader. Read a sample of a commentary before you buy.

Bible Commentary

Over the centuries, many men of God have taken the time to write detailed Bible commentaries, some of which have withstood the tests of time. Renowned Christian figures such as Martin Luther, John Calvin, Charles Spurgeon, Matthew Henry, and John Wesley have all penned Bible commentaries. While there may be differences between them in the interpretation and applications of specific texts, they all have valuable insights for those who make Bible study a part of their daily lives.

Dictionary and Thesaurus

If you're going to study anything in the English language, it is helpful to have a dictionary and thesaurus available. A thesaurus is especially helpful because the Bible text often uses different words to convey what is essentially the same thought or idea.

Writing Supplies

Remember what you did as you sat through class lectures during your high school or college years? If you're like most successful students, you took notes on the lecture of your teacher or professor. Doing that was helpful in two ways: First, it enabled you to go back to your notes so you could be reminded of what the instructor said. Second, it helped brand what he or she said on a particular day into your memory.

But what student has never taken a pen or colored highlighters and marked key passages in a textbook? Obviously, that is an excellent way to remember what is noteworthy and important in the class. The same techniques work when it comes to studying the Bible, and for that reason it is recommended that you have a pen, a notepad, and colored highlighters available when you study your Bible.

Some people are reluctant to mark up their new study Bible with colored pens, but those who are experienced at personal Bible study will tell you that this is an effective way to focus on the keywords in a text, thus giving the reader a leg up in understanding what God is saying through it. You can always keep a second Bible free of all markings if you are distracted by the colored highlighting.

Once you arm yourself with the items listed above, you'll be ready to start a systemized Bible study. The only question then is which method to use. There are many good ways to read and study the Bible, and some are detailed for you in the rest of this chapter.

Reading Through the Bible in a Year

The simplest way to read and study the Bible is to read it very much like you would a novel, meaning starting at "In the beginning" (Genesis 1:1) and ending with "The Grace of the Lord Jesus be with you all" (Revelation 22:21).

There are many excellent study Bibles on the market that can guide the reader through the entire Bible in a year. In addition, there are many outlines available that can take you through the Bible in 365 calendar days—some for sale in the local bookstore and some readily—and freely—available through Internet sources.

Reading the Bible verse by verse from beginning to end in a year is a great way to get an overview of what the Book as a whole has to say, and it is something every believer should strive to do at least once. But there are more effective ways to take from the Bible the personal applications God wants each Christian to have. In order to help you achieve those goals, try one or more of the following tried and true methods of Bible study.

FACT

Without a plan to get through the Bible in a year, it's nearly impossible to keep accurate track of your progress. That's why it's important if you begin reading through the Bible in a year to have a plan or outline and that you stick to it once you've started.

Deductive Bible Study

The deductive method of studying the Bible means picking a certain subject as your starting point, then going through the Bible and finding Scriptures that address it. In short, it is a topical approach to studying the Scriptures.

Most preachers and Bible teachers prepare their materials using the deductive method of study. For example, if a preacher or teacher wanted to give a sermon or teach on the subject of sin, he'd look throughout both the Old Testament and the New Testament to find passages or verses that best fit the point he wanted to make.

One of the advantages of the deductive approach to Bible study is that it gives the reader a good Biblical overview of a particular topic as well as more personal applications. That's because it takes the different things that are said in the Bible on a particular word or topic—all of which you'll find are in amazing harmony—and gives you the bigger picture look at what God has to say about those topics.

Inductive Bible Study

While the deductive method of Bible study involves studying the Bible topically, studying it inductively means taking a passage of Scripture and reading it, pondering it, and asking questions about it until you are able to draw conclusions about what that text is saying in and of itself.

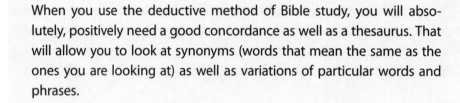

ALERT!

When you use the deductive method of Bible study, you will absolutely, positively need a good concordance as well as a thesaurus. That will allow you to look at synonyms (words that mean the same as the ones you are looking at) as well as variations of particular words and phrases.

If you wanted to do a deductive study on the word *love*, you would search your concordance for that word, as well as variations, and begin looking at the passages and verses that include it. But if you were to do an inductive study, say of 1 Corinthians 13, which has been called the Love Chapter, you would find out how important godly love is and what it looks like—all from reading just one chapter.

The first thing you should do when conducting an inductive Bible study is to simply read what the text says and think about what it means. Ask how this text applies to you and how you can practically and effectively apply this text to your life.

What you observe when you read and study the Bible is absolutely vital because your understanding and application of anything you see or read—including a text of Scripture—will be based upon what you hear it saying. That is why it is so important to take the time during an inductive Bible study to ask God to teach you what He wants you to learn through the particular passage you are looking at.

It is also important that you understand the context of the text you are looking at. Context means everything when it comes to studying anything, particularly the Bible. Without knowing the context, it is impossible to take your studies a step further and understand what a particular passage says in general and what it says to you individually.

When making sense of what a passage of Scripture means, it is always best to look for the obvious. Sometimes what the Bible appears to be saying is exactly what it is saying, and there is no need to read anything else into it. As you read the text, ask the following questions (as well as any others the text might bring to mind):

- Who wrote it, when did he write it, and to whom did he write it?
- Who are the main characters and what are the main events in the text?
- How are the people in the text similar or different from me?
- What is the meaning of the passage?
- What is God telling me and how is He encouraging and strengthening me through this passage?
- What promises can I see in this passage?
- What changes does this passage show me I need to make in my life and how does God want me to make them?
- What sins do I need to be rid of so that I can grow more and enjoy closer fellowship with God?
- What does God want me to share with someone?

When you begin your study of the Bible—no matter what method you use—it is important that you ask God to speak to you through what you are reading and meditating on. So go to the source of all Scripture and ask Him to open your heart, your ears, and your eyes to what it is really saying.

When interpreting a passage in the Bible, ask such questions as how, who, what, when, and where. The answers provide the context and lead to deeper meaning. And in terms of applying the passage, this is where you propose to *do* what God has taught you through these questions and answers.

It is through applying the principles you've learned that God changes your life. God enlightens our minds and we apply it with our wills, and the Spirit of God empowers us to carry out these choices.

As you ask yourself these questions, write them—as well as your answers—down in your notebook. Continued studies may change how you answer those questions later on, but that is a good thing. That just means you are gaining a deeper understanding of what the Bible really says.

FACT

Many people grow up learning about the Bible, however, it is vital that you read it without any preconceived notions. In other words, don't focus on what you think the Bible says but instead let it speak for itself. It has done so just fine for thousands of years and will continue to do so for you!

Devotional Study Method

While all Bible study should have an element of personal devotion to it— meaning that it is with the purpose of deepening one's personal relationship with God—there is one method that makes that aspect of Bible study its primary focus. It's called the devotional study method.

If you study the Bible using this method, you'll need a Bible as well as a notepad and writing utensil. With those items at the ready, go to the passage you wish to study and read it several times over, all the while making notes of observations and questions that come to mind about what you're reading. Then take the time to rewrite the passage in your own words while at the same time personalizing it.

For example, turn in your Bible to Psalm 1:1–3, which reads:

Oh, the joys of those who do not follow the advice of the wicked, or stand around with sinners, or join in with scoffers. But they delight in doing everything the LORD wants; day and night they think about his law. They are like trees planted along the riverbank, bearing fruit each season without fail. Their leaves never wither, and in all they do, they prosper.

After you've read this Psalm several times, rewrite it and personalize it. Your version might read something like this: *God gives me great joy because I choose not to follow the advice of evil people, or spend my time with sinners, or join in when I hear people ridicule or mock the words and ways of God.*

When you study the Bible using this method, its words and messages jump off the pages and become words and messages spoken to you personally. That makes it easier to apply these things to your own life, which in turn brings you closer to God Himself. That's because you're reading the Bible as if God wrote it as a personal letter to you and you alone.

Character, Event, and Place Studies

When God inspired and motivated the writers of the Scriptures to record the words and deeds of those whose names appear in the Bible, He did this so that we could learn from their examples—good and bad—and from how He instructed and responded to them. When you read the Bible and see a name, a place, or an event, you can know that it's in there for a reason. For example, when you study and get to know the story of an Old Testament prophet named Jonah, you find that it's more than a well-known children's Sunday school story of a guy who was swallowed by a fish but also an encouragement and a warning to listen to and obey God, knowing that there is blessing in obedience and folly in turning away from Him.

When you study Bible characters and events, look at the details—the things they said, the things they did, how God instructed and corrected them, the events that took place around them—and ask yourself what significance they all have when it comes to having a better understanding of God's Word and of God Himself. When you do that, you will be able to take personal instruction from things these men and women did and said, as well as the things God did for them.

Keyword Study

If you are adept in the use of modern-day computers, you know how useful it can be to use keywords. In the context of Bible study, keywords are those singular words—and their variations—that give a certain text life and meaning.

Keyword studies are an excellent way to find out what God has to say in the Bible about certain subjects, such as love, forgiveness, sin, and blessing—all of which are important in the believer's life. This is a fairly simple way to study the Bible, because all it involves is going to a concordance and finding out where particular words appear in Scripture.

For example, suppose you were struggling with the idea that God had truly forgiven you for every sin you had committed and confessed to Him. In looking for assurance that you were really forgiven, you would probably want to look up what the Bible has to say about the word *forgive*. You would start your search by looking up that particular word in your concordance, then moving on to variations of the word (*forgive, forgave, forgiving*, and so forth). Next, take out your thesaurus and look up synonyms (different words that mean the same thing) for the word you are studying. For example, one synonym for forgive is *pardon*.

ALERT!

When you do keyword studies, make sure that you look at a word in context so that you aren't looking at a homonym, which is a word that is pronounced the same but means something different. For example, the word *light* can be an adjective meaning "not heavy" or a noun meaning "physical light."

Once you had done that word study, you would know what the Bible has to say about the forgiveness of God. You would know that God's forgiveness is:

- one of His character attributes (Daniel 9:9)
- conditional based on our willingness to forgive others (Matthew 6:14, 15)
- conditional based on our willingness to confess our sins to God (1 John 1:9)
- conditional based on our willingness to repent, or turn away from, our sins (2 Peter 3:9)
- something we can ask Him for (Matthew 6:12)
- available to us through the sacrifice of His Son, Jesus Christ (Ephesians 1:7)

These are just a few of the many Biblical passages dealing with God's forgiveness. And when you take the time to use variations of the word forgive, you will see the provision God has made to forgive sin and the conditions attached to that forgiveness.

A Final Note Before You Start

The Bible tells us that, "All Scripture is inspired by God and is useful to teach us what is true and to make us realize what is wrong in our lives. It straightens us out and teaches us to do what is right. It is God's way of preparing us in every way, fully equipped for every good thing God wants us to do" (2 Timothy 3:16–17).

This tells us that God didn't give us the Bible just so we could have something nice to read before we go to sleep. It means that our goals in studying the Bible are to learn God's truth, to find out what changes we need to make in our personal lives, and to be prepared to do the good things God wants us to do.

As you study the Bible, don't just do it with the goal of learning what might be called "head knowledge." Knowing the contents of the Bible is always a positive, but only if you take its messages and apply them to your life personally.

Chapter 2

Bible Reading and Study: What's in It for You?

One of the most important things you need to remember as you begin reading and studying the Bible is that God wants to use your reading and study as an avenue through which He can do good things in your life. God has given us the Bible so He can show us more about Himself and more about how He wants to relate to humanity as a whole and to individuals.

The Good That Comes from Bible Study

You don't have to attend church or take part in Christian fellowship for long before you hear at least a little something about the importance of reading and studying the Bible for yourself, and doing it daily. If you're in a group study or an accountability group, you may hear questions such as, "What is God showing you through His Word lately?" or "How has God blessed you through your Bible study?"

This is part of the Biblical encouragement for believers to encourage one another in their faith, and it brings up a practical question for the average Bible reader: What good does it *really* do us to read the Bible daily? Or to put it more personally, "What's in it for me?"

You won't have to read and study the Bible for long before you find out that the answer to that question is this: plenty! If you're trying to decide what kind of computer to buy or what to wear to tomorrow's big job interview, you probably won't find anything in the Bible concerning those kinds of decisions. But if you're looking for solid wisdom when it comes to fixing what is wrong in your life or just making your life better, or when you're trying to find out how to be a better person, parent, spouse, friend, or spiritual leader, then you'll find it in the pages of the Bible—*if* you take the time to look for it.

The rest of this chapter details some of the benefits you will most certainly receive if you make daily Bible reading and study a priority in your life. The following sections won't give you all the benefits of reading and studying the Bible—you may find that you come up with a few of those on your own—but they will give you an idea of how God wants to bless you as you place the study of His written Word at the top of your personal daily list of things to do.

Finding Out More about God Himself

If you want to get to know someone very well—if you wanted to find out what makes that person tick and what that person loves, hates, desires, and finds most important—there is no better way to find out than to talk to that person face to face or to read what that person has written himself or herself. That's exactly what happens as you read the Bible.

When you read the Bible, you learn about the person of God. You find out what makes Him tick—what He loves, what He hates, what pleases Him, what angers Him, and what motivated Him to reach out to a lost humanity who had nothing to offer Him in return.

ALERT!

While reading extrabiblical materials about God can be helpful in your spiritual growth (and there are lots of that kind of material around to help you in your study), you should remember that absolutely *nothing* can take the place of reading the Bible itself.

One of the most important things new believers learn early about the Christian faith is that it is not just a set of rules or regulations. It's much more than that. It's a personal relationship—one where you become the friend, child, and servant of God—one that grows and changes over time, just as your relationship with a good friend or your spouse grows and changes.

The apostle Paul expressed the passion that should be within every believer—namely, to know Jesus Christ better and better every new day—when he wrote:

> *Yes, everything else is worthless when compared with the priceless gain of knowing Christ Jesus my Lord. I have discarded everything else, counting it all as garbage, so that I may have Christ and become one with him. I no longer count on my own goodness or my ability to obey God's law, but I trust Christ to save me. For God's way of making us right with Himself depends on faith. As a result, I can really know Christ. (Philippians 3:8–10)*

If your goal as a believer is, like Paul's, to know Christ personally, then Bible reading and study must be a consistent part of your daily life in him. When you read the Bible—Old Testament and New Testament alike—you will learn the purposes for Christ, the thoughts and ways of Christ, and the way to Christ. You will learn that God is more than our Creator, but also a loving heavenly Father who wants more than anything for us to draw close to Him in a personal, loving relationship. When you learn those things, you will make yourself ready to know Him in a deeper and more personal way.

Seeing the History of God's Interaction with People

From the creation story in Genesis 1–2 to the final words of Revelation, the Bible is all about God and His loving interaction with humankind. Scriptures tell us how God has blessed, cursed, loved, and redeemed and saved men and women in spite of their rebellion, and also all about how God brought into the world a Savior who could make that redemption and salvation possible.

But why exactly is it important to know the Biblical history of God's interaction with people? Because those accounts stand as examples—both negative and positive—for us today of how God responds to us as humankind in general and as individuals.

FACT

Remembering is a big theme in the Bible. God wanted His people, the Israelites, to remember how He had brought them out of captivity in Egypt. He continually called them to remember that chapter in Jewish history because He wanted His people to remember His blessings and faithfulness as well as the consequences of their disobedience.

The apostle Paul wrote, "All these events happened to them as examples for us. They were written down to warn us, who live at the time when this age is drawing to a close" (1 Corinthians 10:11). These "events" Paul was writing about were the sins of the Jewish people who had left bondage and slavery in Egypt and were on their way to the Promised Land as well as the punishment they received because of their disobedience.

God wants us to know the history of His interaction with His people. He wants us to observe all the promises, warnings, blessings, and punishments they received and what led to those things. He wants us to observe these things and see what pleases Him, what angers Him, what grieves Him, and what moves Him to action on our behalf.

When we know those things, we get a better peek into the character of God, into what He expects and desires from those who follow Him in faith.

Getting Direction—Straight from the Top!

Anyone who has served in the military knows the importance of following orders. In that culture, it's absolutely essential that servicemen and servicewomen learn how to obey the orders of their superiors to the letter. That's because it's in heeding those orders that each serviceman and servicewoman becomes part of an efficient and smooth-running fighting machine.

The same thing is essentially true of the Christian life. The Bible tells us that when we put our faith in Jesus Christ, we become part of his "body" (1 Corinthians 12), meaning that we have a part to play in making sure that body is healthy and growing. In order to effectively play that part, each of us needs to seek God's direction. And one of the most important ways we seek that direction is through diligently reading God's written Word.

In Psalm 119, the longest psalm among the 150 recorded in the Bible, the psalmist wrote: "How sweet are your words to my taste; they are sweeter than honey. Your commandments give me understanding; no wonder I hate every false way of life. Your word is a lamp for my feet and a light for my path" (Psalm 119:103–105).

ESSENTIAL

It is important when you are looking for direction from above that you not only look to the Bible but also that you pray and ask God to give you the guidance and wisdom to help you apply it to your specific situation. In that situation, pray that God illuminates a passage so that you can apply it.

If you read the entirety of this psalm, you will see that the psalmist thanks and praises God for His law, His commands, His decrees, and His words—all of which we can find recorded in the pages of the Bible. And as you study the Bible, you'll find that it contains God's directions in a variety of situations many of us find in day-to-day life.

Here are just a few examples of where you can find Biblical guidance for specific life situations:

- **marriage** (Proverbs 5:15–19, Matthew 19:5–6, 1 Corinthians 7:1–16, Ephesians 5:21–33, Colossians 3:18–19, 1 Peter 3:1–7, Hebrews 13:4)
- **parenting** (Deuteronomy 6:5–7; Proverbs 13:24, 19:18; Colossians 3:20–21; Ephesians 6:4)
- **when** others hurt or offend you (Matthew 6:12–15, Mark 11:25, Colossians 3:12–15, Romans 12:9–19)
- **work** (Ecclesiastes 5:18–20, Colossians 3:23, 1 Thessalonians 3:7–14)
- **patience** (Psalm 37:7–9, Galatians 5:22, Colossians 1:11, 1 Thessalonians 5:14, Hebrews 12:1, James 1:3–4)

Obviously, there are many more life situations addressed in the Bible. Also, there are more verses and passages that apply to the topics listed above. That tells us something wonderful about the Bible, specifically that it's a book chock full of directions for the Christian life and that each of us benefits greatly when we take the time to find and follow those directions.

In that respect, you can read the Bible as something of a field manual for the Christian life, which we are promised will be a battle in this world. And it's a field manual that will never fail us, simply because we know that God's Word can be trusted and depended upon in all things.

Gaining Practical Insights to the Christian Life

Those who aren't personally familiar with the Bible may not realize it, but it really is a very practical book. It gives us specific instructions and guidelines for every area of the Christian life, and it gives them in a way that we can understand—as long as we are committed to understanding.

As a practical handbook for the Christian life, the Bible tells us everything we need to know in order to live the life God wants us to live, and it also gives us instructions on how to do those things in every situation that faces us. It gives us instructions in what are known as spiritual disciplines, which is really just another way of saying that the Bible tells us how to do the things that are involved in a growing Christian life. For example, the Bible tells us how to:

- **pray** (Matthew 6:9–13, 7:7–11, 18:19–20; Mark 11:24; John 14:13–14; James 5:15; 1 John 5:14–15)
- **worship** God (Exodus 20:4–5, Psalm 150, Matthew 4:10, Mark 7:7, John 4:23–24, Romans 12:1)
- **fast** (Leviticus 16:29, 23:32; Ezra 10:6; Isaiah 58:6; Matthew 6:16–18, 17:21; Acts 13:2–3)
- **demonstrate** Christian love to others (Matthew 5:43–48, John 15:9–13, 1 Corinthians 13)
- **fight** temptation (Psalm 95:8; Luke 22:40, 46; 1 Corinthians 10:13; James 1:2–12; 2 Peter 2:9)

Again, the list above is not a comprehensive one, and the Bible covers many other spiritual disciplines. There are also many other passages not listed here that deal with the subjects listed above. But these examples alone should show you that there isn't anything in the realm of your life with Jesus Christ that isn't covered in the Scriptures.

ALERT!

If you want to read some really practical instructions on the Christian life from Jesus himself, read Matthew 5–7, which records what has come to be known as the Sermon on the Mount. In it, he tells us how to pray, how to give, how to love, and many other practical insights and instructions.

When you study specific areas of the life of faith, it's good to have your concordance and your Bible dictionary on hand. That way you can readily find the passages that deal with the area in question. Also, make sure you read the whole passage surrounding that issue and not just one verse. That will give you some context on that issue.

Growing Spiritually

You don't have to be an experienced parent to know that in order for children to grow they need nourishment—physical, emotional, and spiritual alike. Without proper care and feeding, a child will be stunted in his or her growth and never become what he or she could have been. But with those things, the child grows and becomes a healthy, mature grownup who can function in all ways as an adult.

The very same is true in the spiritual realm. In fact, the Bible uses the comparisons and contrasts between infancy, childhood, and adulthood in teaching us that after God saves us, He wants us to grow and mature spiritually. And it also lets us know that there is a matter of choice and commitment on our parts when it comes to that growth.

That is exactly what the apostle Paul was referring to when he wrote to a bunch of immature believers in a city called Corinth:

> *Dear brothers and sisters, when I was with you I couldn't talk to you as I would to mature Christians. I had to talk as though you belonged to this world or as though you were infants in the Christian life. I had to feed you with milk and not with solid food, because you couldn't handle anything stronger. And you still aren't ready, for you are still controlled by your own sinful desires.*
> *(1 Corinthians 3:1–3)*

In short, Paul is saying, "It's time to start growing up!"

The New Testament is very clear that spiritual maturity is a process and that, though we will all reach a point of maturity, we should never stop growing as long we are on this earth. That was Paul's point when he wrote, "I keep working toward that day when I will finally be all that Christ Jesus saved me for and wants me to be. No, dear brothers and sisters, I am still not all I should be, but I am focusing all my energies on this one thing: Forgetting the past and looking forward to what lies ahead, I strain to reach the end of the race and receive the prize for which God, through Christ Jesus, is calling us up to heaven" (Philippians 3:12–14).

The Bible tells us there are several things we need in order to grow toward spiritual maturity, things such as fellowship with other Christians, prayer, and, of course, Bible reading and study. That was partly Paul's point when he told Timothy, "[Scripture] is God's way of preparing us in every way, fully equipped for every good thing God wants us to do" (2 Timothy 3:17).

There are any number of books, study guides, and multistep programs available for the purpose of helping the believer to spiritual maturity. And while some of them can be very good and helpful, all believers need to keep in mind that nothing can take the place of regular, personal Bible reading and study.

FACT

The apostle Peter, who walked with Jesus during his earthly ministry, wrote of this theme of spiritual growth, "Like newborn babies, you must crave pure spiritual milk so that you will grow into a full experience of salvation. Cry out for this nourishment, now that you have had a taste of the Lord's kindness" (1 Peter 2:2–3).

We also need to remember that maturity doesn't happen overnight, any more than a deep knowledge of the Bible happens overnight. It takes time, personal effort, and, yes, patience for the average believer to see the fruits of true spiritual maturity.

So as you read and study your Bible, remember that you're doing more than filling your mind with some good spiritual material. You're actually feeding the inner part of you that needs nourishment if you are to become a spiritually mature believer.

Having the Joy and Peace of Knowing and Living God's Word Daily

It may come as a surprise to those who haven't yet made Bible reading and study a key part of their lives, but there is a supernatural joy and peace that come from immersing ourselves in the Word of God through daily reading and study.

God's written Word is a source of joy and peace, of inspiration and instruction. When we read, study, and meditate on the words and message of the Bible, we find a joy like no possession or relationship can give and a peace deeper than anything the world has to offer.

When you are down, try reading some of the words of praise and worship recorded in the Psalms. When you need wise direction, try looking through the Proverbs, which give us some of the most profound wisdom ever written. When you need inspiration, try looking at the stories of great men and women whose faith have made them heroes of the Bible. (Start with Hebrews 12 and work backwards.) And when you need peace and joy, focus on the numerous verses and passages in the Bible that give assurance of God's love and compassion for those who call out to Him and ask for it.

When you do those things, when you make the words and messages contained in the Bible your source of comfort, you'll receive every blessing and every bit of wisdom, direction, and peace God has for those who make His written Word a priority in their lives. It's just that kind of book! And, as you will see in the next chapter, it's also the kind of book you can take personally.

Chapter 3
Taking It Personally

A cartoon that appeared in newspapers nationwide showed a preacher standing at the front door of his church sending his flock away for the week. As he shook hands with each of his departing parishioners, he said to each of them, "Nothing personal." That was some good religious humor, but it doesn't at all reflect the reality of what God says to us through the Bible. He *wants* us to take it personally; in fact, that's why He gave it to us in the first place.

The Bible: God's Message to You Personally

God has given His people the Bible so that they can be blessed, challenged, encouraged, warned, loved, enlightened, saved—the list goes on and on. But each of us finds that those things happen to us more profoundly and more powerfully when we take the Bible in our hands and think of it as God's message to us as individuals.

That, after all, is exactly the way God wants each of us to take His written Word.

It has been said that every believer should learn to read the Bible as if it was God's message to him or her personally, as if He had written it to them and them alone. When we do that, we receive personally every blessing He intended for those who love and trust Him.

As you read and study the Bible, learn to take it personally. Learn to see every principle, every promise, every caution, and every blessing as being meant for you personally. And you can do that because God has given not just us but *you* personally His written Word.

He's done that for several very good reasons, and that is what this chapter is about. As you read on, you'll see that the Bible was given as a means for you to know, to become, and to remain everything God wants you to be.

Knowing How to Properly Relate to God

If you know anything at all about the Bible, you know that it is the story of God's interaction with humankind—of the creation of humanity in an environment of perfection, of the fall of humanity into sin, of the consequences of that sin, and of God's plan to redeem and save us all. But perhaps even more important is the fact that the Bible is also a collection of stories of how God related to and interacted with men and women as individuals. That makes the Bible more than a collection of stories about people who somehow figured out what it took to relate to God; it's also a collection of stories that show us through example how to do it for ourselves.

There are many examples in the Bible of men and women who had an understanding of how to relate to God and who acted on that understanding. People like Abraham, Moses, Joshua, and King David stood out as people who, despite their own personal and spiritual flaws and warts, lived the lives and spoke the words that demonstrated their love for God.

The psalmist who wrote Psalm 119 underscored the importance of the Bible in helping people properly relate to God when he wrote, "I used to wander off until you disciplined me; but now I closely follow your word. You are good and do only good; teach me your decrees" (Psalm 119:67, 68).

If you want to read good examples of lives of devotion to God, read more about the people listed above. They were men whose love for and obedience to God guided them in their daily lives and whose love for God always brought them back around to Him when they failed.

But when you want to read of perfect devotion to God in every word and deed, read of the life, the deeds, and the words of Jesus Christ as they are recorded in the four Gospels—Matthew, Mark, Luke, and John. Most of the Bible is devoted to *telling* us how to properly relate to our Creator, but the life and words of Jesus were devoted to *showing* us how. And while we will never in this life attain perfection, we have his life as the perfect example of how to properly relate to God.

There are three parts to properly relating to God, and Jesus demonstrated them all perfectly. They are as follows:

- **love for God** (Exodus 20:6, Deuteronomy 6:5, Joshua 22:5, John 16:27, Romans 8:28, 1 Corinthians 8:3)
- **believe and trust in God** (Genesis 15:6, 2 Kings 18:5, Psalm 31:14, Daniel 6:23, John 14:1, Romans 15:13, 1 John 4:16)
- **obedience to God** (Genesis 26:5, Joshua 1:7, Job 36:11, Psalm 25:10, Luke 6:49, John 3:36, Philippians 2:12)

If you've taken the time to look up the above verses—which are just a few of the many verses and passages containing the messages of love, trust, and obedience to God—you'll see very clearly that we as believers are to love, trust, and obey God. But the question remains: How do we do those things? What actions should we take and words should we speak to show our love, faith, and obedience to God?

That is where personal Bible reading and study come in. It is only through reading God's Word—and especially looking to the example of Jesus Christ—that you'll learn to love Him, trust Him, and obey Him in the way that is due Him. It is only through reading the Bible that you'll find the specifics of what loving God, believing God, and obeying God entails.

Becoming More Like Jesus

In any area of life, it's good to set goals for yourself. Goals are what keep you moving forward simply because they give you something to strive for and attain.

In the New Testament, one of the recurring themes is that believers are to strive to become more and more like Jesus Christ in every area of their lives. For example, the apostle Paul wrote, "So all of us who have had that veil removed can see and reflect the glory of the Lord. And the Lord—who is the Spirit—makes us more and more like him as we are changed into his glorious image" (2 Corinthians 3:18).

"Changed into his glorious image" means we are transformed into something we weren't before, namely the image of Jesus Christ. This means that we are made to be just like him in how we think, talk, and act. This is what Christians call "Christlike," and it's something we are to strive to attain not just in the hereafter but also in the here and now.

We are to be imitators of Jesus Christ in our:

- **approach to temptation** (Matthew 4:1–11)
- **love** (John 13:34–35)
- **humility** (Philippians 2:2–8)
- **attitudes and actions toward others** (1 John 3:18)
- **purity** (1 Thessalonians 4:1–8)
- **compassion** (2 Corinthians 1:3–7)
- **doing good for others** (Matthew 5:16)

This list could go on and on simply because Jesus made himself the perfect example in every area of life.

We don't become like Jesus just by accident or by some sort of supernatural osmosis where we just sit back and let his character and ways be formed in us. If that were the case, then becoming a Christian would mean losing all our free will. And while God wants our wills and thoughts to be submitted to Him, He won't simply take them from us and force us to be like Jesus.

QUESTION?

According to Galatians 5:16–23, who or what is the driving force behind the believer becoming more like Christ?
The Holy Spirit, because it is only he who keeps us walking, talking, and living in the same way Jesus did. It is the Holy Spirit who guides us, directs us, and empowers us to live the way God wants us to live.

Being like Christ only happens when we make a conscious choice to seek and follow him, when we willfully and purposefully ask him to come in and change us from the inside out. It only happens through prayer, worship and praise, spending time in fellowship with other believers, and—you guessed it!—reading and studying the Bible.

But how can we know specifically what the life of Jesus Christ looked like? How can we know how he lived, talked, prayed, and walked? Well, the Bible contains a four-book biography of Jesus's time on earth, with an emphasis on the three-plus years of ministry leading up to the time of the Crucifixion.

As we read the Gospels we see that Jesus did far more than just talk a good game of faith and devotion to God, he played it out every moment of his life. And while we can't—at least in this life—live out those things as perfectly as he did, we can look to him as our perfect example of life, love, faith, and obedience.

Living Within the Family of God

As you read in the last chapter, Christianity is all about relationships, starting with a relationship with God Himself. But the Bible also teaches extensively on the subject of relating well to other people, particularly other believers.

As Jesus prepared to meet with his final earthly destination—the cross—he gave the disciples some final instructions. Among those was this: "This is my commandment: Love each other in the same way I have loved you. There is no greater love than to lay down one's life for one's friends" (John 15:12–13).

Jesus came to earth to live, teach, and die so that he could establish a family, and it's a family of believers who would be tied together by the same kind of love he demonstrated when he gave of himself in every way possible.

The Bible—in both the Old Testament and the New Testament—gives the reader many commands, guidelines, and wisdom on how to lovingly and selflessly operate within that family. Those specific commands can be summed up in the words of Jesus himself: "Love each other."

FACT

The apostle Paul gave the church in Corinth an excellent outline for what Christian love should look like in 1 Corinthians 13. In verses 4 through 7 of that chapter, we are told that love is patient and kind and that it is not jealous, boastful, proud, rude, or selfish.

The word *love* as it is used most often in the Bible doesn't refer to feelings nearly as much as actions. When Jesus told his disciples to "love each other," he wasn't telling them to have warm feelings of friendship for one another. He was telling them to do for one another the things that built up and made each of them better servants of God and to avoid doing those things that could drag one another down and keep them from being all God had called them to be.

Much of the Bible gives instructions on how we are to love one another, but you'll find the most practical and easily applicable guidelines in the proverbs, in the teachings of Jesus (particularly Matthew 5–7), and in the epistles of the apostle Paul, which were more than anything letters of instruction for the operations of churches at that time.

Knowing the Dos and Don'ts of the Christian Life

It has been pointed out that the Christian faith isn't really a religion or a list of dos and don'ts. Instead it is a relationship—a personal, living, growing relationship—with the living God that we enter into through our faith in Jesus Christ.

Unfortunately, too many people view the Bible as a harsh book that does nothing but put limitations on people, that just tells them what they can and can't do. But knowing that our faith is based in a personal relationship, we also need to understand that this relationship—like any we'd have on earth—requires nurturing, care, and work to help it grow and thrive. Another way to put that is to say that there are things we need to do as well as things we need to avoid if we want to fully enjoy a faith-centered, growing relationship with God.

ESSENTIAL

When you are looking through your Bible to find guidelines for living, use your concordance to look for key verbs (action words, such as *give, love, pray*) or adjectives (descriptive words, such as *holy, righteous, blessed*) and it will lead you to some good dos and don'ts of the Christian life as they appear in the Bible.

Yes, that means there are things we should do and things we shouldn't do if we want our relationship with God to continue growing. And the Bible contains many warnings, commands, and bits of wisdom telling us what we should do and what we shouldn't, what we can do and what we can't.

For example, some of the *dos* the Bible tells us to follow are to . . .

- be filled with the Holy Spirit of God (Ephesians 5:18)
- remain in—or stick close to—Christ (John 15:1–11)
- tell others the message of salvation through Jesus (Matthew 28:18–20, Mark 16:15)
- rejoice in the Lord (Philippians 4:4)
- pray about everything (Philippians 4:6)
- resist the devil (James 4:7)

And, for example, the Bible says, *don't* . . .
- do good expecting your reward here on earth (Matthew 6:1–4)
- hang on to anger and bitterness (Matthew 5:22–23)
- steal (Leviticus 19:11, Ephesians 4:28)
- forget to spend time in fellowship with other believers (Hebrews 10:25)
- engage in drunkenness (Ephesians 5:18)

While the Bible contains a lot of instructions for living the Christian life—including some dos and don'ts—it also gives the rewards for doing what we should and the consequences for doing what we shouldn't. God has promised both blessings and protection for those who follow Him in obedience, for those who read what the Bible says and then act on it. (See James 1:22–25.)

Knowing What to Say and How to Say It

After Jesus's death and resurrection, he spent forty days on earth, appearing several times to disciples before he went back to heaven to be with his Father. It was during this time that he gave them some additional teaching and some final instructions.

Probably the most important message Jesus gave the disciples at that time was what has come to be known as the Great Commission, a command that goes like this: "Therefore, go and make disciples of all the nations, baptizing them in the name of the Father and the Son and the Holy Spirit. Teach these new disciples to obey all the commands I have given you" (Matthew 28:19–20).

It was because of the disciples' obedience to this command that Christianity spread throughout the world at that time and why it continues to be the dominant faith of the Western world today. The disciples who heard that command all played a part in taking the gospel to the world around them, and they were later joined by the apostle Paul, a former persecutor of Christians who became the most important and influential Christian missionary of all time.

FACT

The apostle Paul, who wrote much of the New Testament, didn't begin his traveling ministry of preaching, teaching, and writing immediately after he became a Christian—though he did preach in the city of Jerusalem. In fact, he spent three years training in Arabia with Jesus Christ himself before he began his missionary journeys. (See Galatians 1:11–12, 15–18.)

Christians through the centuries have taken Jesus's command to his disciples of that time to apply to all believers, even those who don't go into what we would consider "fulltime ministry." In other words, believers today are charged with the responsibility of making new disciples.

But what does a believer need in order to win converts to Christianity? Obviously, he or she would need to know a little something about the Bible, particularly the works and teachings of Jesus Christ as well as the writings of the apostle Paul. Without that, ministry to others would be all but impossible.

If you're going to encourage fellow believers and influence nonbelievers, you're going to have a good grasp of what the Bible has to say about God, sin, forgiveness, and discipleship. You're going to have to know enough to be able to boldly encourage other Christians and confidently field questions— even objections—you may hear from those who don't yet understand the message of salvation through Christ.

That is what the apostle Peter meant when he wrote that we should always be ready to give an answer to those who ask about the hope we have within us and to do it gently and respectfully. (See 1 Peter 3:15.)

E ALERT!

If you want a good foundation of Biblical truth to present to those who aren't yet believers, a good place to start is the New Testament book of Romans. This book is often referred to as the Gospel according to Paul, and it contains a great overview of the message of salvation.

There are few things more damaging to the reputation of the Christian community than those well-meaning but ill-prepared believers who try to tackle the task of introducing people to Jesus Christ without a good knowledge and grasp of the message of salvation as it is laid out in the Bible. On the other hand, there is nothing more powerful than a believer who is equipped with a solid grasp of the fundamentals of the faith as they are presented in Scriptures.

There are a lot of great reasons to read, study, and know the Bible, one of the best of them being that it gives the believer the ability to present a clear, concise, and (most of all) Biblically accurate picture of the message of salvation through Jesus Christ.

Knowing What Comes Next

There is a common belief among people—even those with a basic knowledge of the Bible—that God will reward us in the afterlife for the good things that we do. And while the Bible is clear that our salvation has nothing to do with our own good works, it does tell us in several places that there are rewards for those who do good things for the right reasons.

Speaking through the apostle John, Jesus tells those who follow him, "Look, I am coming soon, bringing my reward with me to repay all people according to their deeds" (Revelation 22:12). This means that part of God's final judgment of individuals is assessing what their eternal rewards will be.

It's not popular in some Christian circles to talk about rewards as the results for faithfully serving God. And while the Bible indicates that our first priority in serving God is to do so out of love and obedience, Jesus himself talked about rewards for those who do so. In Matthew 5–7, in Jesus's famous

Sermon on the Mount, he makes reference at least nine times to rewards for obedient living.

FACT

Speaking of rewards, the apostle Paul wrote, "Salvation is not a reward for the good things we have done, so none of us can boast about it" (Ephesians 2:9). That is in keeping with the Biblical theme that our salvation is based on the work of God and nothing we can do ourselves.

Even in the Old Testament there are many references to rewards for obedient living. For example, in the book of Genesis we read how God promised Abraham a "great reward" if he would simply trust and obey (Genesis 15:1). Later, King David wrote, "The Lord rewarded me for doing right" (Psalm 18:20).

As you read and study the Bible, you will see that there are great rewards for personalizing what you see, for making the messages of God contained in the Good Book your very own. And, as the Bible itself tells us, the rewards will be both in this life and in the one to come!

Chapter 4

Other Uses for the Bible

To most people, the Bible is like other books in that it can be read, studied, learned, and even applied to their lives if they choose to do so. That, after all, is what the Bible is for. But there are several other ways to use the Bible to enhance and enrich one's life of faith. As you read through this chapter, take some personal mental notes on how you will use the Word of God to help you grow and flourish in your faith.

4

Taking It to Another Level

In an earlier chapter, you read about the different methods of studying the Bible. In this chapter you will find that there are just as many uses for what you study as there are methods of study, and that you can actually add layers to your Bible reading and study experience.

What you are about to read are simply things you can do with what you study or while you are studying the Bible. They are ways to make reading and studying the Good Book a more informative, useful, challenging, and personally rewarding experience.

Before you read on, a couple of notes. First, please understand that the material in this chapter moves Bible reading and study into a more spiritual direction. While simple reading and study of the Bible will touch your mind and spirit, the things in this chapter are meant to actually make the Word of God a part of you in a very real way.

Second, as you endeavor to make the things in this chapter a part of your spiritual life, it's important that you spend time in prayer. Ask God to illuminate to you personally what the Bible says and what it means to you today. Ask Him to indelibly imprint what you read, hear, and see upon you so that it actually becomes a part of who you are. Now, read on and you'll see how the words and messages in the Bible can come alive within you.

Memorizing the Bible

It's no exaggeration to say that memorizing Scripture is one of the most important things a believer can do. It's important for a number of reasons, and it's rewarding and enjoyable to boot.

Having a variety of Bible verses and passages committed to memory can be helpful in many ways. It can help you when you need to remember some good Biblical wisdom or instruction that applies to your own life situation. It can help you minister to other believers who need encouragement. And it can help you to tell others about what exactly the Bible has to say to them as people for whom Christ came to die.

The apostle Peter, who was with Jesus during the entirety of his earthly ministry, explained the importance of knowing Scripture by mind and by heart when he wrote, "And if you are asked about your Christian hope, always be ready to explain it" (1 Peter 3:15).

FACT

The writer of Psalm 119 strongly implied the importance of memorizing Scripture and making it a part of our thinking when he wrote, "I have hidden your word in my heart, that I might not sin against you" (Psalm 119:11). This tells us that memorizing Scripture is a help when it comes to battling temptation to sin.

If you're ever in a situation where someone asks you about your faith—and it's sure to happen eventually—you can more easily explain what you believe, why you believe it, and what it's done for you if you have some of the Bible memorized. But what steps should a Bible reader take to begin effective Bible memorization? Here are some tips and ideas that might help you make memorization a part of your Bible reading and study.

- *Pick a version of the Bible that works for you.* This may not sound like a huge part of Scripture memorization, but you might be surprised to find that the version of the Bible you memorize can make a big difference. Some people find that the more poetic tone of the King James Version is more easily memorable, while others like a more modern-sounding version such as the New King James or the New Living Translation. Pick one you are comfortable with, one whose style and language is easiest for you to connect with. That will help make Bible memorization easier and more comfortable for you.
- *Pick out the verse or verses you want to memorize.* You can do this by topic or by whatever portion of Scripture you are presently studying. (While studying the Bible, some people like to jot down specific verses for memorization.) Read it through several times—silently

and aloud. Focus on the keywords in the verse and pay special attention to the meaning.

- *Write the verse down.* Write it in your study notes, on a note card—anywhere that makes it easy to review later. Many Bible readers are amazed to find out how writing a verse down word for word helps them to memorize it. They also find that writing verses down is helpful for review. If you write the verse on a note card, you can easily carry it with you so that you can look at it and reread it in those spare moments during the day. That goes a long way in helping you memorize particular verses or passages.

- *Don't try to memorize too much at a time.* There's an old saying about the best way to go about eating an elephant: one bite at a time. When you read your Bible, it can seem like a daunting task to memorize enough of it to make a difference. The key is to memorize it in amounts you are comfortable with. Start with three or four verses or passages a week and then see if you can take on more. Remember, different people have different abilities when it comes to memorization. Find your own pace and stick with it.

- *Work with a partner.* Like many other things in life, memorizing Scriptures goes better with teamwork. Memorizing Bible verses with a friend, spouse, roommate, classmate, or any other partner you can count on to consistently help you and challenge you gives you accountability as well as someone to quote Scriptures to when the opportunity presents itself. It's more effective and more fun, too!

Remember learning to spell in grammar school? If you're like most schoolchildren, you used flashcards that contained not just the spelling of a particular word but a picture of it. You can use homemade flashcards to help you memorize Scripture. It's an effective way to help you memorize, especially if you are working with a partner.

Personalizing the Scriptures

The message of the Bible is one of God's love and compassion for a needy, sinful, undeserving world. But have you ever stopped to think that it's also a message God sent just for you?

There is something about taking the Scriptures and personalizing them that makes them come alive, that further opens lines of communication with God and that empowers us to live the way God wants us as believers to live. When we personalize Scriptures, we go from saying "That's a great message" to "That's a great message just for me."

As you study the Bible, take the time to personalize what it says. Take the message of "God so loved the world..." (John 3:16) and make it "God so loved *me*." Think of "...God...will supply all your needs from his glorious riches" (Philippians 4:18) as "God...will supply all *my* needs from his glorious riches."1

When you approach Bible reading and study that way, you will begin to feel more and more connected, not just with the messages in the Bible but also with God Himself.

Meditating on the Bible

In some Christian circles, the word *meditate* (as well as variations of the word) is often greeted with both misunderstanding and fear. That is often because the practice of meditation is associated with Eastern and other religions, many of whose practices are in conflict with sound Biblical teaching.

However, the Bible does teach the practice of meditation, even using that specific word in several places. For example, God told Joshua, the man who would take up the mantle of leadership following the death of Moses, "Study this Book of the Law continually. Meditate on it day and night so you may be sure to obey all that is written in it. Only then will you succeed" (Joshua 1:8).

Also, the book of Psalms, a collection of prayers and songs of praise, starts out with these words: "Blessed is the man who does not walk in the counsel of the wicked or stand in the way of sinners or sit in the seat of mockers. But his delight is in the law of the Lord, and on his law he meditates day and night. He is like a tree planted by streams of water, which yields its fruit in season and whose leaf does not wither. Whatever he does prospers" (Psalm 1:1–3).

ALERT!

When you meditate on the Bible, it's a good idea to do it at a time when you don't have to attend to any other business, particularly the kind that requires your full attention (for example, driving or working with heavy machinery). Meditation requires that you give all of yourself to pondering and dwelling in what you read.

That is just one of many references to the Biblical practice of meditation in the Psalms alone that tells us very clearly and strongly that this is a practice God wants us to take part in—even daily. In fact, the psalmist makes it very clear that there is great spiritual blessing in meditating on God's law.

But what exactly does it mean to meditate on the Word of God? If you were to look up the word *meditate* in your dictionary, you'd find that it means simply to reflect deeply upon something or to ponder it. It means to spend time clearing your mind of everything but what you are thinking about and to think about it from every possible angle. It means asking God to show you personally what He wants you to comprehend.

For example, you can bring to your mind a particular verse or passage, pray over it, and ask yourself the following questions (and others you may think of) about it:

- What was God saying to His people when this was written?
- What is He saying to Christians in general through it right now?
- What is He saying to me personally today?
- What kind of changes should I make in response to what this is saying to me?
- How can I personally and practically apply the message in this Scripture right now?

When you take this approach to the Bible, you will likely find something wonderful happening in your own mind and spirit. You may find that you see and understand things about God and His Word more clearly and from a new angle. You may hear what is to you a new message coming from verses and passages—even some you may have read or memorized before.

QUESTION?

When is the best time and where is the best place to meditate?
You don't have to get under a tree in the middle of a field, cross your legs, and mumble chants to meditate. You can do it just about anywhere you can get alone, clear your mind, and contemplate what God is saying through a certain passage.

This is why prayer is such an important part of Biblical meditation. When you bring your thoughts and contemplations to God and talk to Him about them, He very often will speak back to you, giving you new thoughts and insights. When that happens, you will have "heard" the voice of God.

Praying with the Bible

Earlier in this book you read how the Bible is all about God's interaction with His people. Part of that interaction is the prayers Biblical characters—even Jesus himself—have spoken to the heavenly Father. Probably the most famous of Biblical prayers is what has come to be known as the Lord's Prayer:

Our Father in heaven,
may your name be kept holy.
May your Kingdom come soon.
May your will be done on earth,
as it is in heaven.
Give us today the food we need,
and forgive us our sins,
as we have forgiven those who sin against us.

And don't let us yield to temptation,
but rescue us from the evil one.
—Matthew 6:9–13

The Bible contains many other model prayers, and it is a good practice to read, memorize, and even use these prayers in our own devotional lives. Here are some examples:

What many people don't realize about the Lord's Prayer is that Jesus didn't necessarily instruct us to pray this prayer word for word; it was meant as a model for prayer. He gave these instructions in what has come to be known as the Sermon on the Mount (Matthew 5–7), and he began this prayer by saying, "Pray like this…"

- Joshua's prayer for God's help (Joshua 7:6–13)
- David's prayer for blessing (2 Samuel 7:18–29)
- Solomon prays for wisdom (1 Kings 3:6–15)
- a prayer for prosperity (1 Chronicles 4:10)
- Jesus's prayers for himself, for his disciples, and for others who would believe (John 17)
- Jesus's prayers for deliverance and strength (Matthew 26:39, 42, 43)

These are just a few of the hundreds of prayers found in the pages of the Bible. And in addition to the prayers listed here, there are several different kinds of prayers in Psalms. As you read through them, take note of how the psalmists offered prayers of thanksgiving and praise, prayers for various blessings, prayers for forgiveness, and prayers of faith.

When you read an example of a prayer in either the Old Testament or the New Testament, pay close attention to the tone and the wording of the prayer, and also pay attention to the way God responded to those who prayed the prayers. That way you'll be able to model your prayers after the Biblical ones that were most effective.

Praying God's Word Back to Him

It's one thing to pray the prayers of the Bible or to use them as models, but it's a whole new level of interaction and communion with God to actually pray the words of the Bible to Him.

When you read through Psalms, you're reading some of the most heartfelt, urgent, and loving prayers humankind has ever uttered toward God. It is in Psalms that we read of the writers' love for God, their faith in God, and their questions about God. They even at times express disappointment with God, or at least their perceptions of Him during the time of the writings.

In a very real way the psalmists demonstrate for us a principle concerning the written Word of God, and it's this: God loves it when we pray the very words in the Bible back to Him.

It may sound like a strange thing to do, but the truth is that this is a very Scriptural and effective way to use the words in the Bible. It's a way to access and even claim for ourselves His promises, His encouragements, and His warnings.

What's more, we can know that He will always respond to that kind of prayer. And how do we know this? For one thing, the Bible tells us, "And we are confident that he hears us whenever we ask for anything that pleases him. And since we know he hears us when we make our requests, we also know that he will give us what we ask for" (1 John 5:14–15).

E ALERT!

When you pray God's Word back to Him, make sure you know what you're asking for. Realize that while He will always answer, you can't know for sure how He'll answer. For example, praying for more patience could mean facing a series of situations where your patience is tried and stretched. Pray that way, but be prepared!

In other words, when we pray and request what we know is God's will in a given situation, we can be absolutely certain He hears and responds. For example, if we ask Him to give us more love for our spouses, He's sure to provide an affirmative response only because that fits precisely with the commands in His Word. It may not come in the way we expected, but we can be sure it will come.

Now, knowing that God hears our prayers when we request what pleases Him, is there any source more reliable when it comes to questions of what God wants for us than the Bible? When we read the Bible, we can understand that it contains the absolutely perfect will of God for us. And knowing that, we can pray the very words of the Scriptures to God knowing—not thinking and not hoping—that He'll hear us.

Earlier in this chapter you read about how you can personalize the words of the Bible, making them yours in a very tangible way. Now you can take that a step further, actually using those words as a basis for your very own communication with God Himself.

For example:

- When you feel doubt, you can pray, "Lord, your ways are perfect and you keep all of your promises. You are my shield because I look to you for protection" (based on Psalm 18:3).
- When you feel in need of peace, you can pray, "Lord, I have been made right in your sight by faith, so I have peace with you because of what my Lord Jesus Christ has done for me" (based on Romans 5:1).
- When you are tempted, you can pray, "Lord, the temptations in my life are no different from what others experience. And you are faithful. You will not allow the temptation to be more than I can stand. When I am tempted, you will show me a way out so that I can endure" (based on 1 Corinthians 10:12–13).

The Bible is a book filled not just with promises but promises made by the One who has the power and authority to fulfill all of them absolutely perfectly. You can make those promises a part of your life of faith, and you can also make them a part of your prayers.

The Word as a Weapon of Offense

Have you ever looked at your personal copy of the Bible and thought of it as a weapon? If not, then read on and you'll find out that the leather-covered book you carry with you to church and Bible studies—and, hopefully, that you take time to read on your own—is a devastating weapon when it's used correctly. The Bible is indeed a weapon, but it's a weapon in the kind of fight that a lot of people don't even know is going on right now: in the spiritual world.

All of the steps of Bible reading and study listed in this chapter are important parts of being able to use God's Word as a weapon of offense against the devil. When you make all these things a part of your personal Bible reading and study, you'll be more than equipped to handle anything the devil throws at you.

Paul wrote to the church in a city called Ephesus and told the people that they were to put on what he called "all of God's armor" (Ephesians 6:11) with which they were to do spiritual battle not against humans or human institutions but against "evil rulers and authorities of the unseen world," "mighty powers of darkness who rule this world," and "wicked spirits in the heavenly realms" (Ephesians 6:12).

In that passage, Paul gives the readers a rundown of the armor of God, including the belt of truth and the body armor of God's righteousness (Ephesians 6:14), shoes of peace (Ephesians 6:15), the shield of faith (Ephesians 6:16), and others. The last piece of armor Paul lists isn't really armor at all but is in fact a weapon of offense. It's what he calls "the sword of the Spirit, which is the word of God" (Ephesians 6:17).

It's no accident that God has revealed His written Word as a weapon of offense against the work and wiles of the devil. In fact, that is very clearly demonstrated in accounts in the Gospels that tell us of Jesus himself facing down the temptations of Satan (see Matthew 4:1–11, Mark 1:12–13, and Luke 4:1–13).

In Matthew's account of this story, the devil throws three specific temptations at Jesus, all of which Christ answers with the words "It is written" followed by a direct quotation from the Old Testament. Finally, Jesus completely repels the devil's attacks by telling him, "Get out of here, Satan...For the Scriptures say, 'You must worship the Lord your God; serve only him'" (Matthew 4:10). With that said, the devil had no choice. He left the scene utterly and completely defeated.

FACT

In the scene where Jesus faces down the devil and his temptations, it's interesting—and important—to note that the devil himself quoted Scripture to Jesus in order to tempt him. As believers, we need to keep in mind that the devil not only knows Scripture but also knows how to twist it to suit his purposes.

The Prince of Peace had successfully and decisively fought a spiritual battle against the one who was not just his spiritual enemy but also ours. And he'd done it using a weapon available to us all.

Paul's encouragement to the Ephesians as well as Jesus's victorious encounter with the devil demonstrates something all believers need to understand: When it comes to spiritual battle, when it comes to going toe to toe with the devil, there is no more powerful weapon at our disposal than the written Word of God.

As Christians, we face not only a spiritual enemy (the devil) who is in opposition to everything we do but also a world system that the Bible tells us is also an enemy (1 John 5:4–5). But we have a spiritual weapon that neither can stand against: the Word of God. For that reason we can answer every temptation, every trial, every discouragement, and every battle with the wisdom and truth of what God has already spoken.

- When the enemy says, "You're a miserable sinner," you can answer, "Yes, but I've been washed, sanctified, and justified in the name of the Lord Jesus Christ" (1 Corinthians 6:11).

- When the enemy says, "You're worthless and can't do anything!" you can answer, "On my own that might be true, but I can do everything through Christ who strengthens me" (Philippians 4:13).
- When the enemy says, "How could God love a miserable sinner like you?" you can answer, "While I was still a sinner, Christ died for me!" (Romans 5:8).
- When the enemy tempts you to sin, you can answer, "There isn't one temptation you can throw at me that people haven't seen before. Not only that, God is faithful to show me a way out of it before I give in" (1 Corinthians 10:13).
- And when the enemy starts whispering in your ear, trying to get you to worry, you can answer, "I won't be anxious about anything but instead I'll thank and praise God and pray to him about what I need" (Philippians 4:6).

It is true that our spiritual enemy has more ways to wage war against us than we, in our limited human understanding, can comprehend. But it is equally true that for every thing he can throw at us, we can have an answer, an answer from the very mouth of God.

Chapter 5

Genesis: Abraham's Amazing Faith

From this chapter through the end of this book in an actual Bible study, we are covering the Bible from beginning to end. You will now need your favorite Bible alongside you in order to read the verses, chapters, and larger sections that we comment upon. Just reading the summary is inadequate in terms of accomplishing the study objectives previously set forth. You will also need your Bible to answer the study questions throughout these chapters.

The Beginning of Something Big

Even if you have only a rudimentary knowledge of the Bible, you probably know that it begins, "In the beginning…" (Genesis 1:1). The fact that the book of Genesis, the first book of the Bible, starts with those words is only fitting because Genesis is all about beginnings. In fact, the word *genesis* means "origins" or "beginnings."

This first book of the Bible tells the story of the beginning of our earth and cosmos and of humanity itself (Genesis 1–2), the beginning of human sin and its consequences (Genesis 3–9), and the beginning of human civilization (Genesis 10–11). But the most important beginning in Genesis is the beginning of the Jewish race, the people through whom God would bring salvation to the whole world.

This chapter provides a character study of Abraham, the father of the Jewish and Christian faiths. His story is told in the twelfth through twenty-fourth chapters of the book of Genesis.

Abraham wasn't by any means perfect, but he was a man of obedience to God, full of courage and generosity. He was a man of prayer and a man who, while he made his share of mistakes, was true to his God. Above all, he was a man of tremendous faith.

If you want to know your Bible well and fully understand how it ties itself together, it is important that you know and understand the events in the life of Abraham. That is because he is the man God Himself chose to be the physical father of the great nation of Israel and also the spiritual father of all who put their faith in the God of the Jewish and Christian people.

This book is not going to cover every aspect of Abraham's life—that you'll have to do in your own studies. But it does give you an overview of the events that led to Abraham's becoming the father of God's chosen people, the Jews.

As you read through this chapter—and through the Biblical chapters that tell the story of this great hero of the faith—take note of how Abraham responded to the commands and promises of God, how he related to those God brought into his life, and how God blessed him and those who would come after him.

Abraham's Early Life and God's Calling and Promises (Genesis 12)

Abraham was born around 1950 B.C. in a place called Ur of the Chaldees, which was located about 200 miles southeast of the modern city of Baghdad, Iraq. At birth he was named Abram, which means "God is exalted." Abraham spent his childhood as well as much of his adult life living in Ur. It was there that he married a woman named Sarai (later Sarah).

Later, Abraham traveled with his father, family, and household from Ur to a place called Haran, some 300 miles north of Ur. He lived in Haran until he was seventy-five years old. It was at that time that Abraham received his very special and unique calling from God.

FACT

The book of Genesis doesn't say specifically why Abraham moved from Ur to Haran, but a New Testament reference says, "Our glorious God appeared to our ancestor Abraham in Mesopotamia before he moved to Haran. God told him, 'Leave your native land and your relatives, and come to the land that I will show you'" (Acts 7:2, 3).

After the death of his father Terah, Abraham received this call—and the promises that accompanied it—from God:

The Lord had said to Abram, "Leave your native country, your relatives, and your father's family, and go to the land that I will show you. I will make you into a great nation. I will bless you and make you famous, and you will be a blessing to others. I will bless those who bless you and curse those who treat you with contempt. All the families on earth will be blessed through you." (Genesis 12:1–3)

The Bible tells us that the land God promised Abraham's people would be Canaan, later known as Israel. It also shows us that God made Abraham the father of the great nation of Israel, through which he would bring a blessing to all nations and races in the form of Jesus Christ.

This promise was at the heart of the covenant (or contract) between God and His people, and it was carried through the centuries from Abraham through his descendants, starting with his son Isaac and his grandson Jacob.

Genesis goes on to give the account of the amazing life Abraham lived in service to his God. It wasn't without its stumbles and mistakes, but it was a life dominated by a faith and devotion to the God who called him to a high place in His kingdom and in human history.

Abraham did as God had called him to do, and he spent some time in Egypt before traveling to what would be God's land of promise, Canaan (Genesis 13). But that was just the beginning of an incredible story of Abraham's faith in and obedience to God.

Study Questions

○ What was Abraham's verbal response to God's command? What was his nonverbal response?

○ Read Hebrews 11:8. What did the writer of Hebrews say about Abraham's obedience to God's call to leave his home?

Reassurances and Promises for Abraham (Genesis 15)

Abraham had heard God clearly and believed, and he knew that God was going to make of him a great nation. But like so many believers who have chosen to follow God obediently, Abraham came to a point in his life when he needed some assurance.

First, the Lord gave Abraham what we might consider a general reassurance, telling him, "Do not be afraid, Abram, for I will protect you, and your reward will be great" (Genesis 15:1).

But Abraham needed something more specific, more concrete. "O Sovereign Lord, what good are all your blessings when I don't even have a son? Since I don't have a son, Eliezer of Damascus, a servant in my household, will inherit all my wealth. You have given me no children, so one of my servants will have to be my heir" (15:2–3).

God's answer to Abraham's specific question was itself direct and specific:

Then the Lord said to him, "No, your servant will not be your heir, for you will have a son of your own to inherit everything I am giving you." Then the Lord brought Abram outside beneath the night sky and told him, "Look up into the heavens and count the stars if you can. Your descendants will be like that—too many to count!" And Abram believed the Lord, and the Lord declared him righteous because of his faith. (Genesis 15:4–6)

Now God could have just told Abraham to just trust, obey, and wait for further instructions. But note as you read this passage that He gave Abraham exactly what he asked for, namely some specifics when it came to His promises. Also note that God gave him a concrete illustration of His promises: that his descendants would be more numerous than the stars shining in the nighttime sky.

One of the foundational truths of the Bible—that of the vital importance of faith for those who want to please God—is spelled out in the life of Abraham, of whom the book of Genesis tells us, "And Abram believed the Lord, and the Lord declared him righteous because of his faith" (Genesis 15:6).

After receiving such promises, you would think that Abraham would be willing to wait as long as it would take for God to move on his behalf. But as you will see in the next chapter of Genesis, Abraham made the mistake of moving out ahead of God.

Study Questions

○ Read Romans 4:1–22. What does this tell you about the basis of Abraham's relationship with God?

○ Read Galatians 3:7. Who does God count as the true descendants of Abraham (in other words, God's chosen people)?

Abraham's Big Mistake (Genesis 16)

Lest you believe that God only used the perfect—those who believed Him perfectly, obeyed Him perfectly, and lived their lives perfectly—to accomplish His purposes, just take a look at the actions of Abraham and his wife, Sarah, as they are recorded in Genesis 16.

FACT

It is commonly believed that the descendants of Ishmael are the Arab nations, who over the centuries have been at odds with the people of Israel. That is why the Arab-Israeli conflict has been referred to as the world's oldest sibling rivalry.

God had twice already told Abraham that he would be blessed, that he would be the father of a great nation, but Abraham couldn't leave well enough alone. Instead of trusting in what God had told him, Abraham—as well as his wife—became impatient and attempted to move out ahead of God and do for themselves what He had promised to do for them.

This is the Bible's account of that big mistake:

Now Sarai, Abram's wife, had not been able to bear children for him. But she had an Egyptian servant named Hagar. So Sarai said to Abram, "The Lord has prevented me from having children. Go and sleep with my servant. Perhaps I can have children through her." And Abram agreed with Sarai's proposal. So Sarai, Abram's wife, took Hagar the Egyptian servant and gave her to Abram as a wife (Genesis 16:1–3)

Sarah meant no harm or dishonor to God when she attempted—successfully, it turned out—to persuade her husband to father a child for her through her servant. In her mind, God himself had kept her from having children, and it was up to her to do for herself what God hadn't done for her.

In purely human terms, it's hard to blame Sarah. After all, she was seventy-five years old, had been married for decades, and still had no children. Being in a childless marriage was at that time and in that culture no small matter of dishonor, and Sarah was determined to take care of the situation in the best way she knew how.

However, what Sarah and Abraham did in this case was a big mistake, if for no other reason than it was an act of unbelief. They went ahead of God and attempted to do for themselves what God had promised to do for them. One result was a son God didn't intend for Abraham to father: Ishmael. Another was the conflict that ensued between Sarah and her servant Hagar.

Study Questions

○ What was Abraham's biggest mistake in this account?
○ How were God's promises regarding Ishmael similar to those regarding Abraham's still-to-come child of promise?

A Confirmation and a Name Change (Genesis 17)

In the seventeenth chapter of Genesis, God establishes the Jewish rite of circumcision, but not before again assuring Abraham, by now all of ninety-nine years old, of his calling and promises:

> *This is my covenant with you: I will make you the father of a multitude of nations! What's more, I am changing your name. It will no longer be Abram. Instead, you will be called Abraham, for you will be the father of many nations. I will make you extremely fruitful. Your descendants will become many nations, and kings will be among them! (Genesis 17:4–6)*

God had made a promise, an agreement with Abraham and with all those who would come after him. Abraham's part in the deal was that he and all of his male descendants be circumcised, an act that would have great spiritual significance:

From generation to generation, every male child must be circumcised on the eighth day after his birth. This applies not only to members of your family but also to the servants born in your household and the foreign-born servants whom you have purchased. All must be circumcised. Your bodies will bear the mark of my everlasting covenant. Any male who fails to be circumcised will be cut off from the covenant family for breaking the covenant. (Genesis 17:12–14)

In giving this command, God had appointed circumcision as a special symbol for His chosen people, a badge of their dedication and devotion to Him. And though Abraham was nearly a century old, he and his son Ishmael, who was thirteen years old at the time, were circumcised (Genesis 17:24–27).

ALERT!

The change from the name *Abram* to *Abraham* for the father of the Jewish and Christian faith is very significant because the name *Abraham* means "the father of many" or "father of a multitude." That was in keeping with God's promise that his descendants would number in the millions.

Though there were still episodes ahead in Abraham's life (for example, his intercession for the cities of Sodom and Gomorrah and their destruction as recorded in Genesis 18–19), he would live to one day see the miraculous birth of the son God had promised him.

Study Questions

○ Read 1 Corinthians 7:17, Galatians 6:15, and Colossians 3:11. What is the New Testament approach to circumcision? What, if anything, has taken its place in the life and heart of the believer?

○ Read Genesis 18:23–33. What does this tell you about the importance of praying for others, even those who don't seem to deserve it?

The Long-Awaited Birth of Isaac (Genesis 20–21)

It had been more than twenty years since God had promised Abraham that he and Sarah would have a son, but in an example of how God's timing isn't always our timing, God gave this couple their long-awaited son: "The Lord kept his word and did for Sarah exactly what he had promised. She became pregnant, and she gave birth to a son for Abraham in his old age. This happened at just the time God had said it would. And Abraham named their son Isaac" (Genesis 21:1–3). It was as if God waited to fulfill His promise just because He wanted to show Abraham and Sarah His power and ability to do the miraculous.

FACT

The name *Isaac* means "he laughs." That name has meaning in that it reflects the reaction of unbelief from his mother Sarah when she overheard it said that she was going to have a son in her old age (Genesis 18:10–15). At that time, Sarah was well past childbearing age.

As per God's instructions, Abraham had his son circumcised eight days after his birth. After Isaac was weaned, Abraham threw a huge party to celebrate. It was then that there were more conflicts between Sarah and Hagar, the mother of Ishmael. Sarah wanted to solve the problem by sending Hagar and Ishmael away. That is exactly what God told Abraham to do but with the assurance that Ishmael would be counted among his descendants and, therefore, would be the father of many descendants.

Later in Abraham's life he was confronted with the biggest test of his faith he would ever face, and it would involve his son Isaac. How he fared in that test would determine his place in God's plan to redeem humankind.

Study Questions

○ In what situations in your own life have you been tempted not to hold to your faith in God's promises but instead to run out ahead of God?

○ How do you respond when you read or hear of a promise of God that is a little hard to swallow?

Abraham's Big Test (Genesis 22)

In the Christian life we can talk all we want about our faith and how we are ready to trust God enough to obey His commands, even when they seem strange to us. But sooner or later we're going to have to put some action behind our faith. That is exactly what Abraham was challenged to do in Genesis 22.

After all Abraham had been through prior to receiving his promised son, Isaac, it must have been hard for him to understand what God had in mind when He gave him this command: "Take your son, your only son—yes, Isaac, whom you love so much—and go to the land of Moriah. Go and sacrifice him as a burnt offering on one of the mountains, which I will show you" (Genesis 22:2).

The story of Abraham intending to sacrifice his own son before God is a stark Biblical example of what God wants from each of us: that we be willing to give up to Him anything we have, even those things we very clearly know He has promised us.

Didn't Abraham hear God say that he would have many descendants and that they would be a blessing to all the world? How could this be? How could God ask him to do such a thing? Although what God had commanded him to do probably didn't make a whole lot of sense—and seemed so distasteful—Abraham obeyed God's directions to the very letter.

Early the next morning, Abraham and Isaac set out for Mount Moriah, the place where it seemed God was about to take away what had been promised so long ago. Abraham set up an altar and built a fire, then he prepared to sacrifice his son. But at the very moment of truth, an angel of God stepped in and stopped him, telling him, "Abraham! Abraham!…Don't lay a hand on the boy!…Do not hurt him in any way, for now I know that you truly fear God. You have not withheld from me even your son, your only son" (Genesis 22:11, 12).

> *Then the angel of the Lord called again to Abraham from heaven. "This is what the Lord says: Because you have obeyed me and have not withheld even your son, your only son, I swear by my own name that I will certainly bless you. I will multiply your descendants beyond number, like the stars in the sky and the sand on the seashore. Your descendants will conquer the cities of their enemies. And through your descendants all the nations of the earth will be blessed—all because you have obeyed me." (Genesis 22:15–18)*

From the very beginning this was a test for Abraham, a test to see if he would be faithful and obedient to God. Abraham needed to be tested in order to prove himself worthy to be the father of the people through whom God would bring salvation to all the world.

QUESTION?

According to the New Testament book of Hebrews, what did Abraham believe God would have done if he had actually gone through with sacrificing Isaac?
According to the writer of Hebrews, Abraham, so convinced that Isaac was the son he had been promised, believed that if he had actually slain his son, God would have raised him from the dead (Hebrews 11:17–19).

He passed that test, and because of that he stands as a Biblical example of faith, obedience, and faithfulness. That is also why his descendants were the foundation of the Jewish race and its calling, namely bringing the Savior into the world.

As you continue reading through Genesis, take a close look at the lives of Abraham's descendants, including his son Isaac, his grandchildren Jacob and Esau, and his great-grandchildren (those who would be the fathers of the twelve tribes of Israel), particularly Joseph.

Study Questions

○ How would you respond if God were to tell you to do something that just didn't make sense? How did Abraham respond?

○ What are some of the character qualities in Abraham that you want to emulate in your own life? What are some of his mistakes you want to avoid?

Chapter 6

Numbers: Standing Out from the Crowd

One of the many great things about the Bible is that it tells the stories of some of the great men and women of faith—people who might not have been smarter or more talented than most of us today but who had the nerve to believe God and to act on what they knew. In this chapter you'll read about two early heroes of the faith, Caleb and Joshua, a couple of guys who refused to believe the negative but instead focused on what God had already said.

Standing Alone in Believing God

The book of Genesis closes with the story of Joseph, the fourth-generation patriarch of the Hebrew nation. Exodus, the second book of the Pentateuch (the books of Moses, the first five of the Bible), picks up with the people of Israel living in subjection and slavery to the nation of Egypt.

The books of Exodus, Leviticus, Numbers, and Deuteronomy tell the stories of the leadership of Moses during the Jewish people's flight from Egyptian captivity (known as the Exodus), the giving of the law of God, and the Israelites' journey toward the Promised Land.

This chapter covers a tragic event in the history of the Jewish people: their banishment to the wilderness for forty years due to their own unbelief and disobedience. This story, which is recorded in the thirteenth and fourteenth chapters of Numbers, tells how the people of Israel listened to the negative reports of ten faithless Jewish leaders and ignored the reports of two who dared to believe God and His promises. Worse than that, it's the story of a people who completely rebelled because they just couldn't persevere in believing in a God who keeps His promises.

However, there is a bright side to this story, and it's one we should pay careful attention to as well. It's the story of those two faithful spies, Caleb and Joshua, and the reward they would receive because they dared to continue believing in God despite what they saw.

God's Reconnaissance Mission (Numbers 13:1–24)

God had taken the people of Israel on an incredible journey. Now the time had come for them to claim the land He had promised them. The people were encamped in a place called Kadesh, which was to the south of Canaan, the Promised Land. All that remained for them to do was to follow God's lead, go into the land, and claim it for themselves.

As God prepared His people to enter into the land, He spoke to Moses and gave him these instructions: "'Send men to explore the land of Canaan, the land I am giving to Israel. Send one leader from each of the twelve ancestral tribes.' So Moses did as the Lord commanded him. He sent out twelve men, all tribal leaders of Israel, from their camp in the wilderness of Paran" (Numbers 13:1–3).

FACT

This passage tells us that by the time Moses had sent the twelve spies to check out the land of Canaan, he had changed the name of one of the spies from Hoshea to Joshua (Numbers 13:16). The name *Hoshea* means "salvation," while the name *Joshua* means "the Lord is salvation."

This passage tells us that Moses did exactly as God had told him, sending twelve leaders—one from each tribe of Israel—to Canaan to check out the land. Moses told them to check out the land and the people who lived there. They were to find out if the land was fertile and to see how many people lived in the land and whether they were strong or weak. And while they were at it, they were to bring back samples of the produce that grew there (Numbers 13:17–20).

The twelve spies did as they were told, heading out on a forty-day trip around the land of Canaan. When that journey was finished, two of the men—Caleb of Judah and Joshua (or Hoshea) of Ephraim—would become symbols of faith, while the other ten would become living and dying lessons of the folly of unbelief and unfaithfulness to the commands and promises of God.

Study Questions

○ Who were the twelve spies and what was their significance to the people of Israel?

○ What were the specifics of Moses's instructions to the twelve spies?

It's All a Matter of Focus (Numbers 13:25–33)

When the twelve spies first returned to Kadesh to give their report, it must have appeared that they were about to give the go-ahead for the Israelites to go in and claim the land of Canaan. They brought with them a bundle of grapes so big that it took two of them to carry it, and they brought samples of the figs and pomegranates that grew there. However, they also brought with them a report for Moses that would, unfortunately, frighten and discourage the people of Israel to the point where they were ready to give up and go back to Egypt:

> *We arrived in the land you sent us to see, and it is indeed a magnificent country—a land flowing with milk and honey. Here is some of its fruit as proof. But the people living there are powerful, and their cities and towns are fortified and very large. We also saw the descendants of Anak who are living there! The Amalekites live in the Negev, and the Hittites, Jebusites, and Amorites live in the hill country. The Canaanites live along the coast of the Mediterranean Sea and along the Jordan Valley. (Numbers 13:27–29)*

The problem with this report isn't what the ten spies said about the land. These men freely acknowledged that there was a lot positive to be said about the land God had promised to give His people, that it was everything God said it would be and was a wonderful place to make a home for the people of Israel.

Focusing on the beauty of God's gift and on His ability to keep all His promises, the young spy named Caleb spoke with great confidence and boldness as he attempted to rally the troops for what he was sure would be a successful conquest of the land of Canaan: "We can certainly do it!" (Numbers 13:30).

ESSENTIAL

God had explicitly promised the people of Israel, through Moses, that He would drive the Canaanites out of the land so they could settle in it (Exodus 33:2), yet the ten cowardly spies said, "We can't do it!" Later, the psalmist wrote that the people actually hated the land because they couldn't believe God's promises (Psalm 106:24).

The majority in this group, however, didn't share Caleb's confidence. Instead of focusing on God's promises and on His power to do what seemed impossible, they focused on the giants, fighting men who they thought were unbeatable.

> *But the other men who had explored the land with him answered, "We can't go up against them! They are stronger than we are!" So they spread discouraging reports about the land among the Israelites: "The land we explored will swallow up any who go to live there. All the people we saw were huge. We even saw giants there, the descendants of Anak. We felt like grasshoppers next to them, and that's what we looked like to them!" (Numbers 13:31–33)*

Ten of the spies who had been sent to check out the Promised Land only saw the giants who stood in their way. But Caleb—as well as Joshua—saw the promises of God and His ability to keep those promises. For that reason, he was able to confidently encourage the people to go and take what God had promised them.

Sadly, however, it wasn't Caleb who had the people's ear. Instead of listening to Caleb, who was speaking the very words God wanted them to hear, they listened to the ten spies who were more than ready to give into their fears and stay right where they were—or worse, go back to the slavery and bondage in Egypt.

Study Questions

○ Who were the people that frightened the ten spies so badly that they discouraged the Israelites from entering the Promised Land?

○ What exactly were Caleb's words of encouragement to the people of Israel?

Our Latest Polling Data Shows... (Numbers 14:1–10)

The people of Israel had seen for themselves the miracles God had performed in bringing them out of Egyptian captivity and slavery. They had seen Him bring plagues upon the Egyptians because of Pharaoh's stubbornness, had crossed through the sea on dry land as Pharaoh's army descended upon them, had sung God's praises for their deliverance, had enjoyed His provision, and had heard His promises of a land flowing with milk and honey.

And yet, despite God's awesome demonstrations of love, power, and provision, they grumbled and complained—and rebelled—rather than simply accept and claim what God had already given them. All this because of some reports of giants in the land God had promised them. "We wish we had died in Egypt, or even here in the wilderness!" they wailed. "Why is the Lord taking us to this country only to have us die in battle? Our wives and little ones will be carried off as slaves! Let's get out of here and return to Egypt!" (Numbers 14:2–3).

FACT

Kadesh-barnea, the name of the place where this rebellion took place, is believed to mean "the holy place of the desert of wandering." After this, it remained a camp during the Israelites' wanderings in the desert. This is also where Miriam, the sister of Moses, died and was buried shortly before the Israelites finally entered the Promised Land (Numbers 20:1).

This scene was more than one of people complaining and voicing their fears. It spun far beyond that and became one of open rebellion by the people against Moses and Aaron, the men God had called to lead them out of Egypt and into the Promised Land. In an effort to calm the people and bring them back to a place of trusting God, Caleb and Joshua pleaded with them, first telling them how wonderful the land really was, then begging them, "Do not rebel against the Lord, and don't be afraid of the people of the land. They are only helpless prey to us! They have no protection, but the Lord is with us. Don't be afraid of them!" (Numbers 14:9).

But it was too late to quell the rebellion. The people talked openly about stoning Caleb and Joshua to death, and the only thing that stopped them was an appearance of the glorious presence of the Lord before them.

The object lesson of the account in this passage of Scripture is that it is important for those who want to live a victorious life of faith in God to make sure they are focused on the right things. Sadly, the Israelites focused on the size of the giants in Canaan, not on the bigness and power and ability of their God to keep each and every one of His promises.

Study Questions

○ What more than anything do you think caused the people of Israel to rebel and plot to turn back and return to slavery in Egypt?

○ What qualities did Joshua display to the people of Israel when he pleaded with them not to rebel but to continue on and take what God had promised them?

What Really Offends God: It's Spelled U-N-B-E-L-I-E-F (Numbers 14:11–19)

This passage starts with a demonstration of what God looks and sounds like when He is angry with His people, and it shows us exactly what makes Him angry: "How long will these people reject me? Will they never believe me, even after all the miraculous signs I have done among them? I will disown them and destroy them with a plague. Then I will make you into a nation far greater and mightier than they are!" (Numbers 14:11, 12).

What had God really peeved with His people was their unbelief, which led to their open rebellion. After everything He had brought them through, they still refused to put their trust in Him and move on and claim what was already theirs. Instead, they wanted to go back to lives of bondage and slavery in Egypt.

ALERT!

For a more poetic Old Testament description of this sad episode in Jewish history, read Psalm 95:7–11. The New Testament also makes reference to this event in 1 Corinthians 10:1–12, Hebrews 3:7–11, and Hebrews 4:1–11. All these passages spell out for us the object lessons in this story, and all of them involve lessons about faith.

But Moses had come too far with these people to give up on them. He earnestly pleaded for their lives, reminding God not of the worthiness of these rebellious, unbelieving Israelites but of the goodness and trustworthiness of His name and of His own love, patience, and mercy (Numbers 14:13–19). "Please pardon the sins of this people because of your magnificent unfailing love, just as you have forgiven them ever since they left Egypt" (Numbers 14:19).

In the end, God heard Moses's request and forgave the sins of the people of Israel. However, there would still be consequences for their unbelief and rebellion.

Study Questions

○ According to Numbers 14:13–17, how did Moses plead with God not to destroy the rebellious people?

○ Reread Numbers 14:18–19. According to that passage, what character attributes of God lead him to forgive the sins of those He calls His people?

Close but No Promised Land for the Rebellious Israelites (Numbers 14:20–38)

In one of the more tragic episodes in the Bible, and in the history of the Jewish people, a whole generation was lost in the wilderness simply because they couldn't obey God, which means they couldn't believe God and couldn't remember the things He had done for them previously. God had lost his patience with these wayward people, and it was only because Moses pleaded so ardently with Him that they didn't die on the spot (Numbers 14:13–19). And while God honored Moses's request and forgave these people their individual sins, there were still consequences for those sins:

> Then the Lord said, "I will pardon them as you have requested. But as surely as I live, and as surely as the earth is filled with the Lord's glory, not one of these people will ever enter that land. They have seen my glorious presence and the miraculous signs I performed both in Egypt and in the wilderness, but again and again they tested me by refusing to listen. They will never even see the land I swore to give their ancestors. None of those who have treated me with contempt will enter it." (Numbers 14:20–23)

Later on in this chapter, God tells Moses that no one over the age of twenty—except Caleb and Joshua, who believed God and pleaded with the people to do the same—would ever enter the Promised Land but would instead die in the wilderness. For the next forty years, every man, woman, and child who had left Egypt during the time of the Exodus would wander in the desert around Canaan but would never be allowed to possess it.

While this passages tells us what was to become of all twelve spies—the two who believed and the ten who didn't, Joshua 14:6–15 tells us what eventually became of Caleb because of his faith. Caleb believed God and acted on what he believed, and for that reason he became an example of the kind of faith God honors.

Other than Joshua and Caleb, no one in that throng of millions—not even Moses and Aaron—would ever see the Promised Land. Even those ten spies who came back with a negative report died as a result of their unbelief (Numbers 14:36, 37). The others were sentenced to spending forty years in the wilderness.

Study Questions

○ God pardoned the sins of the people of Israel, yet they still suffered the consequences. What does this tell you about the nature of the sin of unbelief and about the vital importance of taking God at His word?

○ This passage demonstrates the importance of both having faith and putting action behind your faith. What has God challenged you to believe Him for, and what kind of action are you putting behind that faith?

Going It Alone, or Trying to Anyway (Numbers 4:39–45)

Some of the Israelites eventually saw the error of their ways—more or less. Sadly, though, it was too late for them as individuals to receive what

God had promised His people. Still, they made plans to head into Canaan on their own. What's worse for them is that they didn't recognize that attempting to go into Canaan now was suicide. The reason? Moses explained to them:

> But Moses said, "Why are you now disobeying the Lord's orders to return to the wilderness? It won't work. Do not go into the land now. You will only be crushed by your enemies because the Lord is not with you. When you face the Amalekites and Canaanites in battle, you will be slaughtered. The Lord will abandon you because you have abandoned the Lord." (Numbers 4:41–43)

God had kept these people under His protection, given them direction, and provided for them everything they needed to take and keep the Promised Land of Canaan. But in spite of all that, they listened to the voices of those who didn't represent the Lord, gave into their fears rather than trusting in God, and rebelled against God's appointed leaders (and, therefore, God Himself).

FACT

Joshua, one of the two faithful spies who attempted to encourage the Israelites to take the Promised Land, later took the mantle of leadership for the people after the death of Moses. Before his death, Moses gave Joshua a public ceremony to name him leader. (See Deuteronomy 31:23.)

They had everything they could have wanted or needed, and they made the fatal mistake of not staying in that safe, secure place trusting and obeying the God who had proved himself far more than worthy of that trust and obedience. Consequently, not only would all of the adult Israelites who were present at Kadesh end up dying in the wilderness having never seen the Promised Land, but some of them would foolishly try to move into Canaan—despite what the Lord had told them. Again, they would pay a price for their disobedience, this time suffering a humiliating defeat at the hands of the people who presently lived in the land of Canaan.

While Caleb and Joshua would have to spend another forty years in the wilderness with their rebellious and faithless brothers and sisters, they would eventually be among the first of the nation of Israel to actually possess the Promised Land.

In fact, if you read and study the book of Joshua, you will see that he became one of the great spiritual and military leaders in the history of the people of Israel—and a man who holds his place in the faith Hall of Fame.

Study Questions

○ According to Moses's words to the Israelites who were planning to enter Canaan on their own, why was God no longer going to be with them in this endeavor?

○ What "giants" in your life are you focused on that keep you from obeying and enjoying what God has for you?

Chapter 7

Joshua: God Always Finishes What He Starts

One of the dominant themes in the Bible is faithfulness. God identifies Himself as being faithful in every way, and then He goes out time after time and proves it. And God also teaches in His Word that there is great reward in our being faithful, which means that we believe God and then act on what we believe. This chapter is the study of a man who believed God, acted on his faith, and then became one of the heroes of the Jewish and Christian faiths.

Time to Claim the Land

The book of Joshua tells the story of how the people of Israel—the people God had chosen to accomplish His plan of salvation for the whole world—at long last claimed and possessed the Promised Land that God had promised them centuries before.

Joshua (the man and book) picks up where Moses left off. At the end of Deuteronomy, Moses had died and been buried and "Now Joshua son of Nun was full of the spirit of wisdom, for Moses had laid his hands on him. So the people of Israel obeyed him, doing just as the Lord had commanded Moses" (Deuteronomy 34:9).

QUESTION?

Where does the name *Joshua* come from?
The name *Joshua* (originally Hoshea or Jehoshua) is a Hebrew name that means either "Jehovah is his help," "Jehovah the Savior," "the Lord is salvation," or "Jehovah is salvation." The name *Jesus* is a variant of Joshua.

Joshua was going to be God's faithful instrument in finishing what He had started through Moses. While Moses had led the people of Israel out of Egyptian captivity and slavery, Joshua was going to lead them into the Promised Land.

The book of Joshua is an amazing story of faith and obedience. But more than that, it is the story of how God always keeps His promises and how He finishes what He started. Though his people's disobedience, fear, and rebellion delayed their claiming of the Promised Land, God still kept His word. Though the people were forced to wander forty years in the wilderness, God still kept His word. And though their great leader, Moses, had died, God still kept His word.

Words of Encouragement (Joshua 1)

In the very first few verses of the book of Joshua, we see a theme that repeats itself throughout the book as God leads and guides and Joshua follows and obeys. Right away, God calls Joshua and tells him, "Moses my servant is dead. Therefore, the time has come for you to lead these people, the Israelites, across the Jordan River into the land I am giving them. I promise you what I promised Moses..." (Joshua 1:2–3).

And what had God promised to Moses but had been prevented from giving him because of his people's stubbornness? He goes on to tell Joshua:

- Wherever he walked, he would be on the land God had given him (Joshua 1:3).
- No one would be able to stand up against Joshua for as long as he lived (1:5).
- God Himself would be with Joshua and would never fail him or abandon him (1:5).
- He would be the one to lead the people of Israel as they possessed the land God had promised their ancestors (1:6).

There were, however, conditions to these promises, namely that Joshua be strong and filled with courage and that he obey everything God had commanded him and his people to do:

Be strong and very courageous. Be careful to obey all the instructions Moses gave you. Do not deviate from them, turning either to the right or to the left. Then you will be successful in everything you do. Study this Book of Instruction continually. Meditate on it day and night so you will be sure to obey everything written in it. Only then will you prosper and succeed in all you do. This is my command—be strong and courageous! Do not be afraid or discouraged. For the Lord your God is with you wherever you go. (Joshua 1:7–9)

Joshua wasted no time in getting the people ready to move out. First he called together the officers of Israel and told them to go through the camp and tell the people that they would be crossing the Jordan River in three days to take the land. Then he called together the tribes of Reuben, Gad, and the half-tribe of Manasseh and gave them words of encouragement and instruction.

The people didn't argue, question, or resist anything Joshua said. Instead, they enthusiastically told him, "We will do whatever you command us, and we will go wherever you send us" just as they had Moses.

With that, Joshua and the people made final preparations to do what their forefathers had been denied doing themselves because of their rebellion: Take the land God had promised them!

Study Questions

○ What precisely were Joshua's instructions for the people of Israel as he took the mantle of leadership in leading them at long last into the Promised Land?

○ How did the people of Israel respond to Joshua's leadership as he instructed them what to do next?

A Hero Named Rahab (Joshua 2)

One of the recurring themes of the Bible is God using the unlikeliest of people to do great things to further His kingdom and His causes. The second chapter of Joshua provides one of the best examples of this theme in all of Scripture as God gave a prostitute named Rahab a part in his plan to fulfill His promises.

Joshua 2 begins with Joshua doing something Moses had done years earlier: sending out spies (remember, Joshua himself was once a spy) and asking them to scout out the land on the opposite side of the Jordan River, especially around Jericho, which was considered the strongest fortress in the land of Canaan.

When the spies arrived in Jericho, they stayed at Rahab's home where, presumably, they would be safe. But when the king of Jericho was alerted that two men had come to spy on the land, he sent Rahab orders to bring the men out of her home and turn them over.

Rahab had hidden the spies in the house, but she told the king that, yes, they had been at her home earlier but that they had left and she didn't know where they had gone. If they hurried, she told the king's servants, they might be able to catch up with them.

With that threat taken care of, Rahab went to the hidden spies and told them, "I know the Lord has given you this land. We are all afraid of you.

Everyone in the land is living in terror. For we have heard how the Lord made a dry path for you through the Red Sea when you left Egypt" (Joshua 2:9–10).

ALERT!

Rahab's actions in saving the two Hebrew spies earned her mention in the New Testament—in the epistle to the Hebrews and the epistle of James. The writer of Hebrews pointed out that it was by faith that she did what she did (Hebrews 11:31), and James tells us that it was her actions that demonstrated that faith (James 2:25).

Rahab didn't mince words. She and her family and friends in Jericho were terrified because they knew that Joshua's God was supreme. But she then made one request, one the men were happy to grant since she had helped them out: "Now swear to me by the Lord that you will be kind to me and my family since I have helped you. Give me some guarantee that when Jericho is conquered, you will let me live, along with my father and mother, my brothers and sisters, and all their families" (Joshua 2:12–13).

The men swore to her that she and her family would be safe, and Rahab let them out of her home through the window—but only after hearing their terms for keeping her and her family safe. After that, they hid out and waited for three days, avoiding the search party that was looking for them to return. They then returned to the encampment and reported to Joshua what Rahab had told them.

Study Questions
○ What were the spies' conditions for making sure Rahab and her family would be safe when Israel took Jericho? (Read Joshua 2:17–20.)
○ How did the two spies know that the Lord had given the Israelites the land?

Crossing the Jordan (Joshua 3–4)

The people were encouraged by the reports the two spies had brought them, and almost immediately they were ready to cross the Jordan and take what

God had said was theirs. The morning after the spies returned, they left their encampment at a place called Acacia Grove, traveled to the banks of the Jordan River, and set up came there.

Three days after setting up camp on the riverbank, the officers of the Israelites went through the camp and instructed the people to follow the priests carrying the Ark of the Covenant at a distance of about a half mile, making sure they didn't come any closer. Joshua also told the people to purify themselves in preparation for seeing God do great wonders among them the following morning (Joshua 3:3–5).

The next morning everyone did as they had been instructed, and as they headed out the Lord told Joshua, "Today I will begin to make you a great leader in the eyes of all the Israelites. They will know that I am with you, just as I was with Moses. Give this command to the priests who carry the Ark of the Covenant: 'When you reach the banks of the Jordan River, take a few steps into the river and stop there'" (Joshua 3:7–8).

Joshua has been seen in Christianity as a foreshadowing of Jesus Christ (Hebrews 4:8–16). That is because their names mean essentially the same thing and because Joshua brought his people into the Promised Land as Jesus brings his followers into God's heavenly Kingdom. Also, as Joshua's leadership succeeded that of Moses, the gospel of Jesus Christ succeeds the Law of Moses.

Joshua passed along the instructions, including the promise that when the priests' feet touched the water, it would dry up and make a path for them to cross the river. It was the time of year when the Jordan was over-flowing its banks, but when the priests dipped their feet in the water, the water was held back and the people crossed over near the town of Jericho as the priests stood in the middle of the riverbed waiting for them to pass by (Joshua 3:14–17).

With everybody having safely crossed the river, God instructed Joshua to have twelve men—one from each tribe of Israel—set up a memorial to remember the miracle of that day. They were to walk back to the middle of the Jordan River and gather twelve stones to build the memorial. Joshua told them, "In the future your children will ask you, 'What do these stones mean?' Then you can tell them, 'They remind us that the Jordan River stopped flowing when the Ark of the Lord's Covenant went across.' These stones will stand as a memorial among the people of Israel forever" (Joshua 4:6–7).

Having obeyed everything God had told them to do, the people of Israel were now ready to take the land of Canaan. The warriors from the tribes of Reuben, Gad, and the half-tribe of Manasseh were ready for battle. And that day, Joshua was seen in the eyes of the Israelites as every bit the great leader Moses had been.

Study Questions

○ What do you think was God's purpose in having the people of Israel cross the Jordan River in such a miraculous manner?

○ What was God's purpose in having the twelve-stone memorial built?

Taking Down the Walls of Jericho (Joshua 5–6)

What had just happened at the Jordan River crossing wasn't good news for a lot of the kings west of the river and in Canaan. In fact, it was such bad news, that many of them were paralyzed with fear (Joshua 5:1).

But God was about to do even greater things among the people of Israel. After taking the time to re-establish among the people some of the covenant ceremonies, God made the final preparations in the hearts of the people for them to take the land—starting with the city of Jericho.

The people who lived in the walled city of Jericho were terrified of the people of Israel, and all the gates of the city were tightly shut with no one allowed to come in or go out (Joshua 6:1). But walls and gates meant nothing, because God had told Joshua, "I have given you Jericho, its king, and all its strong warriors" (Joshua 6:2). In this passage of Scripture, it's not the fact that God continued to remind Joshua of His previous promises but the way He kept the promise about the fall of Jericho that grabs the reader's attention.

God didn't tell Joshua and his fighting men to just go in and clean up, but instead instructed them to march around Jericho once a day for six days.

Seven priests, each carrying with him a ram's horn, were to walk ahead of the Ark of the Covenant. On the seventh day they were to march around the town seven times with the priests blowing the ram's horns. When the priests gave out a long blast on their horns, all the people were to shout as loudly as they could and the walls of Jericho would collapse, allowing the Israelites to charge straight into town (Joshua 6:3–5).

E ALERT!

The people of Israel were instructed specifically to not take anything from the city of Jericho except for the silver, gold, bronze, and iron—all of which were sacred to God and to be brought into the treasury (Joshua 6:18–19). The consequences of doing otherwise would bring trouble on the camp of Israel.

Again, Joshua didn't question God or try to provide what he thought of as a better plan. Instead, he did exactly as he was told and instructed the people precisely what God had told them to do. On the seventh day, the people of Israel got up at dawn and marched around the city as they had been doing all that week—except this time they went around it seven times. On that seventh lap, the priests sounded a long blast on their horns, the people gave out a shout, and the walls of Jericho came tumbling down. Every living thing in the city—human and nonhuman alike—was destroyed. Only Rahab the prostitute and her family were spared, as Joshua told them to go to her house and bring her out so that she and her loved ones would live. From then on, she lived with the Israelites (Joshua 6:22–25).

With the destruction of Jericho complete, Joshua invoked a curse on anyone who tried to rebuild the city (Joshua 6:26). God was with Joshua, and his reputation grew in the area.

Study Questions

○ Why do you believe God had the people of Israel defeat Jericho in such an unorthodox way?

○ Why do you think Joshua didn't question God when he was given the instructions for the defeat of the city of Jericho?

The Consequences of Not Following God's Instructions (Joshua 7–8)

After what had happened at the bank of the Jordan River and at the walls of Jericho, it seemed like nothing could stop the Israelites. All around the region, people heard what had been happening and they were terrified. But Israel's air of invincibility melted away as quickly as it was established as the Israelites were routed in a battle against Ai, a target the spies who checked it out believed wouldn't take more than a few thousand soldiers to take (Joshua 7:2–5).

FACT

The name of the ancient Biblical city of Ai means "ruins." It was one of the royal cities of the inhabitants of Canaan (Genesis 12:8) prior to the invasion of Israel. After the conquest of Canaan was complete, the city of Ai was rebuilt and inhabited by the Benjamite tribe of Israel (Ezra 2:28, Nehemiah 7:32).

Joshua and the elders of Israel, of course, were distraught over what had happened, and Joshua fell on his face and cried out to God:

Oh, Sovereign Lord, why did you bring us across the Jordan River if you are going to let the Amorites kill us? If only we had been content to stay on the other side! Lord, what can I say now that Israel has fled from its enemies? For when the Canaanites and all the other people living in the land hear about it, they will surround us and wipe our name off the face of the earth. And then what will happen to the honor of your great name? (Joshua 7:7–9)

The problem was spelled out in the first two verses of Joshua 7. A man named Achan had stolen and kept for himself some of the things God had said were to be set apart for Him alone. And because one man had violated God's commands, it was as if the entire nation of Israel had violated His commands.

God commanded Joshua to get up, then told him that the problem was that someone had broken His covenant by stealing and then lying about it (Joshua 7:11). God then told Joshua that in order to set things back on track, the people would have to purify themselves and make things right again.

After going through a process of elimination (Joshua 7:16–18), Joshua discovered that it was Achan who had caused the problems for the Israelites. He had stolen a beautiful robe, 200 silver coins, and a one-pound bar of gold and then hidden them under his tent.

It is in the tenth chapter of Joshua that the city of Jerusalem is first mentioned in the Bible. That city would later become the hub of all Jewish religious activity, the seat of government for Israel, and a place of conflict between Jews and Muslims and Israelis and Palestinians.

Once the wrong had been righted, and once the people of Israel repented for what Achan had done, God instructed Joshua to send the fighting men of Israel back to Ai. When they did, they defeated Ai decisively. After that, the covenant God had made with the people of Israel was renewed (Joshua 8:30–35).

Study Questions

○ What connection can you draw between obedience and God's blessing in this passage?

○ What does the account of the Israelites defeat at the hands of Ai tell you about partial obedience to God?

The Conquest of the South and the North (Joshua 9–12)

With the victories of Jericho and Ai behind him, Joshua then turned his attention toward leading the Israelites in completing the conquests of the peoples who had occupied the Promised Land.

The fame and fear of the Israelite forces was spreading in the area, but in chapter 9 of Joshua we read of the Gibeonites playing a trick on the Israelites that resulted in a treaty between the two. Instead of defeating the Gibeonites, the Israelites were placed in a position of having to defend them.

Chapter 10 begins with Adonizedek, the king of Jerusalem, beginning an alliance of five kings of the Amorites (himself and the kings of Hebron, Jarmuth, Lachish, and Eglon) and attacking the Gibeonites because they see them as traitors. The Gibeonites appeal to Joshua for help, so he attacks the Amorites and eventually defeats their forces and kills the five kings.

Chapter 11 describes the last phase of the Israelites taking the Promised Land. In chapter 10 Joshua had led his forces in conquering the southern part of Canaan, but in chapter 11 he is leading the conquest of northern Canaan.

The northern kings had joined forces in an attempt to stand up to the conquering Israelites, but Joshua led his forces in routing them, leading to the conquest of the entire land of Canaan. For the first time the land would enjoy a rest from war (Joshua 11:23).

Finally, what God had long ago promised the ancestors of the people of Israel had happened. They enjoyed a time of rest and security in their own land. Now all that was left to do was divide the land among the twelve tribes, an event that is recorded in Joshua 13–24.

Study Questions

○ What has God begun in your life that you know He will complete?

○ What tasks has God put before you that you know you must complete before you can fully enjoy His rest?

Chapter 8

First and Second Samuel: The Life and Times of David

While the Bible is filled with great stories and lessons on faith in and obedience to God, it's also a great book of history—especially when it comes to the early part of the history of the Jewish race. The books of 1 and 2 Samuel provide a great historical account as well as lessons we should learn from it. That includes the history of a man named David, the man who would become Israel's model for leadership.

David: A Legacy-Leaving King

One of the best-known and most highly regarded Old Testament characters is David, who reigned as king of Israel for thirty-three years, led his people to many military victories, established Jerusalem as the seat of government for Israel, and wrote many of the psalms that are in our Bible today. David is still seen as the most righteous king in the history of Israel, but as you study his life, you will see that he was far from faultless. Despite his personal weaknesses, problems, and sins, he left behind a legacy that affects the Christian and Jewish faiths to this very day.

While this chapter is by no means a comprehensive study of the man, it guides the reader in a Biblical study of the highlights and key events in David's life, starting with his being chosen to take over for Saul as king of Israel.

David Chosen as Israel's Second King (1 Samuel 16)

The prophet Samuel has just been informed that the reign of Saul as Israel's first king is about to end because he had fallen out of favor with God. As 1 Samuel 15:35 reports: "The Lord was sorry he had ever made Saul king of Israel."

But God had already picked out a replacement for Saul, and He called Samuel to go to Bethlehem and anoint that man. Samuel followed God's instructions to the letter, traveling to Bethlehem and finding a man named Jesse, who had a son who would one day replace Saul.

Samuel met with Jesse's first seven sons, but God let him know that none of them was the one He had chosen to be Israel's second king. Samuel said to Jesse, "The Lord has not chosen any of these" (1 Samuel 16:10). But Jesse had one more son—his youngest—who was out tending his father's sheep and goats. When David arrived, the Lord told Samuel, "This is the one; anoint him" (16:12).

The stage was set for David to become Israel's second—and greatest—king. But before that would happen, David would serve in Saul's court as a musician. King Saul was tormented by a spirit, filling him with depression and fear. Some of his servants suggested that they find a good musician to play the harp so that he could be soothed.

Saul agreed, and his servants told him "One of Jesse's sons from Bethlehem is a talented harp player. Not only that—he is a brave warrior, a man of war, and has good judgment. He is also a fine-looking young man, and the Lord is with him" (1 Samuel 16:18).

One important theme of the Bible—that God looks at the heart and not at outward appearance—is demonstrated in this story: "The Lord said to Samuel, 'Don't judge by his appearance or height, for I have rejected him. The Lord doesn't see things the way you see them. People judge by outward appearance, but the Lord looks at the heart'" (1 Samuel 16:7).

Saul agreed to have David come, and not only did he play the harp for Saul, he also became his armor bearer.

But in time, David would replace Saul in the minds of the people as their leader. That change would start as David faced down and defeated what appeared to be an impossible military challenge.

Study Questions
○ Where was Samuel to find David, and how would he know who he was?
○ Who did Samuel initially think would be David's replacement and what did God say about that man? (See 1 Samuel 16:6–7.)

David Prepares to Fight Goliath (1 Samuel 17:1–40)

Nearly everybody in our culture—especially those who like sports—knows what is meant by a David and Goliath story. That's when an individual or a team who is an impossibly huge underdog goes out and defeats an opponent they had no business beating.

The real-life David and Goliath story is found in the seventeenth chapter of 1 Samuel. It pits the boy-who-would-be-king, David, against a giant Philistine warrior, Goliath, who taunted the Israelites and King Saul, challenging them to send out a man to fight him.

The stakes in this fight were high, but there was no one to answer the challenge. Instead of sending someone out to fight, Saul and the people of Israel trembled in fear. It wasn't until David, only a youth at the time, arrived on the scene that anyone had the nerve to even think about fighting Goliath.

FACT

The Philistines, first mentioned in the Bible in the book of Genesis, were spread over the area of Lebanon and the Jordan Valley as well as Crete and other Mediterranean islands. There were in Biblical times a seemingly endless string of conflicts between the Philistines and the people of Israel.

The Bible tells us that a man named Jesse sent David, his youngest son, to take some food to his older brothers, all of whom were fighting the Philistines. While near the scene of the battle, David heard the taunts of Goliath and saw how the armies of Israel ran from the giant. That was all he needed to hear.

"What will a man get for killing this Philistine and ending his defiance of Israel? Who is this pagan Philistine anyway, that he is allowed to defy the armies of the living God?" David asked the soldiers nearby (1 Samuel 17:26). After a conversation with his brother, David approached Saul and told him, "Don't worry about this Philistine. I'll go fight him!" (17:32).

Saul's response to David was as one might expect. He pointed out that David was only a boy and that Goliath was an experienced warrior. Therefore, there was no way he could go up against him. But David wouldn't take no for an answer. He pointed out that he had been caring for his father's sheep and goats and protecting them from the lions and bears that came to find a quick meal, sometimes even killing them with a club. "I have done this to both lions and bears," David said, "and I'll do it to this pagan Philistine, too, for he has defied the armies of the living God! The Lord who rescued me from the claws of the lion and the bear will rescue me from this Philistine!" (1 Samuel 17:36–37).

King Saul finally relented and gave the lad his own armor—a bronze helmet and a coat. But when David put them on, he realized they wouldn't work for him because he wasn't used to them. So he took off the armor, picked up five smooth stones from a nearby stream, and, armed with nothing more than the rocks, his shepherd's staff, and his sling, headed across the valley to fight Goliath the Philistine.

Study Questions

○ What does the Bible say about Goliath's appearance? How big was he? What kind of armor did he wear?

○ What was the response of David's brother when he heard that David was inquiring about killing Goliath?

David Kills Goliath (1 Samuel 17:41–57)

The description the writer of 1 Samuel paints of David's initial confrontation with Goliath is a frightening one indeed. As the young shepherd approached this battle-hardened giant, he looked at David with utter contempt as demonstrated in the account of what he said to David at that moment: "'Am I a dog,' he roared at David, 'that you come at me with a stick?' And he cursed David by the names of his gods. 'Come over here, and I'll give your flesh to the birds and wild animals!' Goliath yelled" (17:43–44).

The sight of a nearly 10-foot-tall giant sneering down at you promising to turn you into food for birds and animals would be, to put it mildly, intimidating. But David answered Goliath with incredible confidence—the kind of confidence that only comes from absolute faith that his God would give him the victory:

You come to me with sword, spear, and javelin, but I come to you in the name of the Lord of Heaven's Armies—the God of the armies of Israel, whom you have defied. Today the Lord will conquer you, and I will kill you and cut off your head. And then I will give the dead bodies of your men to the birds and wild animals, and the whole world will know that there is a God in Israel! And everyone assembled here will know that the Lord rescues his people, but not with sword and spear. This is the Lord's battle, and he will give you to us! (1 Samuel 17:45–47)

As you read this passage, note that David had absolute and complete faith in God, and because of that he was absolutely sure how this battle was going to turn out. When Goliath began closing in to attack, David ran to meet the giant head on. As he ran, he reached into his shepherd's bag and took out a stone, placed it in his sling, and hurled it at the giant hitting him directly in the forehead.

The stone from David's sling sank into the giant's head, and he stumbled and fell facedown on the ground. David then ran over to Goliath, pulled the sword out of the Philistine's sheath, and cut off his head (1 Samuel 17:48–50).

Goliath had been the champion fighter for the Philistine army, and when the soldiers saw that he was dead, they turned and ran from the army of Israel, which chased them far away, killing many of the Philistine soldiers.

Study Questions

○ What was Goliath's response when he saw the boy David coming at him?
○ What did David say in return after Goliath had finished taunting him?

David and Saul (1 Samuel 18–27)

After David's overwhelming defeat of Goliath the Philistine, King Saul took him into his service permanently. However, it was an uneasy relationship because Saul became jealous of the attention Israel's future king was receiving from the people. What made things worse in Saul's mind was the fact that David developed a very close friendship with Jonathan, Saul's own son (1 Samuel 18:1–4). Also, Saul's daughter Michal fell in love with David and married him (18:20–21).

In a short time, Saul's jealousy turned to hatred, then his hatred turned into attempted murder. Saul, overcome by a "tormenting spirit," twice attempted to kill David by throwing a spear at him (1 Samuel 18:10–13).

ALERT!

The circumstances surrounding the election of Saul as Israel's first king are recorded in 1 Samuel 8–10. Like David, Saul had been anointed by the prophet Samuel and had received three signs confirming his call from God to be king. Saul received the Holy Spirit at that time, which made him "into a different person" (1 Samuel 10:6).

Crazy with fear, jealousy, and anger, Saul went on a campaign of persecution against David, even sending out his servants to find and kill him. David fled to a place called Ramah (1 Samuel 19:12–18), where he stayed for some time with the sons of the prophets. It wasn't long, however, before Saul found out where David had gone and tried to bring him back.

Jonathan, a loyal friend to David, tried in vain to change his father's mind toward David. When David found out that his friend had failed, he fled a greater distance from the king—first to Nob (1 Samuel 21:1–9) and then to Gath (21:10–15), a top Philistine city.

This was only the beginning of Saul's mad obsession with finding and killing David, who seemed only to grow in popularity with the people. Several times Saul seemed to have a bead on David only to have him escape. And on two occasions, David had the opportunity to kill Saul but spared him. "Surely the Lord will strike Saul down someday," David said, "or he will die of old age or in battle. The Lord forbid that I should kill the one he has anointed!" (1 Samuel 26:10–11).

Eventually, Saul's fall from grace led to his death—and the death of his son—at the hands of the Philistines (1 Samuel 31). It was the tragic end of what was once a very promising start for Israel's first king. David, on the other hand, was about to take his rightful place as the one God had anointed to be Israel's king.

Study Questions

○ What was Saul's response when he found out that his daughter had fallen in love with and married David?

○ Why do you think David spared Saul when he knew that Saul would have killed him in an instant if the situation were reversed?

David Takes the Throne of Israel (2 Samuel 1–5)

When David received news of the death of Saul and his son Jonathan—David's close friend—he was genuinely grieved: "David and his men tore their clothes in sorrow when they heard the news. They mourned and wept and fasted all day for Saul and his son Jonathan, and for the Lord's army and the nation of Israel, because they had died by the sword that day" (2 Samuel 1:11–12).

It was a short time later that David prayed and asked God for direction, which he received. God told him to go to Hebron, where he was anointed king of Judah at the age of thirty (2 Samuel 2:1–4). David's ascension to the throne was disputed, however, and that touched off a civil war in Israel. Once that war ended, David was anointed king over all twelve tribes of Israel (2 Samuel 5:1–12).

QUESTION?

What was the Ark of the Covenant?
The Ark of the Covenant was the gold-covered receptacle used to carry the two stone tablets that contained the Ten Commandments, which were seen as the testimony of God's covenant with the Hebrew people. You can find descriptions of the ark in Numbers 7, 10, 19, and 20.

From that time on, the kingdom of Israel, under the leadership of King David, went through a time of incredible expansion. David and his men captured the city of Jerusalem and made it Israel's new seat of government (2

Samuel 5:6–14), defeated the Philistines (5:17–25), and brought the Ark of the Covenant into Jerusalem.

Second Samuel 7 records God's promise to David, spoken through the prophet Nathan. That promise was that although David himself would one day die, his kingdom would, through his descendants, last forever (2 Samuel 7:1–17). After receiving that promise, David prayed a long and beautiful prayer of thanksgiving and praise (2 Samuel 7:18–29).

That was followed by a series of military victories that expanded and strengthened the kingdom of Israel (2 Samuel 8). God had promised David great blessings as Israel's king, and that promise certainly came to pass. However, there came a time when David's own indiscretions and sin could have sunk his monarchy.

Study Questions

○ Why do you think David would mourn at the death of Saul, a man who was his sworn enemy?

○ What was the tone of David's response to receiving God's promise of blessing?

David's Sin with Bathsheba (2 Samuel 11)

There are few Old Testament stories that make the kind of impact as that of David's sin with Bathsheba. In that story we see a man—a man God had called "righteous"—fall into sin so deep and ugly that it's easy to wonder how his name can still be mentioned in the Bible in any kind of positive light.

But the story of David's sin with Bathsheba—which included adultery, murder, and the lies and deceptions it took to try to cover those crimes—is not just one of a man who had fallen but also one of a man God picked up from a self-imposed pit of despair.

This tragic story begins as David, just up from an afternoon nap, looks out from the roof of his palace and spies the very beautiful—but very married—Bathsheba. Without even thinking about it, David sent for Bathsheba, who he is told is married to a warrior named Uriah who is away fighting at the time (2 Samuel 11:1–4).

Bathsheba did the only thing she could when the king of Israel sends for her—she went to him. A short time later she sent him word that she was pregnant. In an attempt to cover up his sin, David sends for Uriah and invites him to go home to his wife for the night before going back to the battlefield. Being a man of amazing integrity and loyalty, Uriah refuses to go home to his wife while his men are still out fighting (2 Samuel 11:5–12).

ALERT!

The story of David's sin is described aptly by the apostle James, who wrote, "Temptation comes from our own desires, which entice us and drag us away. These desires give birth to sinful actions. And when sin is allowed to grow, it gives birth to death" (James 1:14–15).

Since David's plan to cover up his sin has failed, he goes to plan B: have Uriah killed in battle so that no one will be the wiser to what has happened. David sends word to have Uriah placed where the fighting is fiercest so that it will be more likely that he is killed. That is exactly what happens, and when Bathsheba receives word of it, she is sent into a period of mourning over the death of her husband (2 Samuel 11:14–27).

Study Questions
○ Read 2 Samuel 11:2. What do you think was David's first mistake when it came to being tempted to commit adultery with Bathsheba?
○ What character qualities of Uriah do you think helped lead to his death?

The Consequences of David's Sin (2 Samuel 12)

It's likely that once Uriah was out of the way David thought he had gotten away with something. But as you can see throughout the Bible, there is nothing that escapes God's notice, particularly when it comes to his servants falling into sin.

God sent Nathan, a prophet of Israel, to see David and to tell him the story of two men—one rich and one poor—who lived in a certain town. The rich man had all the sheep and cattle he could want, while the poor man had one lamb that he and his children treated like a member of the family. One day the rich man had a guest he wanted to feed, but instead of killing one of his many animals for dinner, he took the poor man's lamb, killed it, and cooked it for his guest (2 Samuel 12:1–4).

David was furious to hear of such an injustice and vowed to Nathan, "As surely as the Lord lives, any man who would do such a thing deserves to die! He must repay four lambs to the poor man for the one he stole and for having no pity" (2 Samuel 12:5–6).

FACT

Psalm 51, one of many written by David, is his psalm of confession and penitence for what he had done in committing adultery with Bathsheba and murder against Uriah. The fourth verse of that psalm reads, "I have done what is evil in your sight. You will be proved right in what you say, and your judgment against me is just."

But what David didn't realize at that moment was that Nathan was talking about him and his sin against Uriah. "You are that man!" Nathan said. "The Lord, the God of Israel, says: I anointed you king of Israel and saved you from the power of Saul. I gave you your master's house and his wives and the kingdoms of Israel and Judah. And if that had not been enough, I would have given you much, much more. Why, then, have you despised the word of the Lord and done this horrible deed? For you have murdered Uriah the Hittite with the sword of the Ammonites and stolen his wife" (2 Samuel 12:7–9).

But this harsh word from God wasn't all King David would have to face because of his sin. In addition, he would face the following consequences:

- his family would "live by the sword" (2 Samuel 12:10)
- his household would rebel against him (12:11)
- his wives would be taken by another man (12:11)

- all of Israel would know about the consequences he faced because of his sin (12:12)

There was nothing else David could do but confess his guilt, which he did. And when he did that, Nathan assured him that God had forgiven him for his sin and that he wouldn't die. However, there was one additional consequence for David's sin—that the child he had fathered with Bathsheba would die. And though David begged God to spare the child, it died.

David then comforted Bathsheba, who was now his wife, and they slept together, again resulting in pregnancy. This time the child born to David would live and grow to be a healthy boy and the next king of Israel: Solomon (2 Samuel 12:24–25).

Study Questions

○ Have you ever committed what you thought was a harmless sin only to see its consequences mushroom?

○ What can you learn from Psalm 51 in terms of your attitude toward God and others in repentance?

Job: With Suffering Comes Wisdom

The Bible contains a lot of teaching about suffering and adversity, and some of that teaching comes in the form of human examples. Probably the best-known of those examples is Job, a man who suffered in every conceivable way. This chapter is a study of Job, the man who suffered loss and physical pain but who at the end came out of it with more than he had before, including a more refined and deeper faith in God.

9

God's Kind of Man

If there is a character in the Bible known for dealing with suffering and adversity, it's Job. The Bible describes him like this: "He was blameless—a man of complete integrity. He feared God and stayed away from evil" (Job 1:1).

Not only was Job a blameless man of integrity who feared God, he was also an incredibly wealthy family man. He had seven sons and three daughters and owned 7,000 sheep, 3,000 camels, 500 teams of oxen, and 500 female donkeys. He was, as the Bible calls him, the richest man in the area where he lived.

That doesn't sound like a man who knows a lot about suffering and adversity. But that is just the beginning of the story—in fact, it's just three verses into the whole book of Job!

ALERT!

The prophetic book of Ezekiel talks about the prehistoric fall from grace of Lucifer, who was one of many of the angels God created (see Ezekiel 28:1–17). This text indicates that Lucifer was expelled from heaven because of his pride and his desire to be like God himself.

Job had it all going for him, and it appeared that nothing could touch him. But out of nowhere came some tests and trials the likes of which Job had never seen. He lost his children, his wealth, even his health. And worst of all, he couldn't for the life of him understand why these things were happening.

Before this story ends, however, Job will again be blessed. And perhaps the best blessing of all will be the wisdom and strength of mind he earns by enduring some of the worst suffering you'll ever read about.

The Testings of a Lifetime (Job 1–2)

The devil believed that Job was a man who lived right and believed right simply because God had given him so much. In short, he was content and had no reason to do anything evil. So the devil challenged God to "reach out and take away everything he has, and he will surely curse you to your face!" (Job 1:11).

God took Satan up on that challenge, allowing him to take from Job everything he had but his health. In short order Job was met with one message of disaster after another. Job lost nearly everything: his livestock, most of his servants, even his beloved children.

Still, Job wouldn't curse or blame God. Instead, he tore his robe in grief, shaved his head, and fell to the ground and worshipped God: "I came naked from my mother's womb, and I will be naked when I leave. The Lord gave me what I had, and the Lord has taken it away. Praise the name of the Lord!" (Job 1:21).

FACT

Job is believed to be one of the oldest books of the Bible—if not the oldest. The authorship of this book is not certain (Jewish tradition credits Moses with writing it), but the story of Job is set during the times of the Jewish patriarchs—Abraham, Isaac, Jacob, and Joseph. The name *Job* means "persecuted."

Job had passed the first test, but the devil wasn't finished. Again he challenged God to let him touch Job's life, and again God allowed him to do it. This time the rules were a little different. Where before the devil wasn't allowed to touch Job's body in any way, this time the only limitation God put on the devil was that he could afflict Job's body but he couldn't kill the man.

Satan left the presence of God, sure that he was going to get Job to curse God. A case of boils covering a man from head to toe will do that to a man, the devil thought, and he was about to give this man of God his very worst.

Study Questions

○ What did God allow the devil to do to Job? What limitations were put in place?

○ How did Job respond to all that had happened to him?

With Friends Like These (Job 2–25)

The scene following Job's physical affliction is a disturbing and discomforting one At the beginning of his case of head-to-toe boils, Job sat in an ash heap, scraping his badly burning and itching skin with a piece of broken pottery. But if his physical agony weren't enough, he then has to deal with some well-meaning but ill-informed people who try to help him out in his misery but don't do much to lift his spirits. The first of those people was his own wife, who offered: "Are you still trying to maintain your integrity? Curse God and die" (Job 2:9).

ALERT!

The word *integrity* appears several times in the book of Job alone and many other times throughout the Bible, so it is obviously an important quality to God. For example: The Lord detests people with crooked hearts, but he delights in those with integrity" (Proverbs 11:20).

But as miserable as Job was—and as much as it must have hurt him to have his own wife advise him to turn away from God—Job maintained his integrity and did not curse or blame God in any way. Instead, he continued praising God through everything. But the situation was about to get more difficult for him, and it was made worse because of the attempted help of some well-meaning friends.

When a man like Job is going through difficult times, it is sure to get people's attention. When three of Job's friends—Eliphaz the Temanite, Bildad the Shuhite, and Zophar the Naamathite, as the Bible identifies them—heard what had happened to him, they traveled from their homes to go and comfort and console him. When they saw him, they hardly recognized him. And when Job finally spoke, it was as if they were the words of a man none of his friends knew: "Let the day of my birth be erased," Job began, "and the night I was conceived. Let that day be turned to darkness. Let it be lost even to God on high, and let no light shine on it" (Job 3:3–4). Job had gone from a man who seemed to have it all—including his integrity and his relationship with God—to a man who not only lost all his financial holdings and his very family, but also his health.

What followed was a series of conversations between Job and his friends. In those conversations they consider and debate the possibility that it is Job's sin that has caused his affliction. They talk about how Job needs to return to his God so that he can be healed.

Job's three friends assumed that Job's suffering was as a direct result of personal sin. Jesus put an end to the notion that all suffering was due to personal sin as he prepared his disciples to witness the healing of a blind man in the city of Jerusalem (John 9:1–5).

As the conversations and debates continue, Job's three friends prove to be little if any help to him. In fact, they are only making him feel worse—largely because they don't understand Job or his God enough to give comfort and sound advice to their miserably suffering friend.

What they end up doing is spouting a seemingly endless list of accusations concerning Job's life. Eliphaz tells Job that since God doesn't make mistakes, then Job must have done something to deserve this. Bildad says, "God is just, so just confess your sin!" And, finally, Zophar tells Job, "God knows you and he is dealing with you justly."

There was, however, a problem with what these men were saying. At least three times in the book of Job, we read that he was an upright man of integrity whose life pleased God. And because the three of them didn't understand Job, they came to some very wrong conclusions about God and about why He sometimes allows suffering.

Obviously, there was another lesson to be learned here. And before this ordeal is all over, Job will have to look someplace other than his three friends to figure out what it is.

Study Questions

○ How did Job respond to his wife's telling him to "curse God and die"?

○ What did Job's friends do with him when they arrived on the scene of his suffering?

The Prosecution Has Rested (Job 26–31)

Eliphaz, Bildad, and Zophar have spoken their last—at least as far as this portion of Job's life is concerned—and have stated in no uncertain terms that Job is at fault for his suffering, that there is some sin in the man's life that brought on all that has befallen him.

Job patiently listens to the accusations and recriminations before he finishes this emotionally charged debate by speaking a long monologue, starting with his thoughts about the nature and person of God. Job even sounds slightly optimistic as he talks about the power and understanding of God (Job 26), the unfailing justice of God (Job 27), and the unsearchable wisdom of God (Job 28).

ALERT!

As you read the book of Job, pay special attention to the contrasts between what Job says about God and how he believes God is dealing with him. Ask yourself how two such differing views of God and of His dealings with the people He so loves can be reconciled in the mind of the believer.

But Job also seems deeply discouraged as he says, "I long for the years gone by when God took care of me, when he lighted the way before me and I walked safely through the darkness" (Job 29:2–3). Obviously, Job felt as if he'd been abandoned by God—or worse.

He continues on in chapter 30 talking about the misery that his life has become. He is discouraged, depressed, and believing that he has been abandoned to his misery:

And now my life seeps away. Depression haunts my days. At night my bones are filled with pain, which gnaws at me relentlessly. With a strong hand, God grabs my shirt. He grips me by the collar of my coat. He has thrown me into the mud. I'm nothing more than dust and ashes. (Job 30:16–19)

Job is sure that God no longer sees him or what he's going through, that he is completely alone, or that, worse yet, God is going out of His way to bring him more harm and misery. Finally, Job closes his monologue by taking a personal spiritual inventory (Job 31) in which he finds that he has indeed lived a life that is pleasing to God.

Yet Job is suffering. As far as he knows he's done nothing to deserve what is happening to him, yet he's in the worst place he could be and still be alive. Why is that? He's close to finding out.

Study Questions

○ Read chapters 26–28. Despite his own terrible suffering, what is Job's view of the person of God?

○ What part does Job believe God Himself plays in his suffering?

Elihu: Some Angry Words (Job 32–37)

With Job's three friends now reduced to silence—and Job still left wondering why he's being tormented—a younger voice speaks up to talk about the situation. Elihu, who is identified as the "son of Barakel the Buzite," is angry and he wants to have some words with Job.

Elihu challenges Job's notion that he is innocent of all sin and that God had counted him as an enemy. He speaks up and defends the justice, the goodness, the mercy, and the righteousness of God—all of which he believes that Job has wrongly maligned, and he tells Job that he has sinned by speaking ignorantly about God (Job 34:1–35:36).

Elihu pointed out something important to Job, namely that God could have been speaking through his suffering: "God speaks again and again, though people do not recognize it. He speaks in dreams, in visions of the night, when deep sleep falls on people as they lie in their beds. He whispers in their ears and terrifies them with warnings" (Job 33:14–16).

Elihu goes to great pains to proclaim the majesty and greatness of God (Job 36:24–37:24), and he encourages Job to, "stop and consider the wonderful miracles of God!" (Job 37:14). At the end of his speech, Elihu tells Job, "We cannot imagine the power of the Almighty, yet he is so just and merciful that he does not oppress us. No wonder people everywhere fear him. People who are truly wise show him reverence" (Job 37:23–24).

Elihu has verbally chastised Job, has tried to correct his notions of the goodness and justice of God, and has tried to remind him that God is a powerful, merciful Creator who doesn't try to harm or oppress His people. While Elihu, like Job's other three friends, wasn't perfect in his scrutiny of Job's situation, it may well be that he prepared Job to hear from the One who could give him the answers he needed—although they weren't necessarily the answers he would have sought.

Study Questions

○ Reread Job 32:3. What was wrong with the counsel Job's three friends had given him?

○ Read Job 33:8–33. How does Elihu believe Job should see his suffering?

Time for Ultimate Wisdom (Job 38–39)

For most of the book of Job, it seems as if God has stood back and silently eavesdropped on the conversations between Job and his wife, Job and his three friends, then Job and Elihu. After listening as others tried in vain to explain what He had allowed to happen to Job, God answered Job directly and in a spectacular fashion: out of a whirlwind. But God had some questions of His own to pose, questions designed to take Job to a place he couldn't have expected.

The first question God posed to Job is, "Where were you when I laid the foundations of the earth? Tell me, if you know so much" (Job 38:4). Over the next two chapters (Job 38–39), God poses one question after another, all of which lead Job to one conclusion: He's talking to his Creator, and He's a Creator filled with power and wisdom.

As the questioning continues, God asks Job some very pointed questions: "Have you ever commanded the morning to appear and caused the dawn to rise in the east?" (Job 38:12). "Have you explored the springs from which the seas come? Have you walked about and explored their depths?" (Job 38:16). "Can you hold back the movements of the stars?" (Job 38:31). "Can you shout to the clouds and make it rain?" (Job 38:34).

FACT

For thirty-seven chapters we have read of the suffering of Job and of the questions that suffering brought to his mind. However, not one of those questions is answered. Instead of giving Job what he wanted and thought he needed—namely, answers to his questions—God gives Job a closeup explanation and look at His person and glory.

Job can only listen as God makes His point. Job can't answer—though he knows the answers to all those questions is "No!"—but he does come to an understanding of who he is talking to. God had reminded Job of some valuable pieces of information, all of which would benefit him over the remainder of his life:

- God is the Creator, and Job was the created one.
- God is in control, and Job is at the mercy of what happens around him.
- God is infinite in his wisdom, and Job cannot understand lofty things.
- God is all-powerful, and Job is limited in what he can do.

With the questioning concerning who was the Creator and who was the created finished, God poses the question: "Do you still want to argue with the Almighty? You are God's critic, but do you have the answers?" (Job 40:2). Of course, Job realized he had spoken out of turn—far out of turn: "I am nothing—how could I ever find the answers? I will cover my mouth with my hand. I have said too much already. I have nothing more to say" (Job 40:4–5).

Study Questions

❍ What criticisms or questions have you had of God, and how did He use them to teach you more about Him and help you to know Him better?

❍ What is your response when you are faced with a situation in which you feel out of control or that makes no sense?

Who God Is in the Midst of All Things (Job 40–42)

God then changes the direction of His questions, leading Job to an even deeper understanding of how big and powerful the Lord is and how small Job really is (Job 40–41).

Job can do nothing but acknowledge what God has been teaching him: "I know that you can do anything, and no one can stop you. You asked, 'Who is this that questions my wisdom with such ignorance?' It is I—and I was talking about things I knew nothing about, things far too wonderful for me" (Job 42:2–3).

Job is an Old Testament example of what God says in the New Testament about how he can use adversity and suffering: "And we know that God causes everything to work together for the good of those who love God and are called according to his purpose for them" (Romans 8:28). Job didn't deserve to suffer, but God used that suffering for his own good.

Finally, God has taken Job where He wanted His servant to go. And while Job may still not understand the reasons or the purposes for his suffering, he knows and understands God as he hadn't before. Job can only respond: "I had only heard about you before, but now I have seen you with my own eyes. I take back everything I said, and I sit in dust and ashes to show my repentance" (Job 42:5–6).

Job has learned what God wanted him to learn through his suffering. And because of that, he is a blessed man. In addition to even greater wisdom, Job was given back the fortune he had lost—twice over! (Job 42:10). Job lived 140 years after his afflictions before dying as an old man who had lived a good life (Job 42:17).

Study Questions

○ What do you think your prayers would sound like if you were angry and frustrated—maybe even at God Himself—at your own misfortune or suffering?

○ Do you believe it is ever right or appropriate to voice objections over your life situation to God?

Chapter 10

Isaiah: A Word Picture of Jesus

This may come as a surprise to a lot of people who don't know the Bible well, but references to Jesus Christ aren't limited to the New Testament. It was as far back as the book of Genesis that the Bible tells us of the coming Savior/Messiah. Probably the richest Old Testament book when it comes to references to Jesus Christ is that of Isaiah, which contains more than one hundred prophecies foretelling everything from the circumstances surrounding his birth to the events leading up to his death on the cross.

Beautiful Reading and a Whole Lot More

In purely literary terms, the book of Isaiah—the twenty-third book in the Old Testament—is hard to beat. It is written poetically and contains many descriptions that are beautiful as well as bleak, frightening as well as encouraging, and gloomy as well as hopeful. It is a book that has been studied, mulled over, and taken apart word by word over the centuries.

But Isaiah's prophetic book is far more than simple literature; it is also a collection of messages about judgment and salvation—both of which come from the same God. The first thirty-nine chapters of Isaiah are filled with pronouncements of judgment on an immoral and idolatrous people, but the final twenty-seven chapters are the declaration of a message of hope and salvation, not just for the people of Judah but also for the whole world.

QUESTION?

What does the name *Isaiah* mean?
The name *Isaiah* literally means "salvation of Jehovah," and the dual themes of the book of Isaiah are the judgment of God on a wayward people and the salvation for those who would turn back to Him.

Isaiah carried out his prophetic ministry to the people of Judah over a period of at least forty years. It was during this time that he warned and encouraged, and he saw not just what was happening in the world around him but also how God would finally accomplish His plan of salvation for all humankind.

The book of Isaiah is the most quoted Old Testament book in the New Testament. That includes many references in the Gospels—Matthew, Mark, Luke, and John. Matthew's gospel contains many references to events in the life of Jesus Christ fulfilling what the prophet Isaiah had written some seven centuries before Jesus's birth.

Isaiah saw in the future a Messiah—a Savior—who would come both as a suffering servant and as a conquering king.

Jesus's Own Family Tree

The Old Testament contains other prophecies concerning the family tree of the Messiah and about his background, which God had foreordained. Included in that list are the following:

- He would be a descendant of King David (2 Samuel 7:16)
- He would be born of the "seed" of a woman (Genesis 3:15)
- He would be born in the city of Bethlehem (Micah 5:2)
- He would be God's own Son (Proverbs 30:4)
- He would be a prophet (Deuteronomy 18:15–19)
- Angels would worship him (Deuteronomy 32:43)

However, it is in the book of Isaiah where we find the greatest number—and the best known—of the prophecies of the coming of Jesus Christ.

Isaiah's prophecies include this passage, which has become a popular one to read around Christmastime: "All right then, the Lord himself will give you the sign. Look! The virgin will conceive a child! She will give birth to a son and will call him Immanuel" (Isaiah 7:14).

ALERT!

Isaiah 9:1–2 tells us the wonderful news that the Jewish Messiah wouldn't be for the Jews only but also for Gentiles. "The people who walk in darkness will see a great light—a light that will shine on all who live in the land where death casts its shadow."

This verse foretells one of the events that is central to the Christian faith, namely that the Messiah—Jesus Christ—would be conceived in a miraculous way and that his mother would remain a physical virgin at the time of his birth. This event is recorded beautifully in the gospels of Matthew (1:18) and Luke (1:26–35).

Isaiah also recorded this prophecy, which we also associate with Christmas celebrations:

For a child is born to us, a son is given to us. The government will rest on his shoulders. And he will be called: Wonderful Counselor, Mighty God, Everlasting Father, Prince of Peace. His government and its peace will never end. He will rule with fairness and justice from the throne of his ancestor David for all eternity. The passionate commitment of the Lord of Heaven's Armies will make this happen! (Isaiah 9:6–7)

When you think of the some of the songs and poems we associate with Christmas or some of the names by which Jesus is known even today, think of the prophet Isaiah who foretold that Jesus Christ would come to earth to be for us.

Study Questions

○ By what name is Jesus referred to in Isaiah 7:14?
○ What are the names of Jesus Christ in Isaiah 9:6–7?

What Kind of Man Is This? (Isaiah 11)

The eleventh chapter of Isaiah begins, "Out of the stump of David's family will grow a shoot—yes, a new Branch bearing fruit from the old root" (Isaiah 11:1). This tells us that Jesus would be a descendant of King David, the fulfillment of which is found in the first chapter of Matthew.

But Isaiah didn't just write in this chapter about the events and circumstances having to do with the earthly ancestors, birth, and life of Jesus Christ. He also wrote about the kind of person he would be and the things he would do.

This passage tells us even more wonderful facts about the Jesus Christ that Isaiah saw centuries before his birth. Isaiah tells us that God's Spirit would rest on Jesus (Isaiah 11:2), that he would have exceptional wisdom and understanding and fear of God (11:2), that he would love obeying God the Father (11:3), and that he would be a righteous and fair judge (11:3–4).

Each of the four Gospels look sat the life of Jesus from different perspectives and focuses on different aspects of his person. The Gospel of Mark presents Jesus as Isaiah did in Isaiah 42—as a humble servant of God and of those he came to save from their sin.

Later on, Isaiah presents a picture of the Messiah who comes to earth to serve God and to serve those who are so desperately in need of the works he was going to perform during his earthly ministry:

Look at my servant, whom I strengthen. He is my chosen one, who pleases me. I have put my Spirit upon him. He will bring justice to the nations. He will not shout or raise his voice in public. He will not crush the weakest reed or put out a flickering candle. He will bring justice to all who have been wronged. He will not falter or lose heart until justice prevails throughout the earth. Even distant lands beyond the sea will wait for his instruction. (Isaiah 42:1–4)

Jesus came to earth and taught a new and radical kind of justice, mercy, and grace, and all those things were in keeping with what God had said centuries before Christ's birth through the prophet Isaiah as well as others.

Study Questions
○ Reread Isaiah 11:1–5. What attributes of Jesus Christ did Isaiah recognize?
○ According to Isaiah 42:1–4, what works will the Messiah perform while on earth?

The Miracle-Working Messiah

If you've studied the life of Jesus as it is recorded in the Gospels, you know that Jesus was a miracle worker who performed great wonders such as turning water into wine (his first recorded miracle), feeding thousands of people with next to no food, calming storms, healing the sick, walking on water, and raising the dead.

Isaiah wrote of the coming Messiah: "And when he comes, he will open the eyes of the blind and unplug the ears of the deaf. The lame will leap like a deer, and those who cannot speak will sing for joy! Springs will gush forth in the wilderness, and streams will water the wasteland" (35:5–6).

QUESTION?

What are the benefits of studying Isaiah's prophecies about Jesus?
There are several, but let's concentrate on two here. First, you get to know who Jesus was and learn to know him better on a personal basis. Second, you build up your faith through knowing that all the things surrounding Jesus's life—including the things he did—had been promised centuries before.

This passage lists a few of the specifics of Jesus's ministry of miracle healing—giving sight to the blind, giving hearing to the deaf, and allowing the disabled to walk—and if you read the Gospels you'll see Jesus performing these miracles repeatedly. Here are a few references for you to look up when you have the time:

- healed people of leprosy (Matthew 8:2, Luke 17:11)
- healed people who were paralyzed (Mark 2:3)
- gave sight to the blind (Matthew 9:27, Luke 18:35, John 9:1)
- gave hearing to the deaf (Mark 7:31)
- raised people from the dead (Mark 5:22, 35; John 7:11, John 11:43)
- healed and freed the demon-possessed (Luke 8:26, Matthew 9:32, Luke 4:33, Matthew 12:22)

While this list is a good starting place to look at some of the miracles of Jesus and how they line up with the prophecies of Isaiah, realize that there are many more examples of Jesus's miracles recorded in the Gospels. In addition to the healing miracles, Jesus also demonstrated power over the weather, over nature, and over earthly events.

Study Questions

○ Read John 10:25 and 14:11. What was the purpose of Jesus's miracles?

○ Read John 2:13–19. How did the Jewish religious leadership approach miracles in that account?

The Rejected Messiah (Isaiah 49)

Jesus came to earth as everything the Jewish people had long waited for. From centuries past came the promises from Isaiah and other Old Testament prophets that a Messiah would come and deliver the people of Israel from oppression.

Yet when Jesus came, he was rejected. He performed great miracles, preached and spoke with incredible power, and demonstrated authority over all things spiritual and physical. And despite all that, his own people rejected him.

ALERT!

Isaiah was far from the only prophet to foretell that the Messiah would be despised and rejected. The Messiah was also referred to as the "stone" rejected by the Jewish people (Psalm 118). Zechariah 11:4–6 also tells us that the Messiah would be rejected in favor of another king, which John 19:13–15 explicitly states is the Roman Emperor Caesar.

That, however, didn't just happen. The Old Testament prophecies tell us that the Messiah, among other things:

- would come at a time of unfit leaders in Israel (Zechariah 11:4–6)
- would not be believed by his own brothers (Psalm 69:8)
- would have national and religious leaders conspire against him (Psalm 22)

Isaiah himself foretold the rejection of the Messiah by his own people: "The Lord, the Redeemer and Holy One of Israel, says to the one who is despised and rejected by the nations, to the one who is the servant of rulers:

'Kings will stand at attention when you pass by. Princes will also bow low because of the Lord, the faithful one, the Holy One of Israel, who has chosen you" (Isaiah 49:7).

Jesus knew the truth of what Isaiah wrote hundreds of years earlier. He knew that part of his earthly mission was to be rejected by a world that wasn't willing or able to understand who he was and what he wanted from all of humanity. And while the Gospels tell us Jesus was welcomed into Jerusalem with a wild celebration just a week before his death, it was only a matter of time before he would face the ultimate rejection by humankind: death on a cross.

Study Questions

○ Why do you think the Jewish people rejected Jesus when he fulfilled so many prophecies of the coming Messiah?

○ According to Isaiah 49:7, what will be the world's ultimate response to the Messiah?

The Suffering and Death of the Messiah (Isaiah 50–53)

Isaiah chapters 50 through 53 refer to Jesus Christ as what has been called "the Suffering Messiah" or "the Suffering Servant." Indeed those four chapters are filled with references to the mistreatment and horrible death of Jesus Christ on a cross of wood.

You read in the last section of this chapter how Jesus's own countrymen rejected him as the Messiah. But there would be more to this story than the people's refusal to believe Jesus and who he claimed to be. This rejection would lead Jesus to his ultimate earthly mission: his sacrificial death.

What is most amazing about this portion of Isaiah's book is the details concerning the Crucifixion of Jesus Christ—details we can easily read of in the Gospels, all four of which give glimpses into the death of the Lord. From a purely human and physical standpoint, it is a brutal picture.

Isaiah 50:6 tells the account of a Messiah who would be brutally—yet willingly—beaten about the face and back, mocked and humiliated, have his beard pulled out, and spit upon: "I offered my back to those who beat me and my cheeks to those who pulled out my beard. I did not hide my face from mockery and spitting."

Later, in chapter 52, Isaiah records that the physical abuse and beating of the Messiah would be so severe that, "many were amazed when they saw him. His face was so disfigured he seemed hardly human, and from his appearance, one would scarcely know he was a man" (52:14).

FACT

Although Isaiah paints a poignant picture of a suffering and dying Jesus Christ, one of the best Old Testament prophecies concerning the crucified Christ appears is Psalm 22, which tells us that the Messiah's hands and feet would be pierced (Psalm 22:16), that he would be mocked (Psalm 22:8), that he would cry out to God but be forsaken (Psalm 22:1).

Isaiah tells us that all these things would happen to the Messiah despite the fact that he was innocent of any crime (Isaiah 53:9), despite the fact that he said nothing to his accusers (53:7). He would suffer great sorrow and grief (53:3), would be oppressed and afflicted (53:7), and would be thought of as cursed by God (53:4).

But all of these things didn't happen to the Messiah Jesus Christ for nothing. Isaiah explains that these things happened so that each and every one of us who put our faith in him can be healed, saved, and forgiven:

Yet it was our weaknesses he carried; it was our sorrows that weighed him down. And we thought his troubles were a punishment from God, a punishment for his own sins! But he was pierced for our rebellion, crushed for our sins. He was beaten so we could be whole. He was whipped so we could be healed. All of us, like sheep, have strayed away. We have left God's paths to follow our own. Yet the Lord laid on him the sins of us all. (Isaiah 53:4–6)

This is the central message of the whole Bible: that God saw a human race so lost and weak and enslaved to sin and corruption that it was completely unable to do anything to improve itself, much less save itself. But because of the amazing love of God, "it was the Lord's good plan to crush him and cause him grief. Yet when his life is made an offering for sin, he will have many descendants" (Isaiah 53:10).

Prophecies aren't really prophecies unless they come true. The incredibly accurate fulfillment of Isaiah's "Suffering Servant" prophecies is found in, among other places, Matthew 26:67 and 27:26, which describe the beatings and abuse Jesus endured.

The New Testament tells us that Jesus willingly gave himself up for our sins, and because of that we are able to find healing and forgiveness, enjoy fellowship with God the Father, and inherit an eternal home in heaven. That is the message Isaiah preached, and it's the message Jesus lived out in every way, including dying a horrible death for all of us on a cross.

Study Questions

○ Read John 3:16 then Isaiah 53:10. How would you describe God's attitude and heart in sending Jesus to live and die for all of us?

○ How does Isaiah's description of Jesus's abuse and death affect your view of sin, forgiveness, and salvation?

Isaiah's Risen Savior (Isaiah 25:8, 53:10)

Absolutely central to the Christian faith is the fact of the resurrection of Jesus from the dead on the third day after his crucifixion. As the apostle Paul wrote, "If Christ has not been raised, then all our preaching is useless, and your faith is useless" (1 Corinthians 15:14).

One of the reasons for Paul's assertion that Christ's resurrection is central to our faith is the fact that the Old Testament prophets foretold not just the death of the Messiah but also his being raised from the dead.

Isaiah 53 contains the predictions of Jesus's arrest and suffering on the Cross, and it also hints that his physical death wouldn't be his ultimate end: "Yet when his life is made an offering for sin, he will have many descendants.

He will enjoy a long life, and the Lord's good plan will prosper in his hands" (Isaiah 53:10).

ALERT!

Probably the best known Old Testament prophecy concerning the resurrection of Christ is this one, written by King David: "No wonder my heart is glad, and I rejoice. My body rests in safety. For you will not leave my soul among the dead or allow your holy one to rot in the grave" (Psalm 16:9–10).

But Isaiah's prophecies concerning Jesus's resurrection go even further—even if they don't do it in chronological order. Back in chapter 25, Isaiah tells us that Jesus's death and resurrection will have the effect of defeating death once and for all for those who would put their faith in him: "He will swallow up death forever! The Sovereign Lord will wipe away all tears. He will remove forever all insults and mockery against his land and people. The Lord has spoken!" (Isaiah 25:8).

Isaiah tells us the same thing about the death of the Messiah that the Gospels tell us: That his death, while cruel and horrible and necessary for the salvation of humankind, wasn't the end—not by a long shot.

The Messiah was going to defeat death once and for all, and he sealed that victory when on the third day after his death he rose from the grave and presented himself to his followers so that they could spread the news of what had happened.

Study Questions

○ How does the fact that Jesus's resurrection was foretold hundreds of years before it happened affect your faith and your approach to telling others his message?

○ Read 1 Corinthians 15. How does the fact of Jesus's resurrection affect your outlook on the subject of physical death?

Chapter 11

Jonah: A Picture of Disobedience Then Obedience

If you attended children's church, you probably remember one of the most popular stories of Jonah, the Jewish prophet who spent three days in the belly of a fish (or whale according to the song; it's not certain which) when he refused to go preach in a city called Nineveh and warn the people that their city was about to be destroyed. This chapter is a more detailed study of what happened to Jonah when he refused to do what God had called him to do and what happened when he finally obeyed.

Jonah's Call from God

The easiest reading of the book of Jonah is that the prophet just didn't feel like going to Nineveh. After all, we don't read of Jonah arguing with God when he was sent, only that he just didn't go. But a closer reading of the history of the people of Israel sheds some more light on the story of Jonah, revealing that he was more than just a rebellious prophet who didn't want to go where God had sent him.

In plain speaking, the mission for which the Lord had sent Jonah was one that, in human thinking anyway, didn't make a lick of sense. God was, in essence, sending Jonah to preach to his enemies. God was sending Jonah to preach to a race of people who were mortal enemies of the Israelites. Jonah knew that the Ninevites were a bloodthirsty, vicious people who posed a very real threat to his own countrymen. On top of that, they were desperately wicked people that Jonah no doubt believed were deserving of God's judgment and wrath.

Jonah just couldn't understand why he should go to a place like Nineveh, and the thought of being called to go there must have galled him. But it didn't matter why he didn't want to go to Nineveh, only that he refused to do what God had told him to do, instead relying on his own human understanding and reasoning. The results of that refusal made a most interesting—and very entertaining—adventure!

You're Sending Me Where? (Jonah 1)

The prophet Jonah was the son of a man named Amittai of Gath-hepher, and his name meant "a dove." The most familiar Biblical story about Jonah begins with this command from God: "Get up and go to the great city of Nineveh. Announce my judgment against it because I have seen how wicked its people are" (Jonah 1:2).

This was a fairly unusual assignment for a prophet of God. Usually when God sent a prophet, it was to the people of Israel with a warning to repent and return to God. This time, however, it was a call to preach to people who, for all Jonah knew, could have killed him on the spot.

But God had a plan for Jonah, and it was a plan to bless him by allowing him to be the vessel through which a generation of people would be saved. It didn't make sense to Jonah; in fact, there was no way he could possibly have understood what God was up to. It wasn't a calling a prophet of God could have expected, but it was God's command—one He expected Jonah to obey.

QUESTION?

Where else is Jonah mentioned in the Old Testament?
Other than in the book that bears his name, the prophet Jonah is not mentioned extensively in the Old Testament. He was a prophet of Israel, and he predicted the restoration of the ancient boundaries of the kingdom (2 Kings 14:25–27). He ministered in the very early reign of King Jeroboam II.

Sadly, however, Jonah did exactly the opposite of what God had told him to do. Rather than head straight for Nineveh, Jonah hopped a boat and headed in the opposite direction. As the book of Jonah tells us: "But Jonah got up and went in the opposite direction to get away from the Lord. He went down to the port of Joppa, where he found a ship leaving for Tarshish. He bought a ticket and went on board, hoping to escape from the Lord by sailing to Tarshish" (Jonah 1:3).

Jonah hoped to get away from God and the very distasteful mission he'd been sent on, and he probably thought he had it made once he boarded the ship. But that was just one of the several missteps Jonah would make before he finally turned around and got his mind and life right. Jonah went nowhere but "down" when he ran from God: down to the port of Joppa (Jonah 1:3), down to the hold of the ship (1:5), down into the stormy sea (1:15), and down into the belly of a giant fish (1:17).

And, as you will see as you study this book, it was only when Jonah looked up that he was pulled up.

Study Questions

○ Why did God send Jonah to Nineveh in the first place?
○ What was Jonah's verbal response to God when he was told to go to Nineveh?

I Think I Know Why This Is Happening (Jonah 1)

There is no more miserable place in life for a Christian to be than running from God and the things He has called us to do. When you turn away from God there is no protection from the devil, there are no messages or comfort from God, there is no peace of mind, and there is no joy or strength from the Lord.

While Jonah probably thought he'd gotten away with something—and away from God—it wasn't long before his sin and rebellion caught up with him. He had purchased a ticket to a place called Tarshish and boarded the boat. He was sleeping soundly in the ship's hold when he was awakened by the terrified and panicked cry of the ship's captain: "'How can you sleep at a time like this?' he shouted. 'Get up and pray to your god! Maybe he will pay attention to us and spare our lives'" (Jonah 1:6).

Jonah really believed he could run from God, and he probably wondered if God knew where he was when he ended up in the belly of the fish. But David the psalmist wrote that it was impossible to hide from God: "I can never escape from your Spirit! I can never get away from your presence!" (Psalm 139:7).

This was no ordinary storm that had struck. It was a storm sent specifically from God (Jonah 1:4) so that He could pull His prophet back to a life of obedience, and it was so violent that it threatened to rip the ship in half. Even the weather-hardened, sea-wise sailors who ran the ship were so afraid they were going to die that they started tossing cargo overboard.

Jonah informed the ship's crew that he was a Hebrew who worshipped the true and living Creator God and that he was on the ship because he was running from God. That, he said, was why they were in the predicament they were in. When they asked Jonah what they should do, he told them very directly and simply: "Throw me overboard" (Jonah 1:12).

But instead of getting rid of the cargo that was causing the problem—Jonah himself—the sailors tried harder to get the ship under control and back to port. When they found that they were helpless against the storm's fury, they threw Jonah overboard and down into the sea.

Just as Jonah had said, the storm ceased immediately and the ship's crew was safe. Jonah, however, had another problem to deal with.

Study Questions
○ How did the sailors respond when Jonah told them that he was a Jewish prophet and probably responsible for what they were enduring?
○ What happened in the hearts of those sailors after they threw Jonah overboard?

A Really Nasty Place to Be (Jonah 1:17)

The Bible tells us that Jonah didn't drown after he was thrown overboard but was swallowed whole by "a great fish" (Jonah 1:17), which the Lord had prepared. While the language in which the book of Jonah was written leaves it open to debate just what kind of creature swallowed the prophet, it is clear that he stayed in the belly of that beast for three days and three nights.

It is difficult to imagine or to try to describe the foulness of such a place. Perhaps one good point of reference is what fishermen refer to as a chum bucket, an onboard receptacle for a mixture of fish heads, blood, and innards, all of which are dumped into the water to help attract fish and bring them closer to the boat so that fisherman can more easily get them to take their bait.

FACT

While many people might look at the story of Jonah and think that it defies plausibility, there is some historic precedence for what the Bible says happened to him. There are several examples of sailors or other men being swallowed whole by sharks or whales and then being rescued hours later.

Being buried head to toe in a bucket of chum would likely be only slightly less unpleasant than being in the belly of the creature God sent to swallow the prophet Jonah. No doubt it was a soaking wet place in which Jonah could hardly move or breathe because it was so enclosed and because it stunk so badly.

But it was a place where a prophet of God, or anybody else, could do only one thing: pray for a way out. That is exactly what Jonah did.

Study Questions

○ What do you think the Bible meant when it said that "the Lord arranged for a great fish to swallow Jonah"?

○ What do you think is the spiritual significance of the unpleasantness of the place where Jonah spent three days?

A Prayer for Deliverance (Jonah 2)

There are a lot of ways God can redirect our focus and bring us back to obedience, but it's hard to imagine one more effective than sending someone to spend three days in the stomach of some kind of giant sea creature. And while Jonah must have wondered if this was how his life would end, he prayed for God's deliverance from the situation.

Jonah's prayer starts out sounding very much like one of the psalms: "I cried out to the Lord in my great trouble, and he answered me. I called to you from the land of the dead, and Lord, you heard me! You threw me into the ocean depths, and I sank down to the heart of the sea. The mighty waters engulfed me; I was buried beneath your wild and stormy waves" (Jonah 2:2–3).

ALERT!

Jesus Christ himself gave the story of Jonah historical authenticity as well as a spiritual application when he said, "For as Jonah was in the belly of the great fish for three days and three nights, so will the Son of Man be in the heart of the earth for three days and three nights" (Matthew 12:40).

As Jonah continued praying, he seems to understand that he had run from God and that God had banished him from His presence because of it. Then he seems to turn back to God, telling him, "Yet I will look once more toward your holy Temple" (Jonah 2:4). Finally, he tells God, "But I will offer sacrifices to you with songs of praise, and I will fulfill all my vows. For my salvation comes from the Lord alone" (Jonah 2:9).

That, apparently, was what God wanted to hear. He removed Jonah from the unpleasantness he had brought on himself through his own disobedience and rebellion: "Then the Lord ordered the fish to spit Jonah out onto the beach" (Jonah 2:10).

But the story was far from finished. There was still that matter of Jonah actually doing what God had called him to do in the first place.

Study Questions

○ Read Psalm 18. How is this psalm similar to Jonah's prayer? How is it different?

○ Does Jonah's prayer sound more like a request for mercy and deliverance or the prayer of a man who knows he is about to die?

Are You Ready to Go Now? (Jonah 3)

While not everyone who spends three days in the stomach of a fish will use that time to get his mind and spirit right, that is exactly what the prophet Jonah did. Once he did that—and once God got him out of that fish's belly—he barely had time to get himself cleaned up when God spoke to him a second time, giving him the same command as before: "Get up and go to the great city of Nineveh, and deliver the message I have given you" (Jonah 3:2).

Jonah had learned his lesson. This time he didn't head "down," but instead he headed out, straight to Nineveh, a city so large that it took three days to see all of it. He still may not have had a clue as to why God had called him to preach to a people like the Ninevites—or why God had chose him to do it—but this time he did as he had been commanded.

And once Jonah was in Nineveh, he didn't pull any punches. He spoke the very message God had given him to deliver.

The book of Jonah doesn't tell us what specific sin or sins the people had committed to bring God's judgment down on themselves, but it does tell us that the situation was dire, so dire that on the very day Jonah entered the city he announced, "Forty days from now Nineveh will be destroyed!" (Jonah 3:4). It was a message Jonah believed with all his heart, and it was a message the Ninevites believed, too.

FACT

Jonah was not the only prophet to foretell the doom and desolation of the city of Nineveh. The book of the prophet Nahum, which is set about a century after the time of Jonah, is taken up almost exclusively with the prophecies of the destruction of the city because of its great sin.

Jonah had spoken from the heart and with passion, because the people of Nineveh—including the king himself—listened and made the changes God had called them to make. Jonah, the reluctant—even rebellious—prophet of God had made a difference, preaching salvation to a people who until that time had been his mortal enemy.

Study Questions

○ What would you do if you knew God wanted you to do something that in your human reasoning just didn't make sense? Would you obey? Argue? Bargain?

○ Why do you think God persisted with Jonah instead of just sending someone else to do the preaching?

The Results of Obedience (Jonah 3,4)

Any doubts Jonah had about the people of Nineveh receiving his message were quickly dispelled. Right away the people of the city—from the most important to the least—heard what he was saying, took heed of the message, and repented.

But there was more. Even the king of Nineveh took Jonah's message seriously. He stepped down from his throne, took off his royal robes, and went into "sackcloth and ashes" repentance. Not only that, he and his nobles passed this decree for the city:

No one, not even the animals from your herds and flocks, may eat or drink anything at all. People and animals alike must wear garments of mourning, and everyone must pray earnestly to God. They must turn from their evil ways and stop all their violence. Who can tell? Perhaps even yet God will change his mind and hold back his fierce anger from destroying us. (Jonah 3:7–9)

Because Jonah had obeyed God—after a three-day side trip—and because he preached the truth that God had given him to speak, the city of Nineveh was spared. God saw how the people had repented and changed their ways, and He changed His mind and didn't carry out the destruction He had earlier threatened.

Jesus himself mentioned Jonah and actually likened Jonah's assigned mission to his own: "The people of Nineveh will stand up against this generation on judgment day and condemn it, for they repented of their sins at the preaching of Jonah. Now someone greater than Jonah is here—but you refuse to repent" (Matthew 28:41).

God had shown mercy, just as He had wanted to in the first place, but that only angered Jonah, who complained, "Didn't I say before I left home that you would do this, Lord? That is why I ran away to Tarshish! I knew that you are a merciful and compassionate God, slow to get angry and filled with unfailing love. You are eager to turn back from destroying people. Just kill me now, Lord! I'd rather be dead than alive if what I predicted will not happen" (Jonah 4:2–3).

This seems like a strange response to the mercy of God, who asks him, "Is it right for you to be angry about this?" (Jonah 4:4). Jonah then went out to the edge of the city and started pouting while he waited to see what would happen to it. Would God do as He had said?

Jonah seems angry that such a wicked city had been saved, that what God had said was going to happen didn't. It seems that he was more concerned that what he prophesied come true than have his warnings lead to the repentance and salvation of a huge city. Finally, God uses a series of miracles to demonstrate the rightness of his mercy on the people of Nineveh.

The book of Jonah ends abruptly, and God has the last word, saying to Jonah, "Nineveh has more than 120,000 people living in spiritual darkness, not to mention all the animals. Shouldn't I feel sorry for such a great city?" (Jonah 4:12).

In the end, it seems that this question is posed for the reader to ponder as there is no answer from Jonah. In fact, that question leaves us only to think about the immense compassion of God—even for those who were not his "chosen" people.

God cares about and loves all people, regardless of what country or race they belong to. The mission of Jonah was an example of that great love and compassion.

Study Questions

○ How would you answer the question that God poses at the end of the book of Jonah?

○ How would you respond if God used you or someone you know to lead someone you thought wasn't worthy to salvation?

Chapter 12

Matthew: Some Tough—and Practical—Teaching

One of the most recognizable sermons of all time came from the mouth of Jesus Christ at the shore of the Sea of Galilee and has come to be known as the Sermon on the Mount. In this sermon, Jesus spoke with a power and authority the likes of which no one had ever seen or heard. This chapter is a study of that sermon, what it meant to the people who heard it straight from Jesus's mouth, and what it means to us today.

Another Look at the Law of Moses

If you've ever read through the first five books of the Bible—known as the Pentateuch or the books of Moses—and wondered what they have to do with your Christian life today, then maybe you should take the time to read and study what has been called the greatest sermon ever preached. It is found in the fifth through seventh chapters of the Gospel of Matthew, and it has been commonly called the Sermon on the Mount. It was delivered by Jesus Christ to a multitude of his followers.

In preaching the Sermon on the Mount, Jesus took the common approach to the law of that time and turned it on its ear. Most of the Jewish religious leadership at that time held to a very black and white application of Jewish law, but Jesus taught a different approach. His was an approach to the law that stressed obedience from the heart and not from a sense of legalism.

Jesus delivered this sermon on a small hill on the shore of the Sea of Galilee. It was different from anything anyone on the scene had ever heard. For those who could hear and understand the message, it revolutionized their lives. The same can happen for those believers who make studying this passage and applying its truths a life priority.

God Blesses Those Who... (Matthew 5:3–16)

Jesus began the Sermon on the Mount by speaking what has come to be known as the Beatitudes, which were simply declarations of blessing to those who follow them. Each of the Beatitudes starts with the phrase "God blesses" (or "Blessed are," depending on what version of the Bible you are reading) and ends with the blessing itself. In the Beatitudes, Jesus tells us that God blesses:

- those who are poor and know how much they need him (Matthew 5:3)
- those who mourn because they will be comforted (5:4)

- those who are humble because they will inherit the whole earth (5:5)
- those who are hungry and thirsty for justice because they will be satisfied (5:6)
- those who show mercy because they will receive mercy (5:7)
- those who have pure hearts because they will see God (5:8)
- those who work for peace because they will be called God's children (5:9)
- those who are persecuted for doing what is right for God's kingdom is theirs (5:10).

Jesus followed this list by telling his followers, "God blesses you when people mock you and persecute you and lie about you and say all sorts of evil things against you because you are my followers. Be happy about it! Be very glad! For a great reward awaits you in heaven. And remember, the ancient prophets were persecuted in the same way" (Matthew 5:11–12).

ALERT!

You can find a more abbreviated version of the Sermon on the Mount in Luke 6:20–49. In that version, there are fewer Beatitudes. Jesus's teaching on loving enemies and judging others is also included in that version.

Jesus went on to tell his followers that they were to be those things and receive those blessings for one reason: because they are the salt and light of the earth, meaning they were to bring the earth light and flavor. Salt is worthless, Jesus said, when it loses its flavor. Likewise, a lamp is useless when it is covered up. For that reason, those who follow Jesus are to do good things for the kingdom of God so that people will see those things and praise God.

Study Questions

○ What did Jesus say it took to "inherit the earth"?

○ Read Matthew 5:12. What are believers to do when people persecute or make fun of them because of their faith?

A New Approach to the Law (Matthew 5:17–47)

Jesus wanted to make sure that his followers didn't misunderstand why he had come and what his relationship to the Law of Moses was, so he told them, "Don't misunderstand why I have come. I did not come to abolish the law of Moses or the writings of the prophets. No, I came to accomplish their purpose. I tell you the truth, until heaven and earth disappear, not even the smallest detail of God's law will disappear until its purpose is achieved" (Matthew 5:17–18).

He went on to encourage them to keep the law, telling them that those who obeyed the law would be rewarded in the afterlife. Where Jesus differed most from the religious authorities and teachers of his day, however, was in his approach to what obeying the law really meant.

ESSENTIAL

Six times in the fifth chapter of Matthew, Jesus used the phrase "But I say," indicating that he wanted to make some changes in how the Jewish leadership of his time had taught and applied the Law of Moses. Five other times he used the phrase, "I tell you." Those are good verses to underline and remember as you study the Sermon on the Mount.

Jesus wanted his followers to understand that obeying God meant more than just doing the minimum and strictly adhering to a bunch of rules. In other words, it's the spirit of the law that mattered more than the letter of the law. That is why he taught such radical ideas about the following subjects:

- **Murder is from the heart** (Matthew 5:21–26). Jesus taught that sin started in the heart and then demonstrated itself in actions. That is why he said in the Sermon on the Mount concerning those who speak hateful words, do hateful deeds, and think hateful thoughts:

  You have heard that our ancestors were told, 'You must not murder. If you commit murder, you are subject to judgment.' But I say, if you are even angry with someone, you are subject to judgment! If you call someone an idiot, you are in danger of being brought before the court. And if you curse someone, you are in danger of the fires of hell. (Matthew 5:21–22)

  Obviously, Jesus wanted his disciples—then and now—to deal properly with their anger at or with one another. That is reflected even more directly in the following verses, where Jesus told them to make sure that they are reconciled with one another before they bother to come to God (Matthew 5:24–25) and to settle their differences with one another before going to court (Matthew 5:25–26).

- **Adultery isn't just about the act** (Matthew 5:27–30). Jesus's teaching on adultery again reflected on the fact that he stressed to his followers the importance of focusing on what was in their hearts and minds. He cited the commandment against committing adultery, but then told the people that any man who looks lustfully at a woman who is not his own wife has already committed adultery with her in his heart.

- **Don't make promises you can't keep** (5:33–37). Jesus addressed the subject of making vows when he said, "I say, do not make any vows! Do not say, 'By heaven!' because heaven is God's throne…Just say a simple, 'Yes, I will,' or 'No, I won't.' Anything beyond this is from the evil one" (Matthew 5:34, 37). In other words, answer with a simple yes or no when someone asks you for something.

- **Revenge is a dish best served not at all** (Matthew 5:38–42). The Law of Moses held that someone who had been wronged or injured by another had the legal right to seek retribution ("an eye for an eye"). But Jesus taught that while people have that right, it is better not to use it.

- **Love your friends but also your enemies** (Matthew 5:43–48). The Law of Moses as outlined in the Old Testament stated that believers were to love their neighbors as themselves. But by the time Jesus arrived on the scene, the meaning of that commandment had become muddled. Jesus wanted his followers to do something really radical—love those who hated and persecuted them: "I say, love your enemies! Pray for those who persecute you! If you love only those who love you, what reward is there for that? Even corrupt tax collectors do that much" (Matthew 5:44, 46).

Study Questions

○ What did Jesus come to do with the Law of Moses?
○ What was different about Jesus's teachings on adultery?

Doing Right for the Right Reasons (Matthew 6:1–18)

By the time Jesus arrived, the approach of most of the Jewish religious leadership in dealing with the law had become very literal. They had lost the spirit of what God had tried to teach them through His law, so they began doing the right things—things God had commanded them to do—but for the wrong reasons.

Jesus wanted to bring people back to doing good for others for the right reasons, which were because they loved God and loved their neighbors. That is why he taught that acts of charity such as giving to the needy, as well as religious acts such as fasting, needed to be done in such a way that only God knew what the believer was doing: "Watch out! Don't do your good deeds publicly, to be admired by others, for you will lose the reward from your Father in heaven. When you give to someone in need, don't do as the hypocrites do—blowing trumpets in the synagogues and streets to call attention to their acts of charity! I tell you the truth, they have received all the reward they will ever get" (Matthew 5:1–2).

He taught essentially the same lesson about prayer and fasting, telling his followers that their prayers should be offered to God in private, not out in the open for everyone to see (Matthew 6:5–6). Furthermore, when they prayed they weren't to just "babble on and on as people of other religions do" (Matthew 6:7), but instead they were to pray according to his words recorded in Matthew 6:9–14, or what is known as the Lord's Prayer (see Chapter 4).

Jesus taught that those who did the things he calls all of us to do—giving, praying, fasting—using the guidelines he gives will receive their reward from God in heaven. However, those who do them with the wrong motivation will receive their reward here on earth.

Study Questions

○ How should Jesus's command/encouragement to do our giving and other acts of charity in private affect how we do those things today?

○ What did Jesus intend when he taught his followers to pray "like this" then spoke what has come to be known as the Lord's Prayer?

A Heavenly Approach to Money and Wealth (Matthew 6:19–34)

Throughout his earthly ministry, Jesus gave some of his most direct teaching when it came to the subject of money. In the Sermon on the Mount, he didn't condemn having money or working to acquire wealth. What he did, in fact, was condemn making money and wealth one's life focus.

"Don't store up treasures here on earth," Jesus taught, "where moths eat them and rust destroys them, and where thieves break in and steal. Store your treasures in heaven, where moths and rust cannot destroy, and thieves do not break in and steal. Wherever your treasure is, there the desires of your heart will also be" (Matthew 6:19–21).

FACT

The theme of God meeting the needs of every one of his people is prominent throughout the Bible. Probably the best known Scripture on that subject is found in Paul's epistle to the Philippians: "And this same God who takes care of me will supply all your needs from his glorious riches, which have been given to us in Christ Jesus" (Philippians 4:19).

Jesus, who obviously understood the negatives of human nature (including greed), taught that it wasn't just difficult but impossible to serve God and money at the same time (Matthew 6:24). In fact, he went so far as to say that attempting to serve both will lead one to hate one or the other.

Jesus also understood that his followers' concerns about money weren't always motivated by greed but simply out of concern for day-to-day living. That is why he encouraged them not to worry about the things they need for everyday life—food, drink, clothing, and the like—but instead to just rely on a God who will give them everything they needed. (Read carefully Jesus's beautiful and inspirational words in Matthew 6:26–30.)

Jesus told them (and us), "So don't worry about these things, saying, 'What will we eat? What will we drink? What will we wear?' These things dominate the thoughts of unbelievers, but your heavenly Father already knows all your needs" (Matthew 6:31–32).

The bottom line when it comes to money and possessions and wealth, Jesus told his followers, is this: "Seek the Kingdom of God above all else, and live righteously, and he will give you everything you need" (Matthew 6:33).

Jesus knew as well as anyone that living this life required certain items, many of which can only be obtained with money. But he also knew perfectly the importance of making God his Father our first focus—with everything and anything else a distant second.

○ In this passage, what does it sound like Jesus's approach to money really is?

○ How should this passage change the believer's approach to money and possessions?

Judging and the Golden Rule (Matthew 7:1–4, 12)

Many of Jesus's teachings—as well as others in the Bible—have become so ingrained into our culture that we know their meaning even if we don't know who said it or in what context. One excellent example of this is from Jesus's Sermon on the Mount and is what has come to be known as the Golden Rule. It goes like this: "Do to others whatever you would like them to do to you. This is the essence of all that is taught in the law and the prophets" (Matthew 7:12).

Jesus's famous Sermon on the Mount very likely wasn't a sermon in the sense that we think of sermons. In that culture, it was very common for teachers to gather their followers for informal question and answer teaching sessions and not preaching in the traditional sense.

On an individual basis, it's not hard to understand what the phrase "do to others whatever you would like them to do to you" means. All of us want to be treated fairly and justly—to be spoken to and treated in a respectful manner, to be paid equitably for our work, to be given what truly is due us. Jesus wanted his followers to understand the importance of treating other people in a manner each of them wants to be treated.

The Golden Rule can be seen as a summarization of the teaching that Jesus had given in the previous few sentences. He started this section by talking about judging others, making the point that we shouldn't judge others if we ourselves don't want to be judged equally as harshly. "Do not judge others, and you will not be judged," he said. "For you will be treated as you treat others. The standard you use in judging is the standard by which you will be judged" (Matthew 7:1–2).

Being the Son of God, Jesus knew better than anyone the frailties and imperfections in humanity, and he also knew that humans would be prone to judging and condemning one another for things as bad or worse as anything they themselves had done. That is partly why he went on to warn people not to worry about removing a "speck" from their friends' eyes while there is a "log" in their own (Matthew 7:3–4). In other words, don't judge or condemn or try to correct someone before you first deal with your own issues.

Study Questions

○ In light of Jesus's teaching not to judge others, what do you think is the appropriate way to respond to those whose lives you can see are out of order?

○ What kind of "logs" do you need to get out of your eye in order to be a better example of Christianity to those around you?

Praying Effectively and Persistently (Matthew 7:7–11)

Earlier in the Sermon on the Mount, Jesus taught what has come to be known as the Lord's Prayer, which is in essence a model prayer containing all the elements of effective prayer, the kind God likes to hear. Later on Jesus picked up again on the theme of prayer (a common theme in his earthly ministry) when he implied very strongly that prayer was a matter of persistence, hard work, and seeking an answer: "Keep on asking, and you will receive what you ask for. Keep on seeking, and you will find. Keep on knocking, and the door will be opened to you. For everyone who asks, receives. Everyone who seeks, finds. And to everyone who knocks, the door will be opened" (Matthew 7:7–8).

Jesus taught his followers that this ask-seek-knock form of prayer is effective because we have a heavenly Father who loves us far beyond what even the most doting mother and father could imagine. As Matthew 7:9–11 illustrates: "You parents—if your children ask for a loaf of bread, do you give them a stone instead? Or if they ask for a fish, do you give them a snake? Of course not! So if you sinful people know how to give good gifts to your children, how much more will your heavenly Father give good gifts to those who ask him."

E ALERT!

The writer of Hebrews echoed this theme of approaching God and asking with confidence and persistence when he wrote: "So let us come boldly to the throne of our gracious God. There we will receive his mercy, and we will find grace to help us when we need it most" (Hebrews 4:16).

Jesus wanted us to realize that God isn't some disinterested celestial personality but a loving heavenly Father who wants to bless those who will come to him and humbly ask for what they need.

Study Questions

○ What in your physical, personal, emotional, or spiritual life do you need to begin asking God to give you today?

○ How does Jesus's teaching that God's love compels him to give good gifts to those who persistently ask him compare with your own perceptions today?

The Narrow Gate and Strong Foundations (Matthew 7:13–28)

As Jesus drew his Sermon on the Mount to a close, he spoke very directly and clearly about who would inherit the kingdom of God and who would not. His teaching in this area—while it was filled with love and compassion—made it very clear that not everyone would be going to heaven, only those who entered by what he called "the narrow gate" in Matthew 7:13–14: "You can enter God's Kingdom only through the narrow gate. The highway to hell is broad, and its gate is wide for the many who choose that way. But the gateway to life is very narrow and the road is difficult, and only a few ever find it."

FACT

The Bible presents a message of salvation to all and tells us repeatedly that there is only one way to see the kingdom of heaven and that is through the "narrow gate" of Jesus Christ, who said, "No one can come to the Father except through me" (John 14:6).

Jesus was teaching those in attendance that day that it was necessary for them to be freed from their sins if they wanted salvation and that they would have to be careful not to listen to those who would come after Jesus with messages to lead them astray: "Beware of false prophets who come disguised as harmless sheep but are really vicious wolves. You can identify them by their fruit, that is, by the way they act. Can you pick grapes from thornbushes, or figs from thistles? A good tree produces good fruit, and a bad tree produces bad fruit" (Matthew 7:15–17).

Jesus intended for his teaching that day—and every day after—to be taken by his followers as the foundational truths by which they would live their lives and by which they would inherit salvation and eternal life in heaven. That is why he said, "Anyone who listens to my teaching and follows it is wise, like a person who builds a house on solid rock" (Matthew 7:24).

He pointed out that a house built on rock won't collapse even in the worst of storms but that one built on sand is a catastrophe waiting to happen. Those who hear and obey his teaching, she said, were like those who built their houses on the solid rock. The ones who don't were building the houses of their lives on sand (Matthew 7:25–27).

Jesus had just preached the greatest sermon ever heard. And when he finished, the people who heard him that day were amazed both at what he had said and at how he had said it: with authority unlike anything the religious teachers of that time could muster (Matthew 7:28–29).

Study Questions

○ How does Jesus's teaching that the gate to heaven is narrow and the highway to hell wide affect your approach to telling others about your faith in Christ?

○ What do you think are some of the "good fruits" you can readily see in those who claim to know the truth about God and the way to get to him?

Chapter 13

John: The Apostle's Account of Holy Week

All four of the accounts of Jesus's time on earth—the Gospels of Matthew, Mark, Luke, and John—describe his final arrival into Jerusalem, his arrest, his trial, his crucifixion, and his resurrection. But John's gospel has a different take on these events, and it's one that emphasizes the identity of Jesus as the Son of God as well as the spiritual implications for those who would believe in him.

Fulfilling What He Had Predicted

For about three and a half years, Jesus Christ traveled by foot around the land of Palestine (now Israel and some surrounding areas) teaching, preaching, performing miracles, and announcing the arrival of the long-awaited Messiah. This was the portion of his life that has been referred to as his "earthly ministry," and it's the time leading up to what some Christians refer to as Holy Week.

QUESTION?

How is John's gospel different from the other three?
The Gospels of Matthew, Mark, and Luke are called the synoptic Gospels because they more or less follow the same chain of events in the life of Jesus. John's gospel is known for a more spiritual focus and for its emphasis on different events in Jesus's life from the other three.

This was the final week of Jesus's life on earth, and it included his final entry into the city of Jerusalem (John 12:12–19), his final teaching, his arrest and trial, his death on the cross, and his resurrection. These were all events he had told his disciples would come, and now that time had come. Jesus was about to fulfill the mission for which he had come to earth in the first place: his death on the cross and his resurrection from the dead.

John's gospel—which was written by the apostle John, who refers to himself in the gospel narrative as "the disciple Jesus loved"—is the last book of the Gospels and it contains several incidents surrounding Jesus's final hours before his death that don't appear in the other three.

A Triumphal Entry (John 12:12–19)

Like most good Jewish men, Jesus had already been to the city of Jerusalem on numerous occasions. It was at that time the custom for Jews in that area of the world to make a pilgrimage from their own homes to Jerusalem to celebrate the Passover.

But there was something different this time as Jesus entered the city. This time he was greeted by a throng of Passover visitors who welcomed him with these words of praise: "Praise God! Blessings on the one who comes in the name of the Lord! Hail to the King of Israel!" (John 12:13).

This scene—which is also recorded in Matthew 21:1–11, Mark 11:1–11, and Luke 19:29–44—was one of near pandemonium as Jesus entered the Holy City. But it was also one with some serious undertones. It was in Jerusalem that the Jewish religious leaders of that time had been plotting and planning to put an end to what Jesus had been doing for the past three years.

If you want a good overview of some of the other things Jesus did and said during that last week prior to the Crucifixion, read Luke chapters 19–22. That will give you a more complete perspective of what Jesus was up against during that week and why it would end the way it did.

If you've read through the entire Gospel of John prior to doing this exercise, then you know that the teaching and deeds of Jesus were often very much in conflict with the religious establishment of that time and place. And while Jesus's arrival into Jerusalem looked like a huge party, it would only be a matter of time before the religious leaders would find a reason to do away with Jesus.

Study Questions

❍ Read John 12:17–18. Why were many of the people coming out to greet Jesus as he entered Jerusalem?

❍ Look at John 12:19, then Luke 19:39–40. How did the Pharisees—the Jewish religious leaders—respond to Jesus's arrival?

A Heart-Wrenching Scene (John 13)

Out of the four Gospels, John's tells us the least when it comes to the things Jesus did and said during his final week in Jerusalem. In fact, all that is really mentioned after he entered Jerusalem and prior to the eve of his crucifixion is a request by some Greek pilgrims to visit with Jesus personally and the sermon he delivered after hearing that request (John 12:20–50).

In the other gospel accounts, we can read of what has come to be known as the Lord's Supper or the Last Supper, but in John's gospel, the events on the eve of the Crucifixion were as follows: Jesus washes the disciples' feet (John 13:1–17), announces that one of the disciples will betray him (13:18–30), then gives the disciples what can best be described as parting words.

The foot-washing scene is an especially touching scene because it is Jesus—the leader, Lord, and Master of the twelve disciples over the previous three-plus years—who takes out the wash basin and towel and begins washing their feet. Of the twelve, only Peter has the nerve to speak up and say what the others were no doubt thinking. But Jesus met Peter's protests with a firm response: "Unless I wash you, you won't belong to me" (John 13:8). Peter, of course, changed his mind and allowed Jesus to wash his feet.

ALERT!

While John wrote of Jesus washing the disciples' feet on the eve of his crucifixion, the other gospel writers record Jesus serving in another way: by presenting them with what has come to be known as the Lord's Supper. In it, the disciples ate the bread that represented Jesus's flesh and drank the wine that represented his blood.

The foot washing was followed by Jesus's very direct announcement to the disciples that one of them would betray him. Judas, who John wrote had been entered by the devil himself, then left the group and disappeared into the night, going to the Jewish religious leaders to betray Jesus.

The stage was now set. Jesus had deliberately and with great purpose put himself in harm's way by coming to Jerusalem. Judas was about to betray him, and that would lead to his arrest, trial, and death. But first, Jesus had some final words for the eleven remaining disciples—as well as what is probably the most amazing prayer recorded in the Bible.

Study Questions

○ How did Jesus demonstrate who his betrayer would be?

○ What did Jesus say Peter would do on the night before his arrest and crucifixion? (See John 13:36–38.)

Some Final Words to the Disciples (John 14–16)

In those final hours before Jesus's arrest, he preached an incredible sermon (this one just to the disciples) filled with words of comfort, promises, encouragements, and warnings. In this sermon, Jesus told the disciples:

- not to be troubled but to trust in him (John 14:1–4)
- that they were to have faith in him as the One sent from God (14:5–14)
- that they were to continue in obedience to him, with the help of the Holy Spirit (14:15–31)
- that they were to remain in him, even though he would be gone soon (15:1–8)
- that they were to love one another the same way he loved them (15:9–17)
- that the world would hate them (15:18–25)
- that he would soon send the Holy Spirit (15:26–16:16)
- that their sorrow and grief would one day be turned to joy (16:17–28)

This section of the Gospel of John is filled with incredible instruction and encouragement for the believer today. It encourages the discouraged, comforts the afflicted, instructs those who aren't sure what to do, and promises that no matter what we go through on this earth, if we remain in Christ we will one day experience joy—all because Jesus remains with us.

Jesus told the disciples that even though he would soon be physically gone, they were to "Remain in me, and I will remain in you" (John 15:4). Jesus wanted the disciples to understand that they had some incredibly difficult work ahead and that the only way they would be able to finish it successfully was to stick close to him. One of the reasons they would need to stick close to Jesus, he taught them, was that they would be going into a world that would hate them—just like it hated Jesus himself—despite the fact that they would be taking with them a positive message of salvation and forgiveness from God.

It is absolutely crucial for a believer to understand that bearing fruit, as Jesus referred to doing positive things for God and for others in his name, can only happen when he or she sticks close to him (John 15:1–4). That theme runs throughout the Bible, Old Testament and New Testament alike.

All of the promises Jesus made in this passage are invaluable to the believer, but it can be argued that the most important of them was his promise to send the Holy Spirit. Jesus went to great lengths to explain to the disciples that the Holy Spirit would remind the world of its need for God's forgiveness and righteousness and would guide them and remind them daily of the things he had taught them while he was on earth with them.

Study Questions

○ What specific things can the believer do to ensure that he or she continues to remain in Christ?

○ Read Acts 2. How does the event in that passage connect with what Jesus told the disciples in this passage?

A Final Word to the Father (John 17)

Just before Jesus went to the olive grove where he was to be betrayed and arrested, he gave the disciples their final marching orders and offered a prayer to God, his Father. It was one of the most beautiful and emotional prayers recorded in the Bible. In this prayer, Jesus prayed for:

- **himself** (John 17:1–6), because the time had come for his divinely appointed death on the cross and he wanted to glorify his Father;
- **his disciples** (17:7–19), because their next few days were going to be filled with pain, disappointment, and disillusionment and because they would be facing the challenge of taking Jesus's message into an unreceptive, even dangerous world;
- **all those who would be believers because of his work and the work of the disciples** (17:20–26), because he wanted them to live in unity with the Father and the Son as well as one another.

As you read this prayer, you get a good idea of the level of commitment Jesus had—and still has—to glorify God in all he did and to the well-being and eternal destinies of those he called to serve God and of those he came to save.

Study Questions

○ According to Jesus's prayer, what is the one way to eternal life?

○ For what specifically did Jesus pray when it came to those who would believe in him?

Jesus's Arrest and Trial (John 18–19:15)

The Jewish religious leaders of Jesus's time didn't like his teaching and interpretations of the Scriptures and their religious traditions. For that reason, he represented a threat to their authority and long-held power structure.

The way they saw it, something had to be done and now the time was right to do it.

After Jesus had finished his final prayer—for himself, for his disciples, and for others who would believe in him—he took his disciples and headed for a nearby olive grove, which we know from other gospel accounts is the garden of Gethsemane.

It was here where Jesus was arrested and taken into custody. While the other three gospels include Jesus's prayers just before he was arrested, John tells us only that Judas showed up guiding some soldiers as well as some representatives sent by the religious leadership. Jesus was taken into custody after a small scuffle that resulted in the wounding of Malchus, a servant of the chief priest. (In Luke's gospel, Jesus healed Malchus.)

Jesus was first taken to a man named Annas, who interviewed him about the things he had been teaching. Jesus declined to defend himself or explain himself, instead only telling Annas that he had spoken and taught openly and that there should be plenty of witnesses to anything he said worthy of death.

FACT

John's gospel is the only one to mention Jesus's meeting with Annas following his arrest. Annas was the former Jewish high priest and the father-in-law of Caiaphas, the high priest at the time of Jesus's arrest. The Roman government of that time had, for purely political reasons, removed Annas from office and replaced him with Caiaphas.

John tells us that Annas sent Jesus away, still bound, to Caiaphas the high priest who then sent him away to Pilate, the Roman governor of Judea. The idea was to accuse Jesus of subversion against the Roman government, a crime the Romans took very seriously and dealt with very harshly.

At first Pilate probably believed that Jesus was no different than a lot of the troublemakers he had faced in his position of authority. But some of the things Jesus said troubled Pilate, and he had a difficult time deciding what to do with him. In truth, Jesus hadn't done anything to deserve the death penalty, and he even said as much to the assembled crowd. In the end, however, after pleading with those who wanted Jesus dead, Pilate gave him over to be crucified.

Study Questions

○ Read Luke's account of Jesus's trial. What additional information does Luke provide to this part of the story?

○ According to John's account, what happened to Peter while this scene was developing?

The Crucifixion (John 19:16–37)

With Jesus's trial finished, it was now time for his appointment with the cross. John tells us that Jesus was led away to a place called Golgotha, or Skull Hill, where he was crucified, or nailed by the hands and feet to a cross made of wood—a common as well as shockingly brutal form of capital punishment in the Roman world of that time.

FACT

The four Gospels' accounts of Jesus's death record him saying different final words. John's account tells us that he said "It is finished!" before he died, while the Matthew and Mark versions record him praying, "My God, my God, why have you forsaken me?" Luke tells us that his last words were "Father, into your hands I commit my spirit."

All four Gospels tell us some of what happened at the Crucifixion scene, with some leaving out what others omit (and vice versa). As you study this passage of John's gospel, it's a good idea to also take a peek at what the other three writers had to say about this scene. When you do that, you will see the complete picture of the most profound act of love in all of human history.

Also notice that John several times points out that events at the Crucifixion scene were direct and specific fulfillments of Old Testament Scripture concerning the Messiah. For example, John 19:23–24 tells us that the soldiers' dividing and throwing of dice for Jesus's clothing fulfilled a prophecy from Psalm 22:28. That was just the first of several of John's references to fulfillments of Old Testament prophecies.

John 19:28–30 tells us that Jesus died only after he was offered a sour wine-soaked sponge to quench his thirst. His last words in this passage: "It is finished!"

○ Look up the Crucifixion accounts in Matthew 27:35–50, Mark 15:25–37, and Luke 23:22–46. What do the words Jesus spoke while on the cross say to you personally?

○ What is the importance to your own spiritual life of the fact that Jesus's crucifixion fulfills so many Old Testament prophecies?

The Resurrection (John 20–21)

The death of Jesus Christ by crucifixion had put the disciples in a deep funk. To them it seemed that everything they had worked for—all that time they had spent following Jesus—was for nothing. Their leader was dead and gone, and the movement they believed he was starting was finished.

ALERT!

The Resurrection is also recorded in Matthew 28:2–15, Mark 16:1–9, and Luke 24:1–12. As you study this passage, look at those three scenes and notice the differences of viewpoint and emphasis in the accounts. For example, Luke gives an account of angels telling the women who followed Jesus what had happened and why.

But this story wasn't finished. Not by a long shot. In fact, on the third day after Jesus's death, God would perform his greatest miracle of all: raising Christ from the dead. John sets up his account of the Resurrection scene by telling about two members of the Jewish religious leadership—Joseph of Arimathea and Nicodemus—who saw to a proper burial of Jesus's body (John 19:38–40).

John tells us that on the morning of the first day of the week (which would have been Sunday according to our calendars), a woman named Mary of Magdala, one of Jesus's followers, went to the tomb only to find that the stone had been removed from the entrance. Mary ran to get Peter and "the other disciple" (John), who both ran to the tomb. When Peter looked into the tomb, all he saw was strips of linen and the burial cloth that had been around Jesus's head.

Although they still didn't understand that the resurrection of Jesus was in keeping with Old Testament prophecies concerning the Messiah, Peter and John both knew something was up (John 20:6–9). They both returned to their homes, while Mary stayed behind grieving over what had apparently happened. It was then that Jesus appeared to her.

The apostle Paul pointed out to the Corinthian church, which was battling some doubts, the centrality to the Christian faith of the literal bodily resurrection of Jesus Christ on the third day after his death when he wrote, "And if Christ has not been raised, then all our preaching is useless, and your faith is useless" (1 Corinthians 15:14).

John points out that Jesus later appeared to all the remaining disciples, including one named Thomas, who had plainly stated that unless he could touch Jesus physically, he wouldn't believe he was alive again.

Study Questions

○ How do you respond when it seems that what God had said would happen didn't happen—at least in the way you'd believed it would?

○ In what instances of your own life have you seen God fulfill a promise you had forgotten he'd made?

Chapter 14

Acts of the Apostles: Paul's Life and Ministry

Historians rank the apostle Paul as one of the most influential and important figures in European and American history. It's small wonder, too, because Paul was the man charged with taking the message of salvation through Jesus Christ to the non-Jewish (Gentile) world, including parts of Europe. This chapter is a study of the accounts of Paul's ministries as they are recorded in the book of Acts—including his call to ministry and all three of his missionary journeys.

Empowered from Above

"But you will receive power when the Holy Spirit comes upon you. And you will be my witnesses, telling people about me everywhere—in Jerusalem, throughout Judea, in Samaria, and to the ends of the earth" (Acts 1:8). These were Jesus's last recorded words before he ascended back to heaven, and they were words the fledgling church—at that point just a group of believers waiting for the arrival of the Holy Spirit—took seriously as it began to move out and spread around the area. One person who wasn't there when Jesus spoke these words was a man named Saul, who was miraculously and spectacularly called to preach the Good News of the message of Jesus Christ to the Gentile world (Greece and Europe) and given a new name as well: Paul the apostle.

The Acts of the Apostles—also known simply as Acts—was written by Luke the physician (who also penned the gospel that bears his name) and tells the stories of the start of the church and of the men who were charged with taking Christ's message of salvation to the world around them. That includes the work of the apostle Paul (Acts 13–28), who took three missionary journeys, all of which resulted in the formation of several new churches in various villages and cities.

Time for a Change in Direction (Acts 9)

Since you've gotten this far in your study of the Bible, you have probably noticed that God often uses the unlikeliest of characters to do His work—people you'd probably never hire to help run your company but that God saw fit to charge with being a part of His plan of salvation for all humankind. The man who would be the apostle Paul was just such a person. Paul was a devout Jew—an expert in Jewish law who at the time of his conversion to Christianity was doing everything he could to wipe out this heretical new movement. The Bible says that he went everywhere, dragging Christian men and women out of their homes and throwing them into prison (Acts 8:3).

His conversion took place as he was on his way to Damascus (in what is now Syria) to persecute Christians. As he approached the city, a bright light from heaven suddenly shone down around him, striking him blind. As he fell to the ground, he heard a voice from heaven say, "Saul! Saul! Why are you persecuting me?" (Acts 9:4).

ALERT!

The first mention of Saul—later the apostle Paul—is in Acts 7, which gives the account of the stoning of a disciple of Jesus named Stephen. While Paul didn't directly participate in this man's death, he did stand by and keep watch over the murderers' garments and later gave approval to the stoning (Acts 7:58, 8:1).

Jesus told Saul that it was him he had been persecuting, then instructed him to get up and go to Damascus where he was to meet with a believer named Ananias, who God had instructed to minister to Saul when he arrived.

Saul remained in Damascus with the believers who lived there. His sight had been restored, and after just a few days he began preaching about Jesus in the synagogues, telling people that he was indeed the Son of God.

Saul's preaching was so powerful and persuasive that the Jewish religious leaders plotted to kill him. But after he found out about the plot, he fled the city and went to Jerusalem where he preached and where the other apostles welcomed him in.

Study Questions

○ What instructions did Jesus give Saul on the road to Damascus?
○ What was Ananias's response when he was instructed to minister to Saul when he arrived in Damascus?

Paul's First Missionary Journey (Acts 13:1–15:35)

The apostle Paul is known to have taken three missionary journeys during which he founded or planted many churches and ministered to many others. All of this took place following his post-conversion preaching, training, travel, and time in Antioch, Syria, which had become the center or base of the Christian church.

FACT

In Acts 13:13, we read of a man named Mark leaving Paul during his first missionary journey. While that isn't a great way to start a life of ministry, Mark finished strong. It is believed that this is the same Mark who penned the gospel that bears his name.

Paul is referred to as the first missionary to the Gentiles, and the start of his first journey is recorded in Acts 13. This journey took place around A.D. 46–48 and was his shortest—both in time and in distance traveled. But it was this first journey that established Paul as a key figure in the spread of the gospel of Christ to the Gentile world. Acts gives this account of Paul and Barnabas's commissioning:

Among the prophets and teachers of the church at Antioch of Syria were Barnabas, Simeon (called "the black man"), Lucius (from Cyrene), Manaen (the childhood companion of King Herod Antipas), and Saul. One day as these men were worshiping the Lord and fasting, the Holy Spirit said, "Dedicate Barnabas and Saul for the special work to which I have called them." So after more fasting and prayer, the men laid their hands on them and sent them on their way. (Acts 13:1–3)

On Paul's first journey he was accompanied by men named Barnabas and Mark. The journey began in Seleucia, the seaport of Antioch in what is now Syria (Acts 13:1–4). From there, Paul, who was still called Saul, sailed to the island nation of Cyprus. They landed in the city of Salamis, where they preached in the Jewish synagogues (13:5). They then traveled the entire southern coast of Cyprus until they reached a place called Paphos (13:6), where the Roman proconsul Sergius Paulus was converted after Paul rebuked a sorcerer there (13:6–12). It was at this time that Paul became the leader in the missionary journey, and also when his name was changed from Saul to Paul (13:9, 13).

From there, Paul and Barnabas visited the following places:

- Perga, where John Mark left them (Acts 13:13)
- Pisidian, Antioch, where many were converted (13:14–41)
- Iconium, where many Jews and Gentiles alike were converted (13:51)
- Lystra, where Paul was stoned (14:8–19)
- Derbe (14:20)

The Bible says that after visiting Derbe, Paul and Barnabas returned by ship to their home base of Antioch (Syria) and that, "Upon arriving in Antioch, they called the church together and reported everything God had done through them and how he had opened the door of faith to the Gentiles, too" (Acts 14:27). Paul and Barnabas stayed in Antioch for a period of time (probably around a year) after that first missionary journey, dealing with various issues and questions in the church there. But it was only a matter of time before Paul had the urge to go and do what God had called and prepared him to do.

Study Questions
○ How was Barnabas referred to when he is first introduced in the book of Acts (Acts 13:1)?
○ While in Salamis, where did Paul and Barnabas preach?

Paul's Second Missionary Journey (Acts 15:36–18:21)

Paul's second missionary journey started like this: "After some time Paul said to Barnabas, 'Let's go back and visit each city where we previously preached the word of the Lord, to see how the new believers are doing'" (Acts 15:36).

Of course, Barnabas was all for a follow-up visit to the cities where he and Paul had preached the gospel message, but that was followed by an unfortunate disagreement. Acts tells us that Barnabas wanted to take John Mark, who had left them on their first missionary journey and returned home, but Paul didn't think it was wise. That led to something of a split between Paul and Barnabas. Although there was no animosity between the two—in fact, Paul later spoke very highly of Barnabas and also made up with John Mark (Colossians 4:10, 2 Timothy 4:11)—the two never traveled together again.

ALERT!

It was during Paul's second missionary journey that Luke, the writer of the book of Acts, personally joined the missionary party. From Acts 16:10 on, the narrative changes and uses the pronoun *we*. ("So we decided to leave for Macedonia at once, having concluded that God was calling us to preach the Good News there.")

The apostle's second missionary trip was far longer than the first. It started around A.D. 49 and lasted for about three years. This time, instead of traveling with Barnabas, Paul was accompanied by a man named Silas. The second trip was over land, through Syria and Cilicia, so that Paul could visit the Asian churches he had established in his first journey.

Among those churches were the ones at Derbe and then the one at Lystra, where a young preacher-to-be named Timothy joined him (Acts 16:1–5). From there they went north through places called Phrygia and Galatia (16:6), the home of the church to which Paul wrote the book of Galatians, which is in the New Testament.

The Biblical account of Paul's second missionary journey is filled with incredible adventures and spiritual visions on the part of Paul, including the following:

- After leaving Galatia, Paul wanted to travel to Bithynia, which is located on the shore of the Black Sea, but he and his companions were stopped when, "the Spirit of Jesus did not allow them to go there" (Acts 16:7). Instead, they traveled to a seaport called Troas, which was on the shore of the Aegean Sea, and preached and taught there (16:8).

- After staying in Troas for a while, Paul had a vision of a man in Macedonia begging him to come and help the people there (Acts 16:9). Realizing that this was a message from God, Paul and his companions set sail for Macedonia, where he worked to establish churches in Philippi (16:11–39), Thessalonica (17:1–9), and Berea (17:10–15).

- Facing threats of death, Paul was sent away from Berea while Silas and Timothy stayed behind. Paul, leaving instructions for Silas and Timothy to rejoin him as soon as possible, was taken to Athens, Greece, a city filled with pagan idolatry. While there, Paul observed a huge altar to "an Unknown God" (Acts 17:23). Paul pointed out to the high council of Athens that they had been worshipping a deity they didn't even know, but he could tell them who God really was and that this God was the one who had power over death (17:24–32). Some who heard Paul's message laughed at him, but some—including a council member named Dionysius and a woman named Damaris—joined him in believing in Jesus Christ.

- From Athens, Paul traveled to Corinth, which was the seat of the Roman government of Achaia. Paul stayed there for a year and a half successfully preaching the message of Jesus Christ to Jews and Greeks alike. While in Corinth, Paul wrote two letters to the church at Thessalonica, which are in the Bible today as First and Second Thessalonians.

To understand the nature of the apostle Paul's missionary journeys, it is vital to understand that they were not without their problems. In the second expedition, for example, Paul and Silas often faced fierce opposition and death threats and were even thrown in jail for casting a spirit out of a fortune teller (Acts 16:16–40).

Following several other visits in the region, many of them quite fruitful, Paul began working his way home to Jerusalem because he, being a devout Jew, wanted to celebrate Pentecost in Jerusalem. Later, he returned home to Antioch (Acts 18:18–23).

Study Questions

○ Read again what Paul said to Barnabas as he prepared him to set out on another missionary journey (Acts 15:36). What was Paul's motivation in visiting those churches again?

○ Read Acts 16:7. What does Paul's change in course tell you about his relationship with God?

Paul's Third Missionary Journey (Acts 18:22–21:16)

Paul's third and final missionary expedition was launched from the same place as the other two: Antioch, Syria (Acts 18:23). The first leg of his third missionary trip was over land in Asia Minor (modern-day Turkey). He visited cities in the regions of Galatia and Phrygia before settling for nearly three years in the city of Ephesus (19:1–41), where he founded a church that would receive one of the letters that later would be included in the Bible.

Like many ancient cities of that time, Ephesus was rife with pagan religious worship and practices. But as Paul preached, taught, and performed miracles for all the people to see—including the healing of sick people and the casting out of demons—many people turned to Christ, including sorcerers who burned very expensive sorcery books (Acts 19:17–20).

FACT

Acts 20:7–12 gives the account of Paul doing what Jesus himself had done: raising a person from the dead. A young man named Eutychus fell three stories from a windowsill to his death. But Paul bent down and took the man in his arms: "'Don't worry,' he said, 'he's alive!'" (20:10). As Paul had said, the young man lived.

While in Ephesus, Paul found himself in trouble from the local idol worshipers. This time, Paul had exposed the fraud of the pagan god Artemis and the craftsmen and artisans who were in the business of supplying the public with the idols. After Paul spoke out, a near riot broke out and he was nearly killed in the melee (Acts 19:28–41).

Paul left Ephesus for Macedonia and eventually arrived in Greece, where he stayed for three months before learning of a plot against his life (Acts 20:1–3). At that time he was preparing to sail back to Syria—most likely Antioch—but decided to return through Macedonia. After arriving in the city of Philippi, he sailed to Troas (20:6). From there, Paul traveled through Assos, Mitylene, Kios, Samos, and Miletus (20:13–16).

While in Miletus, Paul sent for the elders of the church at Ephesus and asked them to come meet him. They did, and Paul told them:

> *You know that from the day I set foot in the province of Asia until now I have done the Lord's work humbly and with many tears. I have endured the trials that came to me from the plots of the Jews. I never shrank back from telling you what you needed to hear, either publicly or in your homes. I have had one message for Jews and Greeks alike—the necessity of repenting from sin and turning to God, and of having faith in our Lord Jesus. (Acts 20:18–21)*

Paul then told them that he would be returning to Jerusalem and encouraged them in their work in their church. In the end, when Paul had finished speaking to the elders, "he knelt and prayed with them. They wept aloud as they embraced him in farewell, sad most of all because he had said that they would never see him again. Then they accompanied him down to the ship" (Acts 20:36–39).

Paul then finished the final leg of his voyage, stopping in the island of Cos, Rhodes, Patara, Cyprus, and then to Tyre, Syria. He then traveled through Ptolemais, Caesarea, and then finally to Jerusalem.

Study Questions

○ What was the tone of Paul's farewell to the elders of the Ephesian church?

○ Read Acts 20:25–35. What specific encouragements did Paul give the elders of the Ephesian church and how do they apply to your life of faith today?

Paul in Jerusalem (Acts 21:17–23:22)

As Paul began his journey back to Jerusalem, he was faced with an ominous prophecy from a man named Agabus. When this prophet visited Paul and his companions, he took Paul's belt and tied his own hands and feet with it, then told Paul that the owner of the belt would be bound likewise by the Jewish leaders in Jerusalem and handed over to the Romans (Acts 21:10–11).

Those words certainly came to pass. Paul was welcomed by the Christian church leaders in Jerusalem (Acts 21:17), who listened as he told them of the things God had done during his travels and who later asked him to deal with some misunderstandings about his teachings among Jewish believers. It wasn't long, however, before he was beaten and nearly murdered in a mob scene near the Temple that arose over the perception that Paul had broken Jewish law. It was only because he was taken into custody by a Roman authority that Paul survived (Acts 21:27–36).

ALERT!

It has been pointed out that this part of Paul's life is very similar to the final few days of Jesus's own life. What was to happen to both was foretold. Both were taken into custody in Jerusalem. Both were falsely accused, and both had to stand trial for crimes they didn't commit.

Some of those opposed to Paul's teachings wanted him dead on the spot, but it was only because of his knowledge of the law of that time that he survived. What followed was an arrest by the Roman authorities and a series of defenses on Paul's own part.

The book of Acts records many instances where Paul defended himself: in front of the crowd who wanted him dead (Acts 22:1–21), before the body of Jewish religious authorities (23:1–10), before Governor Felix, the Roman procurator of Judea at that time (24:10–21), and before King Agrippa (26:1–29).

Study Questions

○ How do you think believers God has called to service should respond in the face of fear and opposition to the work they are doing?

○ How would you respond if you were falsely accused or even punished as Paul was even though he'd committed no crime?

Paul in Caesarea and Rome (Acts 24:10–28:10)

There were plots afoot to have Paul killed, so he was sent away by the Roman authorities to Caesarea, where he stood before Felix, who, in an effort to win favor with the Jewish people, had Paul put in custody. Paul did have some limited freedoms and privileges, but he was left there for two years (Acts 24:22–27).

Two years after Paul's imprisonment there was a change in Roman leadership, and Paul, himself a Roman citizen, appealed his case to Caesar. He did that because there was a plan afoot to have him taken to Jerusalem so that he could be intercepted and killed on the way. For that reason, Paul was sent to Rome to be tried in a Roman court. It was because Paul was a Roman citizen that his appeal was heard.

FACT

It was during Paul's time as a prisoner in Rome that he wrote his epistles to the Colossians, the Ephesians, the Philippians, and to Philemon. Also, if he is the writer of the epistle to the Hebrews (as many believe he is), it was most likely that he wrote that while in Rome as well.

Paul's voyage by sea to Rome was a long and perilous one. At one point, they fought through a long and terrible storm, and no one on the ship had eaten in a long time. Paul, however, received assurance from God in a dream that he would eventually arrive safely in Rome and stand trial before Caesar and bear witness to the gospel (Acts 27:19–25). But that would happen only after the ship was torn apart by a storm off the shore of the Mediterranean island of Malta. Miraculously, everyone on the ship was able to make it to shore, where they stayed for three months and where Paul was able to perform some miracles for some of the locals.

Paul finally made it to Rome, where he was put under what could be considered house arrest. He was allowed to have his own private lodging, but he was under constant guard by a Roman soldier (Acts 28:16). Three days after his arrival, Paul met with the local Jewish leaders and pleaded his case with them, telling them, "Brothers, I was arrested in Jerusalem and handed over to the Roman government, even though I had done nothing against our people or the customs of our ancestors" (Acts 28:17). He went on to explain how the Romans had tried him and acquitted him of any wrongdoing but that when the Jewish leaders protested the decision, he felt it necessary to appeal to Caesar for his own safety. He finished by telling them that he called them together to tell them that the Messiah had come in the person of Jesus Christ (28:18–20).

From that time on, Paul preached the gospel message, telling everyone who would listen that salvation had come to the Jews and to the Gentiles alike. For the next two years he lived in his own rented home, where he welcomed everyone who came to visit him and told them about Jesus Christ. And no one, the final verse of Acts tells us, did anything to stop him.

Study Questions

○ Despite a terrible shipwreck, Paul believed God when he was told that he would one day be in Rome. How do you respond when it appears that the promises God has given you might not come to pass because of some circumstance?

○ Do you believe you would have the courage to preach the gospel of Christ if you were in Paul's situation?

Chapter 15

Romans: The Basics of the Christian Faith

Paul's letter—or epistle—to the Roman Christians is the first of the thirteen letters known to have been authored by Paul to appear in the Bible. (Some ascribe Hebrews to Paul, but that is far from certain.) Romans has been praised as Paul's greatest printed work—mostly because its simplicity and direct approach to the message of the gospel of Jesus Christ makes it accessible and understandable to even the most novice Bible readers.

The Upshot of Romans

The writers of the four Gospels tell us about the words and works of Jesus Christ, but Paul tells us what they mean to those who would put their faith in him after his death, resurrection, and ascension back to heaven. It is through reading Romans that we come to an understanding of the meaning of Jesus's sacrificial death on the cross as well as how that event should change the way we think and live.

FACT

It isn't certain who founded the Roman church, but it is believed that visitors from Rome to Jerusalem for the Passover and Pentecost may have been converted then took the message of Christ back to Rome. Paul's epistle to the Romans is believed to have been written around A.D. 54 or 55.

This chapter provides a study or overview of the first eight chapters of Romans. As you begin reading and studying this epistle for the first time, large portions of the first two or three chapters might seem a little dark—even hopeless. But don't allow yourself to stop just because the early reading might seem like bad news. Make sure you read on so that you can more fully understand the Good News of the salvation God has provided freely through the work of Jesus Christ on the cross.

What Happens to All Sinners
(Romans 1:18–2:10)

One of the most common misconceptions about God is that since He is a God of love, there is no way He would allow anyone to miss out on heaven and end up in the other place. But it is hard—even impossible—to read the Bible and make a case for that kind of thinking.

The apostle Paul—following some greetings to the Roman church, including stating his desire to visit them—points out that there is a price to be paid for all sin, even what we might consider the little ones. He begins this section by stating very clearly that "God shows his anger from heaven against all sinful, wicked people who suppress the truth by their wickedness" (Romans 1:18). Paul goes on to say that sin starts in the heart of humans who won't acknowledge God for who He is or even recognize Him for what He has done.

Because of these things, Paul tells us, God allowed all of humankind to go into every kind of sinful behavior:

Their lives became full of every kind of wickedness, sin, greed, hate, envy, murder, quarreling, deception, malicious behavior, and gossip. They are backstabbers, haters of God, insolent, proud, and boastful. They invent new ways of sinning, and they disobey their parents. They refuse to understand, break their promises, are heartless, and have no mercy. (Romans 1:29–31)

Still, many people might look at the things that Paul has written in Romans 1 and say, "I haven't done any of those things, so I must be doing all right!" But Paul writes, "You may think you can condemn such people, but you are just as bad, and you have no excuse! When you say they are wicked and should be punished, you are condemning yourself, for you who judge others do these very same things" (Romans 2:1).

Then comes the unavoidable truth about the sin for which each and every human being is guilty: "And we know that God, in his justice, will punish anyone who does such things. Since you judge others for doing these things, why do you think you can avoid God's judgment when you do the same things?" (Romans 2:2–3).

Paul gives his readers a hint of the Good News, pointing out that God is kind, tolerant, and patient with each and every one of them and that this kindness, tolerance, and patience is designed to bring them to repentance and away from punishment (Romans 2:4–6) if they will just turn from their stubborn ways. Paul writes, "But he will pour out his anger and wrath on those who live for themselves, who refuse to obey the truth and instead live lives of wickedness" (Romans 2:8).

Paul is coming to the Good News for all of us—Jew and Gentile alike (Romans 2:10), but before he gets to that, he has another point to make when it comes to the sinful condition of all humankind.

Study Questions
○ What does this passage say God has in store for sinners?
○ What kinds of behaviors does the apostle Paul condemn as sinful in this passage?

The Lowdown, Dirty Truth: We're All Sinners (Romans 2:11–3:20)

No one likes to be thought of as a sinner, as someone who has nothing to offer God. We all like to think of ourselves as fundamentally good people who have a good grasp on right and wrong and whose lives are by and large pleasing to God. While most of us know we're not perfect, at least we aren't out doing the really bad stuff.

But Paul is very clear in his letter to the Romans that each and every one of us—Jew and Gentile alike—are all sinners who deserve eternal separation from God. Quoting from the Old Testament, he states, "No one is righteous—not even one. No one is truly wise; no one is seeking God. All have turned away; all have become useless. No one does good, not a single one" (Romans 3:10–12).

ALERT!

When Paul wrote of the universal sinfulness of humankind in Romans 3:10–18, he quoted from several Old Testament sources: Psalms 14:1–3, 53:1–3, 5:9, 140:3, 10:7; Isaiah 53:7–8; Psalm 36:1. Having been a former Pharisee, Paul knew the Old Testament Scriptures very well.

Paul, a Jewish religious leader prior to his conversion and therefore one who knew well the Law of Moses, pointed out in Romans 2:11–16 that all people would be judged the same. Those who sinned without the law would be judged the same as those who sinned under it, he said.

Paul pointed out in Romans 3:19 that the purpose of the law was to show all of humankind that it was sinful, that it had missed the mark when it came to the righteousness of God. He wrote, "For no one can ever be made right with God by doing what the law commands. The law simply shows us how sinful we are" (Romans 3:20).

In citing the writings of Moses (found in the first five books of the Old Testament, also known as the Pentateuch) and the prophets, Paul is pointing out that God's ultimate plan of redemption for humankind through Jesus Christ ran throughout the Bible, starting with the book of Genesis and running through the final book of prophecy.

This is bottom-line preaching, and it tells us that no matter how good we are, no matter how well we keep the letter of the law, no matter how many acts of kindness we take part in, we are still sinners in the eyes and by the standards of a holy God.

So what is the good news in all this? Paul goes on to tell us that it is the fact that God justifies us or makes us righteous through our faith in Christ, not in following the letter of the law.

Study Questions
○ Read Romans 3:10–18. What does this tell us we as humans lack when it comes to being righteous?
○ What is the true purpose of the law of God, according to Paul?

Now for the Good News! (Romans 3:21–31)

If you take them alone, most of the first three chapters of Romans can seem kind of bleak. Paul is essentially telling his readers that keeping the law of God even to the very letter isn't going to do them any good when it comes to being truly righteous—not to mention truly saved.

But the apostle isn't going to leave his readers hanging over a pit of despair. He has set them up to see the beauty and wonder of God's plan of salvation for Jew and Gentile alike, a plan that has nothing to do with keeping the law or with our own acts of goodness: "But now God has shown us a way to be made right with him without keeping the requirements of the law, as was promised in the writings of Moses and the prophets long ago. We are made right with God by placing our faith in Jesus Christ. And this is true for everyone who believes, no matter who we are" (Romans 3:21–22).

Paul has gone to great pains to establish the fact that all men and women—no matter what their background, ethnic heritage, or religious pedigrees—are sinners on their way to eternity in hell. "For all have sinned; all fall short of God's glorious standard," he summarizes (Romans 3:23), then concludes, "Yet now God in his gracious kindness declares us not guilty. He has done this through Christ Jesus, who has freed us by taking away our sins. For God sent Jesus to take the punishment for our sins and to satisfy God's anger against us. We are made right with God when we believe that Jesus shed his blood, sacrificing his life for us" (Romans 3:24–25).

FACT

One of the key themes in Paul's letter to the Romans is the Good News of salvation in Jesus Christ. That phrase appears in Romans sixteen times in all, compared with twenty-six times in the four Gospels. That is one of the reasons this book has been referred to as the Gospel according to Paul.

This passage brings to mind a courtroom scene in which each of us as individuals stand absolutely 100 percent guilty before God. We not only don't have adequate defense, we have no defense at all. God is well within His rights to pronounce judgment on us, but His Son, Jesus, steps between the Father and us and pronounces us not guilty. Yes, we've sinned, but because Jesus willingly took the punishment for our sins on the cross, God sees us as pure and sinless.

Some people may believe that God judges people on a scale that weights the good things we've done against the bad things we've done. If the good outweighs the bad, then we've punched our own ticket into heaven.

However, Paul points out that this kind of thinking is completely wrong and backward: "Can we boast, then, that we have done anything to be accepted by God? No, because our acquittal is not based on our good deeds. It is based on our faith. So we are made right with God through faith and not by obeying the law" (Romans 3:27–28).

That's the Good News in a nutshell: Each of us is guilty—guilty as sin, as it were. But because of God's incredible graciousness and mercy, we are made right with Him. And that's not because of anything we are or anything we do. It's all because of who God is and what He is like.

Study Questions

○ According to Romans 3:24, on what basis does God save sinners?
○ According to Romans 3:25, what exactly did Jesus do in order to bring salvation to those who believe in him?

Justified Through Faith (Romans 3:29–5:1)

A beloved humanitarian and the lowliest nobody who never lifted a finger in his life to help his fellow man have one thing in common: Without faith, neither of them will see the kingdom of God.

Forgiveness means that God has removed from us the stain of our sin so that He can't see it anymore. Justification means that He's made us right before Himself through the work of Jesus Christ on the cross. Those two things—which are absolutely essential to the one who wants to inherit God's heavenly, eternal kingdom—are accessed through faith and faith alone.

Faith can be defined simply as taking God at His word. It means that you believe Him when He tells you that He's taken care of everything it takes for you to be made right with Him. Again, for Jew and Gentile alike, faith is what it takes to be made right before God. As Paul points out, God is the God of all people—Jew and non-Jew alike—and He has made faith the common denominator for everyone to approach Him.

"There is only one God, and there is only one way of being accepted by him. He makes people right with himself only be faith, whether they are Jews or Gentiles" (Romans 3:30). And that faith, Paul points out, doesn't replace the law but in fact fulfills it (Romans 3:31).

ALERT!

The theme of justification through faith is hardly unique to the New Testament. In the book of Genesis, Abraham is said to have believed God and been justified through his faith. Paul cites that passage of Genesis in several other of his epistles to the various churches.

Paul pointed out that Abraham, who was the earthly father of the Jewish people, wasn't declared righteous through anything he did but because of who he believed: "Abraham believed God, so God declared him to be righteous" (Romans 4:3). Paul tells us that Abraham, while he wasn't a perfect man, never wavered in his faith. He continued through his life to believe God in all things, and because of that the life of Abraham was a benefit to all of humankind (Romans 4:16–17). It was through Abraham's people that God brought into the world the Messiah, Jesus Christ, who died for the sins of all humanity.

That is why Paul wrote, "Therefore, since we have been made right in God's sight by faith, we have peace with God because of what Jesus Christ our Lord has done for us" (Romans 5:1). Being made right in God's sight is a wonderful place to be. It's a place of forgiveness and justification, and a place of many other benefits.

Study Questions
○ What part does faith play in personal salvation through Jesus Christ?
○ What "works" make us worthy in God's eyes of salvation?

The Benefits of Being Made Right with God Through Faith (Romans 5:1–5)

Paul echoed what the book of Genesis said about Abraham, the father of the Jewish people, namely that he believed God and was declared righteous because of that faith. That is the number one benefit each and every one of us who place our faith in Jesus Christ receive: being right with God.

It has been said that the word *justified* as Paul uses it in his letter to the Romans means that when God looks at those who have put their faith in Jesus Christ, He sees perfection because He sees only His own righteousness, which was lived out perfectly in the life of His only begotten Son.

But there are many other side benefits that flow out of that one, and they are all important for us to enjoy as we grow and mature in our faith in Christ. According to Paul in his letter to the Romans, when we are "made right in God's sight" by placing our faith in Jesus Christ, we have the benefit of:

- being at peace with God (Romans 5:1);
- being in a position to receive undeserved blessing and freedom (5:2);
- confidently and joyfully looking forward to sharing in God's eternal glory (5:2);
- knowing that everything we go through, including trials and problems, helps us to mature (5:3);
- knowing that all we endure develops character, which strengthens our confidence in our salvation (5:4);
- knowing how dearly God loves us, simply because He's given us His own spirit (5:5);
- being called "friends of God" (5:10–11).

All of these things flow out of God's unmerited favor, which has been seen as the very definition of His grace. It is also reflected in these words

Paul wrote about the sacrificial death of Jesus Christ: "When we were utterly helpless, Christ came at just the right time and died for us sinners. Now, most people would not be willing to die for an upright person, though someone might perhaps be willing to die for a person who is especially good. But God showed his great love for us by sending Christ to die for us while we were still sinners" (Romans 5:6–8).

Romans tells us that when Christ did those things for us, he made us right with God, and that he will certainly save us from the condemnation that has come upon all humankind because of the sin of Adam.

Study Questions

○ What does it mean to you to be at peace with God?
○ What benefits have you personally received through your faith in Jesus Christ?

A New Life in Christ (Romans 6–7)

The sacrifice of Jesus Christ on the cross ensures that each and every person who puts their faith in him is forgiven, justified, and guaranteed a place in God's eternal kingdom. But a change in eternal destination isn't the only way our lives are altered. In addition, Paul tells us that we are given the freedom over the effects and bondage of sin.

ALERT!

Romans 5:12–19 outlines what is known as the doctrine of original sin, which states that sin entered the human race through one man, Adam, and that all of his descendants (which are all of us) are born with that sin. This doctrine further states that through one man, Jesus, that sin is removed.

In Romans 1–5, Paul outlines how we can be saved, but in Romans 6–8 he tells us what that means to our lives in the here and now. This passage is, in other words, instructions on how to live the Christian life.

In these three chapters, Paul tells us that we have the potential to live holy lives because we know Christ (Romans 6) but that we find living those kinds of lives impossible through our own efforts because we still live in sinful bodies (Romans 7). The answer to this problem is spelled out in chapter 8, which tells us that we are empowered to live godly lives because God gives each of those who put their faith in Jesus Christ His Holy Spirit to aide and guide them.

Chapter 6 begins, "Well then, should we keep on sinning so that God can show us more and more of his wonderful grace? Of course not! Since we have died to sin, how can we continue to live in it? Or have you forgotten that when we were joined with Christ Jesus in baptism, we joined him in his death?" (Romans 6:1–3).

Paul then goes on to explain that those who have received Christ have, through baptism, symbolically and spiritually died with him, been buried with him, and been raised from the dead with him (Romans 6:4–11). When we died with him, our sinful natures died and were buried. What was raised was a new person, one who has had the power of sin broken in his or her life.

Because of that, we are no longer slaves to sin, as we once were. Instead, we are slaves to God, and that means we are free to live lives that lead to holiness and eternal life (Romans 6:20–23).

Study Questions

○ How does God's grace affect how you view sin in your personal life?

○ How has your faith in Christ changed how you view sin?

Power for Godly Living (Romans 8)

The eighth chapter of Romans begins with this powerful message: "So now there is no condemnation for those who belong to Christ Jesus. And because you belong to him, the power of the life-giving Spirit has freed you from the power of sin that leads to death" (verses 1–2).

This tells us that although we will never be completely free of sin while we live in these mortal bodies (see Romans 7), we are freed from the power of sin over our bodies and free from the control of indwelling sin—meaning sin within us. Paul tells his readers that the law—meaning the Law of

Moses—could do nothing to release us from the power of sin, that it could only show us how sinful we really are. The power of the life-giving Spirit of God, on the other hand, has freed all who believe "from the power of sin that leads to death." Yes, even those who have put their faith in Jesus Christ are prone to sin at times, but they are never to be controlled by or dominated by the sin that once so cruelly ruled over them.

Romans 8 opens by telling us that there is no condemnation for those who belong to Christ Jesus, and it ends by telling us that there is nothing that can separate us from his love:

> *And I am convinced that nothing can ever separate us from God's love. Neither death nor life, neither angels nor demons, neither our fears for today nor our worries about tomorrow—not even the powers of hell can separate us from God's love. No power in the sky above or in the earth below—indeed, nothing in all creation will ever be able to separate us from the love of God that is revealed in Christ Jesus our Lord. (Romans 8:38–39)*

This is what the life in Christ is all about. We aren't condemned, but we are loved and freed to live a godly life. And no matter what happens—no matter what kind of opposition comes our way—nothing can remove us from God's love, which was demonstrated through Jesus Christ.

Study Questions

○ How does knowing that there is no condemnation for you affect your life for and in Jesus Christ?

○ What part do you think God's Holy Spirit plays in your personal daily walk with Jesus Christ?

Chapter 16

Ephesians: Engaging in Spiritual Warfare

Jesus came to earth as the Prince of Peace, but what he left behind after going back to his Father in heaven was a people he had called to go to war on his behalf—spiritual war that is. This chapter is a study of a section of the apostle Paul's letter to the Ephesian church in which he encourages them to go to spiritual war but to make sure they are fully equipped to fight before they go.

The Look of the Church (Ephesians 1–5)

The apostle Paul, writing to a group of Christians (also called "the church") in a city called Ephesus, wrote about the blessings they had received in Jesus Christ, how they were to be united in Christ, and the mission Christ had performed when he was on earth. He followed that by writing about the diversity of the church and what holiness within the church looked like.

One of the main themes of the book of Ephesians is that all Christians have been given "every spiritual blessing in the heavenly realms, because we belong to Christ" (Ephesians 1:6). One of those blessings is listed in Ephesians 6, and it's probably the best known in this particular epistle. It is in this section that Paul writes about what has come to be known as spiritual warfare.

Paul wanted the believers in Ephesus to understand that they have tremendous power in Christ—power they had hardly even begun to harness and use to their advantage—and that their victory in the spiritual realm was absolutely guaranteed, simply because Jesus had delivered them the victory. This section on spiritual warfare was Paul's final message of encouragement to the Ephesians, and it started like this:

> A final word: Be strong in the Lord and in his mighty power. Put on all of God's armor so that you will be able to stand firm against all strategies of the devil. For we are not fighting against flesh-and-blood enemies, but against evil rulers and authorities of the unseen world, against mighty powers in this dark world, and against evil spirits in the heavenly places. (Ephesians 6:10–12)

Before telling the Ephesians what the weapons for spiritual warfare are, Paul tells them to put on the "full armor of God" so that they will be able to withstand evil and stand their ground (Ephesians 6:13).

Belt and Body Armor (Ephesians 6:10–14)

After telling the believers in Ephesus to put on every piece of their spiritual armor, and after telling them who the battle is really against, he goes on to tell them what those pieces are. He starts that section by saying, "Stand your ground, putting on the belt of truth and the body armor of God's righteousness" (Ephesians 6:14).

You don't have to be an expert on all things military to know that the belt and body armor are used to protect a warrior from a frontal assault—not to protect him from behind. That is why Paul starts this section by telling the Ephesians to stand their ground.

There are only a few things God cannot do, simply because they would violate His perfect nature. Among them is telling an untruth: "So God has given both his promise and his oath. These two things are unchangeable because it is impossible for God to lie" (Hebrews 6:18).

The belt of truth means God's truth. God speaks only truth. It is not in His nature to lie in any way. If He has said it in the pages of the Bible, you can bank on it!

On the other hand, the enemy and his cohorts are liars and deceivers. Of course, we would expect them to lie and deceive in order to win a war by keeping us from seeing the truth about ourselves, about the power we have in Christ, about the authority of God's written Word, and about God Himself. But Paul tells us that the truth of God will keep us from being blinded, deceived, or confused by the devil or by the worldly influences he attempts to use in spiritual war.

The breastplate of righteousness refers to God's righteousness. That's because God has declared all believers righteous—meaning right or justified before him—because of what Christ has done for us on the cross. (See Romans 5:18–19 to read about that wonderful truth.) That declaration makes our souls and spirits untouchable as far as Satan's attacks are concerned. Yes, he may harass us and try to keep us from doing the things God calls all believers to do, but as long as we are protected by God's body armor, he can never strike anything coming close to a mortal blow. Paul wanted to remind the Ephesian Christians that they possessed an impenetrable piece of armor that would protect them as they went on the offensive against the devil and against the ungodly world around them.

Study Questions

○ What are believers to do as they put on the belt of truth and the body armor of God's righteousness?

○ What is the purpose of the belt of truth and the body armor of God's righteousness?

Wearing the Shoes of Peace (Ephesians 6:15)

Paul's "full armor of God" includes weapons of defense and weapons of offense. And it also includes shoes. Paul wrote, "For shoes, put on the peace that comes from the Good News so that you will be fully prepared" (Ephesians 6:15).

ALERT!

The word *peace* is one that has many meanings in the Bible. It's used in a spiritual, emotional, and sometimes even physical sense. All of these meanings are important to God, but it is still important you use a concordance and a Bible dictionary and that you pay close attention to how the word is used when you study it.

At a glance, shoes might seem a little out of place when you're talking about dressing for war. But think about it for a minute. What a soldier wears on his feet may be just as important as what he uses to cover his torso or head. If you don't believe that, try hiking ten miles in one day in a really uncomfortable pair of boots. Furthermore, if the Bible tells us to put on shoes or other footwear, that means God intends for us to be on the move.

And that would tell us that we are to be moving forward in an offensive against the devil, not sitting back just playing defense. It would also tell us that we are to walk on and in the peace we have as Christians because we have received the Good News of salvation through faith in Jesus Christ.

One application of that idea of peace is found in Paul's epistle to the Romans: "Therefore, since we have been made right in God's sight by faith, we have peace with God because of what Jesus Christ our Lord has done for us" (Romans 5:1). There are many other references to the word peace in the Bible, some of which refer to our peace with God, others that talk about the inner peace Christians are to have, and still others that talk about peace with one another.

Thinking of peace as one of the pieces of armor for spiritual war may seem a little backward, but it implies that being at peace with God means being in a war of offense against the ungodly elements of our world and, of course, against the devil.

Study Questions

○ What part do the shoes play in the full armor of God?
○ According to Ephesians 6:15, where does peace come from?

A Shield of Faith (Ephesians 6:16)

No first-century soldier in his right mind would have headed out for battle without his shield. Without that all-important piece of equipment, he would be easy prey for his well-armed counterpart, who was probably carrying spears, swords, and other projectile weapons.

FACT

The apostle Peter also warned people to be on the alert for the devil, but he used a different metaphor: "Stay alert! Watch out for your great enemy, the devil. He prowls around like a roaring lion, looking for someone to devour" (1 Peter 5:8). While the wording was different, the idea was the same: Be alert and ready!

Likewise, no Christian would dare head out and attempt to do spiritual war without taking along the shield of faith. That is why Paul wrote, "In addition to all of these, hold up the shield of faith to stop the fiery arrows of the devil" (Ephesians 6:16).

Paul knew that while the devil was defeated by what Jesus did on the cross, he wasn't about to lie down and acknowledge his defeat without trying to take down as many people with him as possible. He is an angry adversary who still had some fight left in him, even if the outcome of the battle was settled.

The devil has an array of weapons he likes to use against believers: fear, doubt, lust, anxiety...the list goes on and on. But Paul says that God has given us a means to repel the devil's use of those weapons: faith. Having faith—meaning taking God at his word and believing He keeps His promises, and knowing that God Himself is bigger and more powerful than anything the devil can throw at us—renders the devil's weapons of offense against the believer absolutely worthless.

Study Questions

○ What specific spiritual weapons has the devil been trying to use against you?

○ In what areas of your spiritual life is God challenging you to have more faith today?

The Helmet of Salvation (Ephesians 6:17)

Very few soldiers can survive a direct shot to the head. Paul wanted his readers to understand that a great deal of the war they were engaged in would be taking place between their ears—in their minds. And he wanted them to understand that the devil wanted nothing more than to take their thinking away from the kind of thinking God wanted them engaged in.

ALERT!

Paul also wrote, "For God has not given us a spirit of fear and timidity, but of power, love, and self-discipline" (2 Timothy 1:7). Other versions of this same verse use the term "sound mind" interchangeably with "self-discipline," which tells us of the importance to God of our right thinking, or putting "on salvation as your helmet."

Furthermore, Paul wanted the Ephesians to understand that they had a means of protection for their heads and their minds: "Put on salvation as your helmet" (Ephesians 6:17). That meant making sure that their minds were fixed on what God had done for them through Jesus Christ and on what it meant to them in their present lives.

But a helmet—be it one used in war, one used in sports, or one used on a construction site—won't do its owner a bit of good unless it is worn. So how do we put on the helmet of salvation?

It's by keeping in mind who you are in Christ—that you have been saved and are on your way to heaven, that you have been given the ability to serve God, and that you are given the authority over the devil and the ability to battle him and win. It's knowing that no matter what you have to endure in this life, God has your very best in mind and that He won't allow you to be tempted beyond your ability to withstand it and that He'll cause everything to work for your best. (See Romans 8:28.)

It is knowing with absolute certainty that in Christ, you are:

- a child of God (John 1:12)
- chosen and enabled to do good things on this earth for God (John 15:16)
- a prized possession of God (1 Corinthians 6:19–20)
- forgiven of all your sins (Colossians 1:13–14)
- able to do all things through the strength of Christ (Philippians 4:13)
- on your way to heaven (Philippians 3:20)

During times of spiritual attack, the devil loves to try to get inside our minds and tell us that we aren't some or any of the things listed above, but when we put on our helmet of salvation, he is unable to sway our minds away from who and what God says we are.

Study Questions

○ Look up the word *salvation* (and its variations) in the New Testament. What do these messages say to Christians about their salvation?

○ Use your concordance and find instances in the New Testament where it says, "You are." What does the New Testament say about who and what Christians really are in Christ?

God's Word: The Sword of the Spirit (Ephesians 6:17)

Earlier in this book, you read that one of the uses of the Word of God, the Bible, was as a weapon of spiritual warfare. That is why Paul referred to it as "the sword of the spirit."

God wants us to understand that the truths and promises contained in the Bible, when they are illuminated by the Holy Spirit—and when we are empowered to receive and apply them—are tremendous weapons in the spiritual battle that is going on this very day. Remember, it was Jesus himself who repelled the devil and his temptations by using the Scriptures correctly (the devil had twisted them in an attempt to tempt Jesus into something God hadn't sent him to do), answering each temptation with the words, "It is written...."

ESSENTIAL

The book of Psalms starts out saying this of those who hold to the Word of God: "Oh, the joys of those who do not follow the advice of the wicked, or stand around with sinners, or join in with mockers. But they delight in the law of the Lord, meditating on it day and night" (Psalm 1:1–2).

The power of God's Word to repel the attacks of the devil didn't end when Jesus went back to heaven. In fact, because God later sent His Holy Spirit to help remind us of the things Jesus did and taught and to shed some light on the Scriptures themselves, we have all the power we need to use the Bible the same way Jesus did. Here are some of the things the Bible says about the Scripture:

- that it will not return to God unfulfilled (Isaiah 55:10–11)
- that it is like a consuming fire and a hammer (Jeremiah 23:29)
- that it will never pass away (Matthew 24:35)
- that it is quick, powerful, and sharp (Hebrews 4:12)
- that it is "inspired by God" (2 Timothy 3:16)

Knowing all these things about the Bible, it's hard to imagine living the Christian life—including fighting spiritual battles against the devil—without reading, studying, and meditating on the Bible. In fact, it can't be done!

Paul is encouraging us to take up our swords by making the Bible a regular and consistent part of our daily lives. When we do that, we will be able to wield a weapon of offense against the devil.

Study Questions

○ In what ways have you personalized the Word of God and used it as a weapon against the devil?

○ Is there anything in your life today toward which you can use the Word of God in order to take victory? What is it and what step will you take next to claim that victory?

Don't Forget to Pray! (Ephesians 6:18–19)

One of the themes we find throughout the Bible is that nothing we attempt to do on God's behalf or to further His kingdom is going to go anywhere unless we have His blessing. And how do we get his blessing? Through prayer!

Paul finishes his spiritual call to arms for the Ephesian Christians by telling them, "And pray in the Spirit at all times and on every occasion. Stay alert and be persistent in your prayers for all believers everywhere" (Ephesians 6:18).

FACT

Paul told us who to pray for when he wrote to the young pastor named Timothy: "I urge you, first of all, to pray for all people. Ask God to help them; intercede on their behalf, and give thanks for them" (1 Timothy 2:1). When you do spiritual warfare and pray for people, pray for everyone God brings to your mind.

Over the centuries, there has been much debate about what exactly it means to "pray in the Spirit," but there can be little question that Paul is reminding believers that if the weapon of choice against the devil is the

Word of God, then prayer should be the fasteners that hold the armor of God in place.

We are encouraged throughout the Bible to pray in all situations and for all things. We are encouraged to pray privately and publicly, in groups or alone. There are many models for prayer in the Bible, but the apostle Paul himself wrote this about prayer: "Don't worry about anything; instead, pray about everything. Tell God what you need, and thank him for all he has done" (Philippians 4:6).

Paul is telling us to pray according to the teaching of the Word of God and through the power of the Holy Spirit. When we are in the midst of spiritual warfare, we must pray for ourselves and for other believers who are in the midst of the very same battles we are fighting.

Paul wants believers to understand that the devil is our spiritual enemy and that we will only be successful in defeating him through using all the weapons at our disposal, including prayer.

So if you forget anything today—your lunch, your car keys, your driver's license—make sure you remember to pray.

Study Questions
○ What kinds of spiritual battles are you fighting now, and how are you praying about them?
○ What groups of people and which individuals do you believe God through his Holy Spirit is asking you to pray for today?

Chapter 17

Philippians: Real Joy in the Midst of Suffering and Adversity

One of the recurring themes you will find in the Bible—particularly in the New Testament letters from Paul, John, and the others—is that of the believer having joy in the midst of suffering and trials. This chapter is a study of Paul's letter to the Philippian church, focusing on his encouragements to live and think in terms of joy—even when times are tough, which they certainly were for the first-century church.

What the Bible Really Says about Suffering

Right now you may be scratching your head and asking yourself, "Does the Bible really say that I'm supposed to be happy because I'm suffering?" Well, that's not exactly what the Bible teaches.

God doesn't expect us to look at difficulties in our lives, such as the loss of jobs, broken relationships, sicknesses, injuries, and the like, and be happy that they are happening to us. In fact, he knows that there is absolutely no way we can be happy about those kinds of things. What God does want, however, is for us to be able to acknowledge that we are hurting and suffering but at the same time know that He is doing something good in us and for us through those times of suffering.

The apostle Paul knew a little bit about suffering. He went through arrests, beatings, imprisonments, shipwrecks, threats, and just about every other difficulty you can imagine. Even as he wrote his letter to the Philippian church, Paul sat in chains in a Roman prison, not knowing whether he would ever see freedom again or if he was going to live or die. Yet in the midst of all that, he was able to say from the heart, "always be full of joy in the Lord" (Philippians 4:4).

ALERT!

In the short letter of Philippians, the apostle Paul uses the word *joy*—or variations—no fewer than eight times and the word *rejoice* no fewer than five. Obviously, Paul wants to convey the idea that our relationships with God through Jesus Christ give us many reasons to feel joy in our hearts.

It was the fact that Paul wrote these things while in stocks and chains in a Roman prison that makes his letter to the Philippians not just a beautiful letter to a church he loved but also a study in rejoicing in even the worst of times and situations.

Always be full of joy in the Lord. That is exactly what Paul himself was. In spite of his present circumstances, he writes a joy-filled love letter to his friends, his brothers, and his sisters in Philippi. For that reason, this book of the Bible is in itself an encouragement to all believers to live in the joy of the Lord no matter what circumstances they face. In his letter to the Philippians, Paul has many things to teach us about joy in the midst of adversity and suffering.

There Is Joy in Jesus Christ, Even When We Suffer

If you were to read a letter someone had written while being confined to a jail cell with only the bare essentials for survival, it's very likely that the tone of the letter would be very dark and dismal. That is exactly the situation Paul was in when he wrote the letter to the Philippians, but his tone is filled with joy and without even a hint of darkness, complaining, or suffering. That is because Paul had learned to have joy in Christ, no matter what his present circumstances.

In fact, as Paul sits in his prison cell, all he can think to say about his situation is that it is benefiting others by bringing them the message of salvation and by emboldening those who are already Christians: "And I want you to know, my dear brothers and sisters, that everything that has happened to me here has helped to spread the Good News. For everyone here, including the whole palace guard, knows that I am in chains because of Christ. And because of my imprisonment, most of the believers here have gained confidence and boldly speak God's message without fear" (Philippians 1:12–14).

FACT

The apostle Paul, along with his co-missionary Silas, founded the Philippian church during his second missionary journey (Acts 16:12–40). Their first convert was a woman named Lydia and her family, followed by a jailer in Philippi (who heard the message of Christ while guarding Paul and Silas) and his family.

This is far more than optimistic thinking. It's a man who seems to take no thought of his suffering other than in what it can do for the good of the kingdom of God. It is a man who, humanly speaking, had every reason to complain and feel sorry for himself but who could do nothing but thank God that his imprisonment had helped further his own missionary work.

As you read through the first chapter of Philippians, ask yourself if you could be as positive and filled with joy as Paul obviously was if you were going through the kind of suffering he was going through.

Study Questions

○ How specifically does Paul describe his feelings for the believers in Philippi?

○ Who did Paul say heard the message of Christ through his imprisonment?

Joy in Our Relationship with Christ (Philippians 2)

A common misconception is that being a Christian means being protected from any physical harm, any kind of sickness or injury, or from persecution at the hands of those who don't like what Christianity stands for. Paul wants his readers—his friends in Philippi—to know that this just isn't the case. He's in what any right thinking person would consider a negative situation, and yet he constantly and repeatedly speaks positive words, words that convey his joy.

ESSENTIAL

It may be tempting to think of the words *joy* and *happiness* as interchangeable—that they mean the same thing. But in the Biblical context, the word *joy* refers to a deep feeling of contentment and satisfaction that has nothing to do with our present circumstances and everything to do with the fulfillment we have in our relationship with God.

In the first chapter of Paul's letter to the Philippians, we read that there is joy not just in knowing Christ but also in suffering for Christ. True Christian joy, which emanates from within the person who knows Jesus Christ as his or her Lord and Savior, will always triumph over even the worst suffering.

In the second chapter of this letter, Paul tells us that it is also the fact of our salvation in Christ that gives us joy, even in the worst of times. This means that no matter what happens to us, we can rest assured that we have been welcomed in as one of God's own children and that we have been marked among those who will spend eternity with Him in heaven.

The second chapter of this letter starts with Paul asking three rhetorical questions: "Is there any encouragement from belonging to Christ? Any comfort from his love? Any fellowship together in the Spirit? Are your hearts tender and compassionate?" (Philippians 2:1)

Paul wants his readers to see that the obvious answers to all three are a resounding "Yes!" But he goes on in verses 2–5 to show the Philippians how that inner joy should show itself both within the church and to the outside world.

Study Questions

○ According to Philippians 2:1, what do we as believers receive from Christ, in good times and bad alike?

○ Read Philippians 2:2–5. What should be the outward, visible effects of a believer's joy in his or her salvation?

Joy in Being Made Truly Righteous Before God (Philippians 3:1–11)

When you're sitting in a prison in chains, not sure if you'll ever again see the light of day, you do a lot of reflecting about your life—where you've been, the things you've done, and what those things mean to you now. Paul writes to the Philippian church about those things:

Yes, everything else is worthless when compared with the infinite value of knowing Christ Jesus my Lord. For his sake I have discarded everything else, counting it all as garbage, so that I could gain Christ and become one with him. I no longer count on my own righteousness through obeying the law; rather, I become righteous through faith in Christ. For God's way of making us right with himself depends on faith. (Philippians 3:8–9)

Paul lists the "everything else" in verses 4–7, in which the apostle writes of his earthly pedigree and lists his credentials as a religious leader. Paul explains that he had followed all the Jewish laws to the letter, that he was from the "right" family, and that he had even been educated as a Pharisee, the Jewish religious leaders who were known for their zealous and strict obedience to the Law of Moses and other legal traditions.

ALERT!

The story of Paul's (his name was Saul before he became a Christian) conversion is told in the ninth chapter of Acts. Amazingly enough, he was on his way to Damascus to aid in the persecution of Christians. It was on the road to Damascus where was struck down, converted, and called to be the messenger of Christ to the non-Jewish world.

Those things, he said, could have given him reason to boast in his own accomplishments and credentials. But he also wanted the Philippian Christians to understand that as far as he was concerned, those things meant nothing to him now. He had renounced his own pedigree and credentials—as far as their having anything to do with his righteousness before God—and had placed his trust completely in the work of Jesus Christ.

Paul took great joy in knowing that he belonged to Jesus Christ and that no matter what happened to him, his ultimate destination in heaven was sealed forever. But not only that, he took deep joy and great encouragement in the fact that his own suffering helped him identify with the sufferings of Jesus Christ, who had died on a cross of wood for him and who was raised from the dead (Philippians 3:10–11).

Study Questions

○ According to Philippians 3:8–9, what are the results of Paul's laying aside his own credentials as a Jewish religious leader and committing himself in every way to Jesus Christ?

○ Reread Philippians 3:10–11. In what event should all believers draw encouragement and joy, especially in times of adversity and suffering?

Joy at Looking to Future Perfection in Christ (Philippians 3:12–16)

When a man is imprisoned and not sure if he'll ever be released alive, he's not prone to think or talk a lot about the future—unless it's to wonder if he has one. But Paul, in the midst of the suffering and persecution he's going through in that Roman prison, takes a forward-looking approach to his faith:

> *I don't mean to say that I have already achieved these things or that I have already reached perfection. But I press on to possess that perfection for which Christ Jesus first possessed me. No, dear brothers and sisters, I have not achieved it, but I focus on this one thing: Forgetting the past and looking forward to what lies ahead, I press on to reach the end of the race and receive the heavenly prize for which God, through Christ Jesus, is calling us. (Philippians 3:12)*

Essentially, Paul is saying that he knows that God has a plan for him to reach spiritual maturity, which was what He had called Paul to in the first place. And Paul speaks as if finishing that race is a certainty. Paul wants his readers to understand that what lay behind them is nothing compared with what is ahead, and that is the heavenly prize God has called each believer to receive at the end of the race He has for each of us to run.

Focusing on the future God has for us is a recurring theme in the Bible, and it's the subject of one of the best-known and most beloved Old Testament verses: "'For I know the plans I have for you,' says the Lord. '"They are plans for good and not for disaster, to give you a future and a hope'" (Jeremiah 29:11).

For that reason, the apostle stands as an example to us modern-day Bible readers of looking forward to what is ahead, not looking back longingly at better days or regretfully at what used to be. This passage shows us that Christianity is very much a religion of looking forward and not backward. God calls each of us to keep our eyes focused ahead and not behind as we press on.

Study Questions

○ What kinds of things in the past do you believe God wants believers to put behind them as they "press on to reach the end of the race and receive the heavenly prize"?

○ Why do you think Paul strongly implies that it's not a good idea to focus on the past but a great idea to focus on the future?

Joy in God's Provision (Philippians 4:1–7)

"Always be full of joy in the Lord," Paul tells the Philippians. He then punctuates that command by writing, " I say it again—rejoice!" (Philippians 4:4).

In times of suffering, adversity, or need, it's difficult for us humans to allow ourselves to feel much of anything good, let alone feel joyful. But Paul isn't just telling his readers to feel joy in the midst of suffering, adversity, and need, he's doing it in writing for them!

Paul wrote: "Don't worry about anything; instead, pray about everything. Tell God what you need, and thank him for all he has done. Then you will experience God's peace, which exceeds anything we can understand. His peace will guard your hearts and minds as you live in Christ Jesus" (Philippians 4:6–7).

FACT

Jesus was teaching something very similar to what Paul is saying in this passage, "When you pray, don't babble on and on as people of other religions do. They think their prayers are answered merely by repeating their words again and again. Don't be like them, for your Father knows exactly what you need even before you ask him" (Matthew 6:7–8).

This sounds like a simple formula, and in some ways it is. Paul is telling his readers that when they are in a tough spot or in a time of need, just do the following:

1. Stop worrying.
2. Pray and tell God what you need.
3. Thank God for what He's already done and for what He's going to do.
4. Rest in the peace of God, which is itself beyond human understanding.

That sounds like a tall order for a lot of believers, especially those who are going through difficult times. It's hard not to worry when you or a loved one is sick and you don't know what's going to happen next. It's hard sometimes to tell God what you need, especially when you may not know specifically what kind of difficulty you are looking at. It's hard to be thankful when things aren't going well. And it's hardest of all to rest in the peace of God when life is anything but peaceful.

But Paul tells us it can be done, and he tells us that there is something of a supernatural intervention on the part of God himself when we simply take the steps laid out for us in Philippians 4:6–7. Again, this is all coming from a man who knew all too well the need for inner peace in the face of trials and tribulations. So if you're looking for someone with some credibility when it comes to such things, look at the apostle Paul, who in all things, no matter how difficult or insurmountable they may have seemed, knew to look to his heavenly Father who always provided what Paul needed when he needed it.

Study Questions

○ Can you think of times when God provided—maybe even miraculously— for something you needed but didn't see any way of getting? How did you respond?

○ What seemingly impossible trial or test are you facing right now? How are you responding to it?

Joy in Focusing on the Right Things (Philippians 4:8–9)

Paul finished his encouragements to the Philippian church by telling them: "And now, dear brothers and sisters, one final thing. Fix your thoughts on what is true, and honorable, and right, and pure, and lovely, and admirable. Think about things that are excellent and worthy of praise. Keep putting into practice all you learned and received from me—everything you heard from me and saw me doing. Then the God of peace will be with you" (Philippians 4:8–9).

ALERT!

Paul had plenty of opportunity in Philippi to put what he taught into practice. It was shortly after he led a woman named Lydia to Christ that he and his companion, Silas, were arrested, severely beaten, bound in stocks and chains, and thrown in prison. Despite everything, Paul and Silas sang songs of praise in prison (Acts 16:16–40).

This was many centuries before anyone talked about anything like the power of positive thinking, but Paul pointed out the importance of right thinking. He encouraged the Philippians to put their focus on what is:

- true and not on what is false
- honorable and not on what is dishonorable
- right and not on what is clearly wrong
- pure and not on what is polluted
- lovely and not on what is horrible
- admirable and not on what is unworthy

Today, the question remains: How do we know what are good things to think on? Simply put, those are the things that God Himself thinks on, and we can find that out by reading, studying, and memorizing the Bible. It is there that we find out what God thinks about every subject important to our faith—where we learn truth, where we learn right from wrong, where we see what is honorable, where God shows us what is pure, lovely, and admirable.

Paul learned that in the midst of suffering, it's important to make sure that you fix your thoughts on the things that will fill your mind and heart with joy—even when your present situation might make joyful thinking humanly difficult or even impossible. That is his final word to the Philippians, and it's his message of hope and joy in Jesus Christ that has withstood 2,000 years of time.

Study Questions

○ What do you tend to think of when life seems difficult or even unfair? What do you think God wants you to think of?

○ Reread Philippians 4:8–9. What specific things should you think on at all times, particularly difficult times?

Chapter 18

Hebrews:
The "Betterness" of Jesus

The writer of the epistle to the Hebrews (it isn't certain who wrote it and exactly when) was writing to Jewish people who had become Christians but who later wanted to reverse course in order to escape persecution by their Jewish brothers and sisters. The theme of the book of Hebrews is the superiority of Jesus Christ over the Jewish system of priesthood, laws, and sacrifices. Jesus, the writer tells them, is better than angels, better than Moses, better than the established Jewish priesthood, better than the Law of Moses.

Encouragement Toward Maturity

Hebrews paints a word picture of Jesus that is specially designed for the Jewish people, and it gives all readers an overview of who Jesus really is—to them and to other believers who would come behind them. The writer's goal is to keep these Jewish Christians on course toward spiritual maturity. As he wrote, "So let us stop going over the basic teachings about Christ again and again. Let us go on instead and become mature in our understanding. Surely we don't need to start again with the fundamental importance of repenting from evil deeds and placing our faith in God" (Hebrews 6:1). That he does by explaining to them—in unmistakably Jewish terms—who Jesus was, is, and will always be and how he was better than anything or anyone who had come before him or would come after him.

Jesus: Better Than the Angels and Other Created Beings (Hebrews 1:5–14)

Jesus lived and ministered in a time when the people of Palestine had what can only be seen as an unhealthy and unbalanced view of angels. The believers of that time had some understanding of the role that angels played in bringing about the plans of God, and that was a good thing. But there were many people—especially in the Jewish community—whose ideas about angels had become superstitious or even idolatrous. They had come to believe that angels were mediators between God and man, the position Jesus held himself.

This gave the writer of Hebrews the opportunity to set the people straight about what angels really were. In doing that, he set Jesus apart as being far above any created thing—including the angels and the humans to whom angels would be subject.

The writer spells out that the relationship between God the Father and His Son was infinitely superior than the relationship between God and the angels simply because it was a father-son relationship and not a creator-created relationship: "For God never said to any angel what he said to Jesus:

'You are my Son. Today I have become your Father.' God also said, 'I will be his Father, and he will be my Son.' And when he brought his firstborn Son into the world, God said, 'Let all of God's angels worship him'" (Hebrews 1:5–6)

Indeed, there were several examples in the Gospels of angels doing what they had been created to do: minister to Jesus and to those he loved. In fact, it was an angel who first announced the coming birth of Christ (Luke 1:26–38) and an angel who announced his resurrection from the dead (Luke 24:1–7).

QUESTION?

Who was the writer of the epistle to the Hebrews?
It is believed that the apostle Paul wrote the book of Hebrews, but that is not certain. Other candidates are Barnabas (a leader in the early church), Luke (the writer of the Gospel of Luke and Acts of the Apostles), Apollos (a believer mentioned in Acts and in the epistles of Paul), and several others.

Angels are wonderful creations of God, the writer of Hebrews tells us, but they are just that—creations. And God doesn't call us to worship what He has created, He has called us to and allowed us the privilege of worshiping Him by worshipping His Son.

Study Questions
○ What does Hebrews 1:5–14 tell us is the true place of angels in God's kingdom?
○ According to Hebrews 2:9, what place did Jesus hold in comparison with the angels at his death on the cross?

Jesus: Better Than Moses (Hebrews 3:1–6)

In first-century Jewish culture, there were a few men of the past who qualified as heroes of the culture and of the faith. One of those men was Moses, who answered—although somewhat reluctantly at first—God's call to lead the people of Israel out of captivity in Egypt. The first-century Jews had a very high opinion of Moses, and rightly so. And while the writer of Hebrews doesn't downplay the faithfulness or faith of Moses or the importance of what he did, he wrote that "Jesus deserves far more glory than Moses, just as a person who builds a house deserves more praise than the house itself. For every house has a builder, but the one who built everything is God" (Hebrews 3:3–4).

FACT

Jesus himself didn't downplay the importance of Moses's part in God's plan of redemption. In his famed Sermon on the Mount, Jesus said, "Don't misunderstand why I have come. I did not come to abolish the law of Moses or the writings of the prophets. No, I came to accomplish their purpose" (Matthew 5:17).

In other words, Moses, just like every other human being, was created by God, the same God Jesus represented perfectly in everything he did. But still, Moses played his part in the plan to bring salvation to the world: "Moses was certainly faithful in God's house as a servant. His work was an illustration of the truths God would reveal later. But Christ, as the Son, is in charge of God's entire house. And we are God's house, if we keep our courage and remain confident in our hope in Christ" (Hebrews 3:5–7).

Moses was called to fulfill his part in God's plan of redemption for all of humankind, and he played that part. While he wasn't perfect in everything he did and said—as Jesus was—he faithfully and obediently did as God had called him to do.

Jesus, on the other hand, was perfect in everything he said and did—perfect in his obedience to God and in his service to humankind. He was everything that Moses and other servants of God had been before him as they prepared the world for his arrival. But he was far, far more.

While Moses was a great leader of the Jewish people and a man who is to be revered, he was only a foreshadowing of what Jesus Christ would be.

Jesus is our Savior, the One sent of God to seek out and save the lost (Luke 19:10). He is God in the flesh, and as such he is worthy of infinitely higher praise and reverence than Moses.

Study Questions
○ How did the writer of Hebrews describe Moses?
○ How did the writer of Hebrews compare and contrast Moses and Jesus?

A Better Rest in Jesus Christ (Hebrews 3:7–4:11)

The first eleven verses of Hebrews 4 are about a new and better kind of rest that God gives those who believe Him, who take Him at his word, and who have the kind of faith it takes to enjoy God's salvation. This passage is a continuation of the latter parts of Hebrews 3, which recount the tragedy of the deaths of untold thousands of Israelites in the desert outside the Promised Land of Canaan. They died there, the writer tells us, because they "rebelled against God, even though they heard his voice" (Hebrews 3:16). In this passage, the Hebrew believers are warned and encouraged to continue on in their faith so that they could enter into a much better rest even than the one the people of Israel missed out on because of their unbelief and rebellion. (See Chapter 6.)

When the writer of Hebrews wrote, "So in my anger I took an oath: 'They will never enter my place of rest,'" he was quoting Psalm 95:11, which refers to the generation of Israelites who, because of their unbelief and rebellion, died in the wilderness without seeing the Promised Land.

Hebrews 4:1–2 says, "God's promise of entering his rest still stands, so we ought to tremble with fear that some of you might fail to experience it.

For this good news—that God has prepared this rest—has been announced to us just as it was to them. But it did them no good because they didn't share the faith of those who listened to God." But there is one condition for entering into this rest, the better rest in Jesus Christ: We have to believe! (Hebrews 4:3).

The writer of Hebrews tells us, "So there is a special rest still waiting for the people of God. For all who have entered into God's rest have rested from their labors, just as God did after creating the world" (Hebrews 4:9–10). This is a different rest, a better rest, because it is an everlasting rest. It is the rest Jesus gives us that allows us to cease from all work when it comes to earning our salvation, and it is the rest we have in knowing that we don't need to rely on our own strength to live the lives God wants us to live.

Study Questions
○ What does the writer of Hebrews tell us is God's reaction to unbelief?
○ What is the condition we must meet before we can enter into and enjoy God's perfect rest?

Jesus: A Better High Priest (Hebrews 4:14–5:11)

Jesus is referred to in the Bible by dozens of names, one of which appears late in the fourteenth chapter of Hebrews: "So then, since we have a great High Priest who has entered heaven, Jesus the Son of God, let us hold firmly to what we believe" (Hebrews 4:14). In speaking of Jesus as a newer, better high priest, the writer of Hebrews is speaking the language of the Jews. The Jewish people understood that they just couldn't walk into the tabernacle or temple and approach God. They needed to approach through the high priest, who was in their system of worship the only one through whom they could approach God and offer their prayers and offerings.

That all changed with this new high priesthood of Jesus Christ, the one Hebrews tells us is vastly superior to the old one, first, because he was like us in all ways except that he never sinned, and also because he gives us direct access to God: "This High Priest of ours understands our weaknesses, for he faced all of the same testings we do, yet he did not sin. So let us come boldly to the throne of our gracious God. There we will receive his mercy, and we will find grace to help us when we need it most" (Hebrews 4:15–16).

The apostle Peter pointed out that believers are to join Jesus as priests in this life and to this world: "You are royal priests, a holy nation, God's very own possession. As a result, you can show others the goodness of God, for he called you out of the darkness into his wonderful light" (1 Peter 2:9).

Hebrews 5 starts where chapter 4 left off, explaining to the reader the duties and qualifications of the high priesthood. It tells us that the office of high priest wasn't one someone could have simply because he wanted it. Rather, it was an office to which God Himself had to call someone—just as He called and appointed Jesus to it (Hebrews 5:1–5).

But there is more to the superiority of Jesus' priesthood. Hebrews tells us: "And in another passage God said to him, 'You are a priest forever in the order of Melchizedek'" (Hebrews 5:6).

By that, God meant that Jesus wasn't just priesthood but royal priesthood. Melchizedek was the king-priest mentioned in Genesis 14:18–20, and he came long before the Jewish priesthood had been established. His priesthood was considered timeless—without beginning and without end. Hebrews ends this section this way:

While Jesus was here on earth, he offered prayers and pleadings, with a loud cry and tears, to the one who could rescue him from death. And God heard his prayers because of his deep reverence for God. Even though Jesus was God's Son, he learned obedience from the things he suffered. In this way, God qualified him as a perfect

High Priest, and he became the source of eternal salvation for all those who obey him. (Hebrews 5:7–9)

In other words, this passage is saying that Jesus was a perfect example in all he did, including how to pray and how to live a life of perfect obedience to God. That is why he is a high priest who is not only better than any who came before him, but he is a perfect high priest.

Study Questions

○ What, according to Hebrews 5:1–3, were the duties of the high priest and how do they compare with what Jesus does for us today?

○ How should knowing Jesus as our high priest change how we approach God?

Jesus: The Bringer of a New—and Better—Covenant (Hebrews 8:1–9:10)

We've already seen that Jesus brought with him a priesthood that was better than the one established centuries before him. But he also brought with him—and purchased through his sacrificial death on the cross—what the epistle to the Hebrews referred to as a "new covenant" (Hebrews 8:8), meaning a new promise or agreement with his people.

ALERT!

Jesus spoke of the "new" aspect of worship that the writer of Hebrews seems to refer to when he said, "But the time is coming—indeed it's here now—when true worshipers will worship the Father in spirit and in truth. The Father is looking for those who will worship him that way" (John 4:23).

The writer of Hebrews wrote of those who worshipped under the old covenant:

They serve in a system of worship that is only a copy, a shadow of the real one in heaven. For when Moses was getting ready to build the Tabernacle, God gave him this warning: "Be sure that you make everything according to the pattern I have shown you here on the mountain." But now Jesus, our High Priest, has been given a ministry that is far superior to the old priesthood, for he is the one who mediates for us a far better covenant with God, based on better promises. (Hebrews 8:5–6)

This tells us that Jesus brought us something new when it comes to worshipping God, something the writer stated very directly when he wrote: "When God speaks of a 'new' covenant, it means he has made the first one obsolete. It is now out of date and will soon disappear" (Hebrews 8:13).

And what was it that God made obsolete? What is now out of date and will soon disappear? The writer of Hebrews goes on to explain that it was the complex system of worship—the places and ways people could worship God—that was a part of the Law of Moses.

This new covenant means that no longer would God pay attention to where people worshipped Him or whether they followed rigid rules of worship. Now He would focus on the hearts of those who came to Him and would write His laws and His ways in their hearts and not on tablets. This would be a covenant based not on laws and regulations but on a personal one-on-one relationship with a God who extended His grace to the people of Israel—the Hebrews—and the rest of the world.

Study Questions

○ What do you think studying and understanding this new covenant will do to your relationship with Jesus Christ?

○ How would you describe your Christian faith when it comes to the personal relationship with God through Jesus Christ?

Jesus, a Better—Perfect—Sin Sacrifice (Hebrews 9:11–10:18)

The target audience of this epistle—Jewish converts to Christianity—were no doubt aware of the system of animal and grain sacrifices set up during the time of Moses in order to deal, temporarily anyway, with sin. But the writer of Hebrews pointed out that the sacrificial system was temporary and nothing more than a precursor to what Jesus would do on the cross: "The old system under the law of Moses was only a shadow, a dim preview of the good things to come, not the good things themselves" (Hebrews 10:1).

FACT

The laws concerning the sin offering are given in detail in the book of Leviticus (4:1–6:13; 9:7–11, 22–24; 12:6–8; 15:2, 14, 25–30; 14:19, 31) and in Numbers (6:10–14). Sin offerings were presented on the Day of Atonement and on the five annual Jewish religious festivals (Numbers 28, 29).

The tenth chapter of Hebrews points out that the sacrifice of Jesus Christ was superior to the old system of animal and grain sacrifices in the following ways:

- Under the old system, the sacrifices were done yearly, but Christ's was done once and for all (verse 1–3).
- Under the old system, the sacrifices made someone "clean" enough to be able to worship, but the sacrifice of Christ completely cleanses us from all sin and guilt (verse 2–3).
- The blood of animals can't completely take away sins, but the sacrifice of Christ has done just that (verse 3–6).
- Under the old system, there were several different sacrifices for different occasions, but Christ willingly offered himself so that we could be made holy and pure (verses 11–12).
- Christ's sacrifice negates any need for further sacrifices (verse 18).

The sacrifice of Jesus Christ is infinitely superior to those spelled out under the Law of Moses. That is because what Jesus did on the cross provided not just forgiveness of sin but also power against it. Jesus destroyed once and for all the works of the devil, and he has made those who would put their faith in him right before God.

Study Questions

○ How do you personally approach the Law of Moses as it is written in the Old Testament?

○ What is your response to knowing that the work of Jesus on the cross completed what was started in the Law of Moses?

Chapter 19

First Peter: The Look of the Christian Life

The apostle Peter, the man who spent three-plus years traveling with Jesus during his earthly ministry and the man Jesus charged with taking the gospel message of salvation to the Jewish world, wrote his first epistle to the Christians in the Black Sea coastal area. These believers were facing intense suffering and persecution over their faith, and Peter wants them to know that they should not be surprised or alarmed because of the opposition that was coming their way.

The Importance of Gladness

Peter's first epistle—one of two bearing his name—is amazingly practical in how it sets forth guidelines and offers wisdom for living the Christian life in the midst of a corrupt, evil, and sometimes violent world. Peter tells these believers:

> *So be truly glad. There is wonderful joy ahead, even though you have to endure many trials for a little while. These trials will show that your faith is genuine. It is being tested as fire tests and purifies gold—though your faith is far more precious than mere gold. So when your faith remains strong through many trials, it will bring you much praise and glory and honor on the day when Jesus Christ is revealed to the whole world. (1 Peter 1:6–7)*

As these Christians go through the faith-testing trials, Peter wants them to know about the joy that is ahead and the life Jesus Christ has for them right now. That is the focus of this chapter, which is a study of the principles found in the book of 1 Peter.

Growing in the Faith (1 Peter 2:1–11)

One of the most daunting questions a new Christian faces is how to properly live now that he or she has left behind a life in the world and in the flesh and joined God's eternal family through faith in Jesus Christ. In his first epistle, Peter explains how Christians are to live: "So get rid of all evil behavior. Be done with all deceit, hypocrisy, jealousy, and all unkind speech. Like new-born babies, you must crave pure spiritual milk so that you will grow into a full experience of salvation. Cry out for this nourishment, now that you have had a taste of the Lord's kindness" (1 Peter 2:1–3).

Another way of looking at this passage is that believers are to abandon all those things we know are sinful—dishonesty, jealousy, unkindness, and the like—and replace them with the things that help us to grow to maturity. That is what Peter meant when he wrote, "crave spiritual milk so that you will grow into a full experience of salvation."

Peter starts with the assumption that when we are first saved through our faith in Jesus Christ, we are immature believers—newborn babies who have nothing to offer God or anyone else. If you've ever been around an infant, you know that it is completely incapable of doing anything for itself. A little girl or boy is completely dependant on others to be fed, clothed, and changed. You also know that there is nothing that infant craves more than its own mother's milk.

E ALERT!

The writer of the epistle to the Hebrews (chapters 5–6)—as well as other New Testament writings—indicates that while we are all born again as spiritual babies, we should still undertake a process of spiritual maturity throughout the rest of our earthly lives.

If you were to try to feed a newborn infant steak and potatoes, then the poor little thing would likely starve within a few days. That's because that sort of food isn't appropriate for a baby; babies aren't meant to eat those kinds of foods.

As Christians, especially new Christians, God doesn't intend for us to be feeding on our old ways of life, on behavior and thought patterns we know to be unhealthy for our spiritual lives. Instead, we are to abandon all those things and make sure that we nourish ourselves with the milk of God's Word, which can be found in the pages of the Bible.

Study Questions

○ What kinds of behaviors does Peter tell believers to rid their lives of?

○ What does Peter tell us is necessary to grow into the "full experience of salvation?"

A Life Worthy of a Priest (1 Peter 2:4–11)

If someone were to ask you how a priest lives, how would you answer? Most of us think of priests as people who hang around the local parish, who can't marry, who listen to people confessing their sins all day long, and who wear funny-looking collars.

But there is more to being a priest than doing all those things. Being a priest—or any other kind of minister for that matter—means living under a higher standard of conduct, making sure that everything said and done properly reflects the position entrusted to the person. The very same thing applies to those who have been welcomed into God's eternal family through their faith in Jesus Christ.

Peter points out in this passage that there will be people who "stumble" because they don't obey God's Word, and the consequences are that they meet a fate other than the one reserved for those who have put their faith in Jesus Christ (1 Peter 2:8). True believers, on the other hand, are different because: "you are a chosen people. You are royal priests, a holy nation, God's very own possession. As a result, you can show others the goodness of God, for he called you out of the darkness into his wonderful light. Once you had no identity as a people; now you are God's people. Once you received no mercy; now you have received God's mercy." (1 Peter 2: 9–10).

Peter's teaching on the priesthood of the individual believer was one of the assertions made by Martin Luther and other reformers during a sixteenth-century event in the history of Christianity known as the Protestant Reformation. Luther believed that the Catholic Church at the time was going against this teaching by asserting so much control over individuals.

As God's chosen people—as those who are royal priests and members of a holy nation—God has called us all to live in this world as "temporary residents and foreigners" (1 Peter 2:11). That means we are to "keep away from worldly desires that wage war against your very souls. Be careful to live properly among your unbelieving neighbors. Then even if they accuse you of doing wrong, they will see your honorable behavior, and they will give honor to God when he judges the world" (1 Peter 2:11–12).

In other words, since God has taken us as His own possession and called us "royal priests," we are to live lives befitting those God has called to such a high spiritual position. We are to live lives that people around us will see as different, as above reproach. And when we do that, others will see Jesus Christ in us.

Study Questions

○ Who does Peter tell us we are in relation to God because of the work of Jesus Christ?

○ What does Peter say God has called believers into?

Properly Responding to Authority (1 Peter 2:13–17, 3:1–7)

Peter wrote that good Christian behavior included submission to and respect for those in authority over us, including those in civil positions. Peter used the example of kings and his officials, but the modern-day application of this principle would include local, state, and federal authorities as well as those we've put ourselves under in the spiritual sense.

The reason for doing that is simple: "It is God's will that your honorable lives should silence those ignorant people who make foolish accusations against you. For you are free, yet you are God's slaves, so don't use your freedom as an excuse to do evil. Respect everyone, and love your Christian brothers and sisters. Fear God, and respect the king" (1 Peter 2:15–17).

FACT

The apostle Paul also had something to say about how husbands and wives were to relate to one another. In Ephesians 5:21, Paul indicates that wives and husbands are to submit to one another "out of reverence for Christ." He later instructs wives to submit to their husbands and husbands to love their wives (Ephesians 5:22–28).

Peter also directed wives to submit to the authority of their husbands because in doing so they may through their examples win over an unbelieving spouse to the faith (1 Peter 3:1). He also encouraged them not to be concerned about their outward appearance—fancy hairstyles, expensive jewelry, beautiful clothes, and the like—but to "clothe yourselves instead with the beauty that comes from within, the unfading beauty of a gentle and quiet spirit, which is so precious to God" (1 Peter 3:4).

Peter also commanded husbands to honor their wives and to treat them with understanding and respect. He told them, "She may be weaker than you are, but she is your equal partner in God's gift of new life. Treat her as you should so your prayers will not be hindered" (1 Peter 3:7).

While this might sound older than old school by today's standards, it was quite radical for that time and in that culture. Back then, wives were considered just barely above personal property and servants.

Study Questions

○ How does the preceding passage apply to how believers are to respond to authority today?

○ How can this passage be applied in marriage today?

Patiently Endure Wrong Treatment (1 Peter 2:18–25)

One of the most amazing aspects of Jesus Christ going to the cross in order to pay for our sins is that he did it willingly and without complaint. As the prophet Isaiah said about the Messiah Jesus, "He was oppressed and treated harshly, yet he never said a word. He was led like a lamb to the slaughter. And as a sheep is silent before the shearers, he did not open his mouth" (Isaiah 53:7).

There are few things that demonstrate to the world the transformation Jesus Christ has done in believers more than their following his example of patiently enduring being wronged and treated unjustly. When Christians do that, people clearly see that there is something different about them.

ALERT!

Peter's teaching in this passage is consistent with that of Jesus: "You have heard the law that says the punishment must match the injury: 'An eye for an eye, and a tooth for a tooth.' But I say, do not resist an evil person! If someone slaps you on the right cheek, offer the other cheek also" (Matthew 5:38–39).

That is the more modern application of Peter's encouragement to slaves of that time: "You who are slaves must accept the authority of your masters with all respect. Do what they tell you—not only if they are kind and reasonable, but even if they are cruel. For God is pleased with you when you do what you know is right and patiently endure unfair treatment" (1 Peter 2:18–19).

Today, slavery is seen as a dark part of the Western world's past, but we know that there was a time when humans were allowed to own other humans and that those precious human souls who were held as slaves were sometimes subjected to abominable treatment. Apparently, the same thing was true in Peter's day.

While none of us in our culture today are held as slaves, it is still possible that we may have to sometimes endure cruel mistreatment at the hands of people God has put in our lives. Sometimes that mistreatment is in the form of cruel words or actual wrongs committed. Either way, Peter tells us that as believers we are to "patiently endure unfair treatment."

God doesn't credit us for being punished for doing wrong, but if we patiently endure mistreatment when we are innocent of any wrong, then God is pleased with us. Why? Because in doing so, we follow Jesus's example and reflect him to the world around us (2:20–21).

Study Questions

○ How do you respond when people speak wrongly about you or treat you in a way you think is unfair?

○ How do you think you are to respond when people don't treat you fairly or justly?

Living for God So That Others Will See (1 Peter 4:1–6)

Jesus told his followers, "Let your good deeds shine out for all to see, so that everyone will praise your heavenly Father" (Matthew 5:16). And so began the New Testament theme of believers living lives that brought glory to God and caused nonbelievers to see the differences Jesus has made in our lives.

One of the subthemes in Peter's first epistle was that of allowing people in the world to hear in our words and see in our attitudes and actions the transformation Jesus Christ has done within us. And one of those differences is fairly obvious for all to see: "You won't spend the rest of your lives chasing your own desires, but you will be anxious to do the will of God. You have had enough in the past of the evil things that godless people enjoy— their immorality and lust, their feasting and drunkenness and wild parties, and their terrible worship of idols" (1 Peter 4:2–3).

ALERT!

The apostle Paul provided the church at Corinth a list of the sins and behaviors that people are to leave behind when they become Christians. He also warns that those who practice those things have "no share in the kingdom of God" (1 Corinthians 6:9–11).

Of course, Peter points out, some of our former friends will be surprised at the changes in our lives, and some may even insult or slander us. But he wants us to remember that each of us will have to face a God who will righteously judge everyone and call to account the things they have done.

God doesn't save people so that they can go on living as they once did. Being a part of God's eternal family means allowing Him to make changes in your thoughts as well as your deeds in this life. Some will notice and laugh, but others will see the changes in your life and be drawn to what God can also do in their own lives (1 Peter 4:4).

Study Questions

○ What effect do you think your behavior and attitudes have on those who know you are a Christian?

○ What attitudes or behaviors do you believe God wants you to give up so that you can glorify him in front of others?

Serving the Body of Christ (1 Peter 4:7–11)

Peter told his readers that the end of the world was coming soon, and for that reason they needed to be both "earnest and disciplined" in their prayer lives. But more important than that, he said they needed to show love for one another. Peter himself heard Jesus tell the disciples, "Your love for one another will prove to the world that you are my disciples" (John 13:35), and he wanted his readers to understand the importance of believers having deep love for one another, "for love covers a multitude of sins" (1 Peter 4:8). He even gave believers a practical way to demonstrate that love when he told them to cheerfully share their homes with those who needed a meal or a place to stay (1 Peter 4:9).

Peter also said that believers are to use the spiritual gifts God has given them in service of one another. Be it speaking, helping others, or whatever gifts we have, we are to use them with all the strength God gives us so that everything we do will bring glory to God through Jesus Christ (1 Peter 4:10–11).

Study Questions

○ Read 1 Corinthians 12. What are some of the abilities the Holy Spirit gives us so that we can serve the body of Christ more effectively?

○ What gifts do you believe God has given you to serve his kingdom and the body of Christ?

Glorifying God in Our Suffering (1 Peter 4:12–19)

Peter lived and served in a time when just being a Christian could subject you to unspeakably harsh treatment. Believers were routinely rounded up, imprisoned, tortured, and killed—all because they practiced a religion different from that of the Roman world.

Peter teaches the importance of glorifying God in our suffering—or to put it another way, suffering the right way. And what is the right way? The way Jesus himself suffered as those who persecuted and murdered him looked on. Peter wrote in 1 Peter 4:1: "So then, since Christ suffered physical pain, you must arm yourselves with the same attitude he had, and be ready to suffer, too."

ESSENTIAL

> Thriving and growing in our faith in the midst of suffering is one of the main themes, if not the main theme, of 1 Peter. The word *suffer*, or variations of it, is used no fewer than seventeen times in this epistle, while the word *trial* is used five times.

Just hours before he was about to endure some of the most brutal physical punishment ever inflicted, Jesus told his disciples, "If the world hates you, remember that it hated me first....Do you remember what I told you? 'A slave is not greater than the master.' Since they persecuted me, naturally they will persecute you. And if they had listened to me, they would listen to you" (John 15:18, 20).

One thing those who have suffered for their faith can tell you is that persecution, opposition, and other kinds of suffering have a way of either killing you or making you stronger. That is partly why Peter, who was with Jesus when he gave the above warning, wrote, "Dear friends, don't be surprised at the fiery trials you are going through, as if something strange were happening to you. Instead, be very glad—for these trials make you partners with Christ in his suffering, so that you will have the wonderful joy of seeing his glory when it is revealed to all the world" (1 Peter 4:12–13).

We live in a world where most people can avoid any kind of suffering or discomfort. It's also a world in which even the most outspoken Christians have to endure little more than verbal abuse. But Peter, who lived in a place and time of incredible danger for Christians, encouraged his brothers and sisters in the faith of that time to:

- not be surprised at the "fiery trials" they were going through
- be glad about the suffering, because they make them partners with Jesus Christ in his suffering.
- know that suffering in a way that glorifies God gives them the privilege of seeing God's glory revealed to the world

In other words, when we suffer for Christ in any way, enduring it without complaining but with a sense of joy, peace, and faith, it is sure to get the world's attention and reflect positively on the faith you have and on the One in whom you have that faith.

FACT

The first chapter of James gives an excellent overview of the purpose God has in our spiritual lives for trials and suffering. In that passage, James points out that suffering produces endurance and endurance produces strength of character (James 1:2–4).

In this passage, Peter does give his readers a small addendum to let them know that while there is no shame but only joy and reward for suffering for Christ, it is important to make sure we are suffering for the right reasons. He wrote, "If you suffer, however, it must not be for murder, stealing, making trouble, or prying into other people's affairs" (1 Peter 4:15).

This is in keeping with making sure that our lives continue to be a reflection of the Christ we serve. And Peter seems to indicate that if we suffer because of our own ungodly, unacceptable actions, then there is no reward in that—only the consequences of our own shameful behavior.

However, Peter tells us that there is no shame in suffering for being a Christian, so we can praise God for the privilege of being called by His name. And if we suffer in a way that pleases God, if we keep doing the right things, if we keep trusting in our Creator, He will never fail us—no matter what we have to endure (1 Peter 4:16–19).

Study Questions

○ How do you typically respond when you are criticized or chided for being a Christian? In light of Peter's teaching, how do you think you should respond?

○ What behaviors and thought patterns do you think cause you to suffer needlessly?

Chapter 20

First John: A Life of Love

Central to the message of the gospel of Jesus Christ is love. Jesus explained his presence on earth beginning with, "God so loved the world" and later left his disciples with the command that they "love one another." The message of the Bible is that God loved us so we are to love Him in return. Not only that, we are to love one another just as He has loved us—in a sacrificial, selfless way. That is the message of this chapter, which is a study of 1 John.

20

John's Central Message: Love

The apostle John, who spent three-plus years of his life following Jesus—watching him perform miracles, preach powerful sermons, and demonstrate love—was the writer of the gospel that bears his name and the three letters that appear late in the New Testament (First John, Second John, and Third John), as well as the book of Revelation. In his first letter—or epistle—John writes very caringly and lovingly about what the Christian life should look like, giving emphasis to the kind of love Jesus repeatedly taught about when he was on earth.

It was John who recorded these words of Jesus just prior to his arrest, trial, and crucifixion: "So now I am giving you a new commandment: Love each other. Just as I have loved you, you should love each other" (John 13:34). And it is in the apostle's first letter that we read of what that love looks like.

Jesus wanted his disciples to know that what they were about to embark on—taking the message he had preached to the world around them once he was gone—could only be done if they were bound together in the kind of love Jesus showed them every day. That is why John so strongly echoed in his first letter the teachings of Jesus when it came to love.

In 1 John, we read of our love for God and what that means, and we read how our love for him motivates, encourages, and empowers us to love one another. The book of John, then, is a love letter to believers throughout the centuries.

Why We Obey God's Commandments (1 John 2:4–6)

You can't have marriage—not a good one, anyway—without love. The very same thing is true when it comes to our love for God. If we love God, we will prove it because we obey His commandments. That is what John meant when he wrote, "If someone claims, 'I know God,' but doesn't obey God's commandments, that person is a liar and is not living in the truth. But those who obey God's word truly show how completely they love him. That is how we know we are living in him" (1 John 2:4–5). Love and obedience: You can't have one without the other!

Jesus himself spoke of the keeping of God's commandments as proof of our love for him when he told his disciples, "If you love me, obey my commandments" (John 14:15). This tells us that our love for God and our obedience to God are inseparable. You truly can't have one without the other.

John goes on to tell his readers that they are to live out their lives of love for God in the very same way Jesus did (1 John 2:6). Jesus was perfectly obedient to God, and that was because he loved God and communed with God intimately. Everything Jesus said and did were perfect reflections of a deep and abiding love for his Father in heaven.

And while we can't in this life and on this earth be perfect in our love for and obedience to Jesus, we can follow Jesus's example and continue growing in our love for God. As our love for Him grows, so does our ability to obey Him better and better.

Study Questions

○ What kind of person, according to 1 John, claims to love God but lives a life of disobedience?

○ What does this passage tell us is the proof of our love for God?

Why We Are Called Children of God

The third chapter of John 1 begins, "See how very much our Father loves us, for he calls us his children, and that is what we are! But the people who belong to this world don't recognize that we are God's children because they don't know him" (1 John 3:1).

The theme of believers being children of God is repeated throughout the Bible and is especially prevalent in 1 John. In that epistle, John repeatedly refers to his readers using the obvious term of love and affection: "dear children."

John wanted his readers to know that as Christians we weren't just saved from going to hell, but we were also given the privilege of being called God's children, a point he also made early in his gospel (John 1:12–13).

FACT

The apostle Paul echoed this theme of the loving Fatherhood of God when he wrote, "And because we are his children, God has sent the Spirit of his Son into our hearts, prompting us to call out, "Abba, Father" (Galatians 4:6). The word *Abba* implies a familiar, loving father/child relationship similar to the English word *Daddy*. (See also Romans 8:15.)

God did that out of a love that fallen, sinful humanity can't fully grasp. It is in many ways a complex love, but it is also simple in many ways, too. It is a love that:

- moved God to reach out to a lost and sinful world (John 3:16)
- was given to us directly through Jesus Christ (John 15:9)
- is radiated out of us through the Holy Spirit (Romans 5:5)
- is a source of comfort to the afflicted (2 Corinthians 1:3–6)
- existed before we even knew God through Christ (Romans 5:8)
- causes God to discipline His children (Hebrews 12:1–13)

These are just a few examples of what God's love for His people really looks like. There are dozens and dozens of other examples and descriptions of God's love of those He refers to as His children in the Old and New Testaments.

As you study the love of God in the Bible, you'll find that it is a love that comes with a variety of rights and privileges. And it is also a love that comes with some responsibilities, all of which God empowers us to carry out as we demonstrate His love to the world around us—just like Jesus did so perfectly.

Study Questions

○ What does God call those who belong to Him?

○ Why don't people in the world understand that believers are actually God's own children?

The Proof That We Are Really Born Again (1 John 3:10–15)

John taught that the love that Jesus showed would be an outgrowth of someone who had made him his or her Savior. "So now we can tell who are children of God and who are children of the devil. Anyone who does not live righteously and does not love other believers does not belong to God" (1 John 3:10).

John goes on to say that loving one another is the message his readers had heard from the very beginning (1 John 3:11). But then he tells them that brotherly Christian love is the proof that someone has really been saved: "If we love our Christian brothers and sisters, it proves that we have passed from death to life. But a person who has no love is still dead. Anyone who hates another brother or sister is really a murderer at heart. And you know that murderers don't have eternal life within them" (1 John 3:14–15).

QUESTION?

How exactly do we demonstrate Christian love?
The apostle Paul gives some of the best examples and instruction when it comes to loving one another in the thirteenth chapter of his first letter to the Corinthian church—also known as the Love Chapter. In that passage, he tells us that love is, among other things, patient and kind and that it is not jealous, vain, proud, rude, or selfish.

John's teaching about love being the proof of one's Christianity fits in with what Jesus told his disciples late in his earthly ministry: "Your love for one another will prove to the world that you are my disciples" (John 13:35).

In other words, love is proof to the world, to ourselves, and to other believers that we really are children of God.

Study Questions

○ What, according to John, are the two proofs that someone is a child of God?

○ What does John say about those who don't love other Christians?

Jesus: A Perfect Example of Love (1 John 3:16–17)

One of the great things about love is that the Bible shows us a perfect example of how to do it every day and in every way. This perfect example is what John was referring to when he wrote, "We know what real love is because Jesus gave up his life for us" (1 John 3:16).

Jesus himself said, "There is no greater love than to lay down one's life for one's friends" (John 15:13). And that is exactly the kind of love Jesus demonstrated to his "friends"—those who had made a lifetime commitment to follow him.

But how, according to John, do we imperfect humans reflect God's perfect love? Most of the time, it's just a matter of being practical. John goes on to write, "So we also ought to give up our lives for our brothers and sisters. If someone has enough money to live well and sees a brother or sister in need but shows no compassion—how can God's love be in that person? (1 John 3:16–17).

ESSENTIAL

Sacrificial love is central to the Christian faith and was demonstrated perfectly by Jesus, who "gave up his divine privileges; he took the humble position of a slave and was born as a human being. When he appeared in human form, he humbled himself in obedience to God and died a criminal's death on a cross" (Philippians 2:7–8).

In other words, love, in order to be love, must be demonstrated through actions, not just through feelings and words. And while there are numerous references in the New Testament letters to feelings of affection and friendship from one believer to another, real love—the kind of love Jesus had for his followers—has to be demonstrated and not just felt.

Jesus demonstrated his love for others by speaking soothing words of comfort as well as difficult words of truth, by meeting people's physical needs through some of his miracles, and by healing those who were sick or injured. But his greatest act of love—the greatest act of love in all of history—was when he willingly gave himself up to die a horrible death on a cross of wood.

From the very beginning of his life, Jesus, John tells us, is our perfect example of love. While it is highly unlikely that any individual believer is going to have to die for another, it is a certainty that we all will have opportunities to "give up our lives for our brothers and sisters" by demonstrating the kind of compassion Jesus demonstrated every day.

Study Questions

○ What should it mean, practically speaking, to the believer today to love as Jesus loved when he was on earth?

○ Why do you think Jesus spent so much time meeting the physical needs of people through his many miracles when his ultimate mission was to save people's souls?

God the Father: Another Perfect Example of Love (1 John 4:8–12)

John tells us that it is God's nature to love. But he goes a step further in telling us that God Himself is love (1 John 4:8). That means that God in His very essence is love, and it's a love that needs to be displayed and given away: "God showed how much he loved us by sending his one and only Son into the world so that we might have eternal life through him. This is real love—not that we loved God, but that he loved us and sent his Son as a sacrifice to take away our sins" (1 John 4:9–10).

FACT

In what may be the best-known verse in all of the Bible, Jesus told Nicodemus, a Pharisee with whom he had engaged in a deep spiritual conversation, "For God loved the world so much that he gave his one and only Son, so that everyone who believes in him will not perish but have eternal life" (John 3:16).

The one who knows God knows that it is in His nature to love, to give of Himself, and to extend kindness to even the most lost and hurting sinner. That is what moved Him to send Jesus Christ to earth to die on the cross so that we could be freely forgiven for our sins and adopted into the family of God. It is beyond human ability to fully and adequately explain this love of God, but it is simple to point others to the ultimate display of that love: Jesus Christ on the cross, dying a sacrificial death for unworthy sinners.

When we respond to God the Father's love—and to the expression of that love through Christ—we become His children and inherit eternal life with Him. But there is a here-and-now aspect to this love. Since God has so loved us and given His Son for us, John says, we should be willing to love one another. After all, he states, if we in whom God lives love one another, God is alive in us and has expressed our love in and through us (1 John 4:11–12).

It has been said that love isn't love until it is given away. And our heavenly Father has given us a perfect example of what giving away love looks like.

Study Questions

○ In light of 1 John 4:11–12, what specifically should be your response to the love of God?

○ How do you think your loving others can more perfectly express the love of God for humankind?

Living and Growing in God's Love (1 John 4:17)

Christianity isn't just a system of beliefs or something we carry with us like an identification card. It's a life of faith in God, a life that changes as we grow stronger and more mature in our faith. And it's a life of love that brings us to maturity in all areas of our lives, including how we love God and others.

The apostle John points out that the love that is within us—and that radiates out of us—will grow toward perfection as we grow more perfect in our relationship with God: "And as we live in God, our love grows more perfect. So we will not be afraid on the day of judgment, but we can face him with confidence because we live like Jesus here in this world" (1 John 4:17).

The point John makes here is that there will be a day when each of us will appear before God, a day when we will give an accounting of what we did and didn't do. And this verse tells us that when we grow in our love, when our loves becomes "perfect"—meaning more like the love of Jesus—then we'll have every reason to face God Himself with confidence because we know and love His Son—our Savior—Jesus Christ, and because we allowed him to love others through us.

E ALERT!

The apostle Paul wrote of the centrality of love to the Christian life: "Three things will last forever—faith, hope, and love—and the greatest of these is love" (1 Corinthians 13:13). Love, then, is the beginning and the end and everything in between when it comes to our relationships with God. That's because we get to love God and love others because God loved us first.

When Jesus was asked which commandments were most important, he replied that the two most important were to love God with all of our being and to love our neighbors as we do ourselves (see Matthew 22:35–39). Jesus finished his point by saying, "The entire law and all the demands of the prophets are based on these two commandments" (Matthew 22:40). That means that there is nothing we can do in the Christian life—no kind word, no act of charity, no religious performance—that can please God if it isn't done with a pure heart of love, both for Him and for others.

When we love God, our obedience to Him comes not out of a dread of God or out of fear that He will punish us—although we are told in the Bible that it is a good thing to fear God—but out of a heart of love for Him and for our brothers and sisters in Christ. When we do those things willingly and joyfully, it is a sign that we are maturing spiritually, that we are becoming, in John's words, "more perfect" in our love.

We aren't to love God because we're afraid not to, and we aren't to love the people He has put in our lives because we know there is eternal reward in doing so. While outside the love of God is certainly a scary place to be, and while there is reward in performing those acts of love for our brothers and sisters, we are to love from our hearts without worrying about the costs of not loving and without concern for the rewards of loving.

The Christian life is a life of faith in and obedience to God, but more than anything it is a life of love. And when we respond to God's love by loving Him in return, we will find that our lives become fountains of love to God Himself and to the people He puts around us.

Study Questions

○ What does it mean to you to be "more perfect" in God's love?

○ What steps are you taking now to grow "more perfect" in God's love? What other steps can you take?

Chapter 21

Revelation: How It All Ends Up

Back in Chapter 5 you studied Genesis, the book of beginnings. Now you will study the book that closes out the Bible, the book of Revelation, the book on how it all ends up—how God's divine plan of redemption is finally brought to completion. The meaning of much of Revelation may be difficult to decipher, but it is still filled with messages that are as relevant today as they were when they were written two thousand years ago.

John's Prophetic Message

Written by the apostle John (the writer of the gospel and the epistles that bear his name) during a time of exile on the island of Patmos, the book of Revelation is the only New Testament book whose focus is primarily on prophetic events. John wrote Revelation near the end of the first century, a time of terrible suffering and persecution for a lot of Christians. It was a time when Roman emperors demanded deitylike worship, and Christians and Jews who refused to worship these emperors were routinely pressured economically, tortured, and even put to death. John himself was banished to Patmos.

Before you delve into reading and studying the book of Revelation, a warning or caution is in order. This book is filled with oftentimes strange and mystifying imagery whose meanings have been a source of debate for centuries. As you study this book, it is especially helpful to purchase a study guide—or several for that matter—to give you a leg up in deciphering this book. Even at that, it is likely that you will find contradictory interpretations on what this book really means and what context it should be read under. When you read and study the book of Revelation, do it with an open heart and mind that takes what it sees at face value.

Christ and the Seven Churches (Revelation 1-3)

The book of Revelation begins with a stunning description of someone that John identifies as the glorified Jesus Christ. John was one of the men who spent three years with Jesus during his earthly ministry, but his description of his Lord is nothing like what we think of when we read John's gospel account. In John's vision, he saw seven gold lampstands:

And standing in the middle of the lampstands was someone like the Son of Man. He was wearing a long robe with a gold sash across his chest. His head and his hair were white like wool, as white as snow. And his eyes were like flames of fire. His feet were like polished bronze refined in a furnace, and his voice thundered like

*mighty ocean waves. He held seven stars in his right hand, and a
sharp two-edged sword came from his mouth. And his face was
like the sun in all its brilliance. (Revelation 1:13–16)*

When John saw this vision, he goes on to say: "I fell at his feet as if I were
dead. But he laid his right hand on me and said, 'Don't be afraid. I am the
First and the Last. I am the living one. I died, but look—I am alive forever
and ever. And I hold the keys of death and the grave'" (Revelation 1:17–18).

Then John received the meaning of the mystery of the seven gold lampstands, namely that they were the seven churches who would be addressed
in Revelation 2–3.

> While the meaning of some of John's imagery in the book of Revelation
> is open to debate, what isn't open to debate is the main theme of the
> book: remain true to Jesus Christ, even in the face of persecution, even
> in the face of suffering, even in the face of losing all you have, even in
> the face of death.

The next two chapters of the book of Revelation are a collection of let-
ters to seven churches in Asia Minor (modern Turkey)—the churches of
Ephesus, Smyrna, Pergamum, Thyatira, Sardis, Philadelphia, and Laodicea.
Here is what Jesus had to say to those churches:

- **Ephesus:** This church received praise for doing good things but was
  also criticized for not loving Christ or one another as much as it
  did at first (Revelation 2:4). Christ called this church to turn back to
  doing the things it did at first.
- **Smyrna:** Though this church was in poverty and being slandered by
  the outside world, it was a church of great spiritual riches (Revelation 2:9).
- **Pergamum:** This church is praised for remaining true to Christ,
  even in the face of intense persecution, but it is also chided for

compromising when it came to the kind of teaching it received (Revelation 2:12–27).

- **Thyatira:** Jesus spoke highly of this church's love, faith, service, and endurance. The problem, however, was that idolatry and sexual immorality had crept its way into the church (Revelation 2:18–29).
- **Sardis:** Jesus's message to this church indicated that it was spiritually dead and in need of a reawakening (Revelation 3:1–6).
- **Philadelphia:** This church also received high praise for its faithfulness and perseverance—even in the face of persecution by "Satan's synagogue," or false Jews who were making life rough for these believers (Revelation 3:7–13).
- **Laodicea:** This church was a spiritual mess. That is because they were "neither hot nor cold" but lukewarm. Jesus wanted them to decide which they wanted to be. "But since you are like lukewarm water, neither hot nor cold, I will spit you out of my mouth!" (Revelation 3:14–22). The word *spit* in this context means "vomit," meaning that Jesus was saying, in effect, "You make me sick!"

Jesus's final words in this message for the churches were these:

Look! I stand at the door and knock. If you hear my voice and open the door, I will come in, and we will share a meal together as friends. Those who are victorious will sit with me on my throne, just as I was victorious and sat with my Father on his throne. Anyone with ears to hear must listen to the Spirit and understand what he is saying to the churches. (Revelation 3:20–22)

This was quite a promise to those believers who lived during such a dangerous time. It assured those who put their faith in Jesus Christ that, no matter how bad things got for them, their endurance would mean incredible blessings to come.

Study Questions
○ What are some of the things Jesus praises his church for in Revelation 2:4-3:22?
○ What are some of the things Jesus chides his church for?

Christ's Throne and the Seven Seals (Revelation 4–5)

Chapter 4 of Revelation opens with an invitation to view the throne of God and the scene surrounding it: "Then as I looked, I saw a door standing open in heaven, and the same voice I had heard before spoke to me like a trumpet blast. The voice said, 'Come up here, and I will show you what must happen after this' (Revelation 4:1).

John, now in the Spirit, saw a throne with a figure on it who was as brilliant as gemstones. The glow of an emerald circled the throne like a rainbow, and twenty-four thrones surrounded it. On the thrones were "twenty-four elders"—all of whom were clothed in white and wearing gold crowns. From the main throne came lightning flashes and thunderclaps. In front of the throne were seven torches with burning flames, which represented the sevenfold Spirit of God. Also in front of the throne was a shiny, sparkling sea of glass.

There were four living creatures—each of them covered with eyes front to back—in the center and around the throne. One of them looked like a lion, another like an ox, the third like a human, and the fourth like an eagle in flight. Each of them had six wings, which were also covered with eyes. Day in and day out, night in and night out, these creatures spoke these words: "Holy, holy, holy is the Lord God, the Almighty—the one who always was, who is, and who is still to come" (Revelation 4:8).

John saw that whenever one of these beings gave glory and honor to the one sitting on the throne, the twenty-four elders fell and worshipped him also and laid their crowns before the throne.

ALERT!

The number seven, which appears repeatedly in the book of Revelation—seven churches, seven seals, seven trumpets, seven signs, seven plagues, seven dooms, seven new things—is important in Jewish tradition because it represents God's own perfection as He rested on the seventh day.

John also saw in his vision a scroll in the right hand of the one sitting on the throne—Christ, the Lamb of God. There was writing on both sides of the scroll and it was sealed with seven seals that no one on heaven or earth was able to open and read.

John was bitterly distraught that no one was worthy to open the scroll, but one of the elders told him, "Stop weeping! Look, the Lion of the tribe of Judah, the heir to David's throne, has won the victory. He is worthy to open the scroll and its seven seals" (Revelation 5:5). John saw a vision of a lamb looking as if it had been slaughtered but which was standing. It had seven horns and seven eyes (which represented the sevenfold spirit of God). As the lamb stepped forward and took the scroll, the four living beings and the twenty-four elders fell down before him. They sang a "new song."

Study Questions

○ What did the one sitting on the throne look like?

○ What are the words of the "new song" being sung in this scene (Revelation 5:9–13)?

The Breaking of the Seals (Revelation 6–7)

Revelation 6 begins with John's vision of the lamb breaking the first of the seven seals on the scroll. When he broke the first seal, John saw a white horse with a rider wearing a crown and holding a bow. He rode out to win many battles and "gain the victory" (Revelation 6:2).

When the lamb broke the second seal, a red horse appeared who brought horrible war and death on the earth (Revelation 6:4). He was followed by the black horse of famine and scarcity (Revelation 6:5–6). Finally, the pale green horse of pestilence and death is brought forth as the fourth seal was broken (Revelation 6:7–8).

At the opening of the fifth seal, John saw a vision of the souls of those who had died on account of their faith and heard their voices asking how much longer it would be before God avenged their deaths and set things on earth right (6:9–11). The sixth seal brings earthquakes, environmental catastrophes, celestial occurrences, and such chaos that everyone on earth would hide themselves in the caves and such places, wishing for the mountains to fall on them so that they could avoid the wrath of God (Revelation 6:12–15).

Before the seventh seal was broken, John saw four angels who held "back the four winds so that they did not blow on the earth or the sea, or even on any tree" (Revelation 7:1). He also saw another angel coming from the east carrying the seal of the living God and telling the four not to harm the land or sea or the trees until they had placed the seal of God on His servants' foreheads (Revelation 7:2–3). John saw a throng of 144,000 people— 12,000 from each of the tribes of Israel—who had been marked with that seal (Revelation 7:4–8).

The time of tribulation described in Revelation is commonly accepted to be the same event described by Jesus, who referred to it as a time of "greater anguish than at any time since the world began" and said that "unless that time of calamity is shortened, not a single person will survive." (Matthew 24:21–22).

John also saw a crowd so huge that it was impossible to count—from every nation, tribe, and language—standing in front of the throne and in front of the lamb, all shouting, "Salvation comes from our God who sits on the throne and from the lamb!" (Revelation 7:10).

Finally, the lamb broke the seventh seal, and there was silence in heaven for about half an hour. After that, John saw seven angels standing before God, and each of them were given seven trumpets. This was the calm before the storm!

Study Questions

○ What did the first seal reveal when it was broken?
○ How were the other seals different from the first?

The Trumpets (Revelation 8–11)

The seven angels with the seven trumpets were ready to blast away, and when they did all hell breaks loose upon the earth. After the first angel blew his trumpet, a mixture of hail and fire and blood showered the earth, setting a third of its surface on fire (Revelation 8:7).

The second trumpet blast brought with it a mountain of fire, which was thrown into the sea, turning a third of the water the color of blood and killing a third of all things in the sea and destroying a third of the ships.

The third trumpet blast brought a huge star, which burned "like a torch," falling from the sky, turning a third of the water on earth so "bitter" that it killed people who drank it (Revelation 8:10–11). When the fourth angel blew his trumpet, a third of the sun's light and a third of the moon's light was struck, and a third of the stars became dark. "Then I looked," John writes in Revelation 8:13, "and I heard a single eagle crying loudly as it flew through the air, 'Terror, terror, terror to all who belong to this world because of what will happen when the last three angels blow their trumpets.'"

ALERT!

The time described in this section of Revelation is one of incredible suffering, destruction, and pain. It is a time when the devil, knowing his days are numbered, will attempt to spread as much hate and fury as he can on the whole world but especially on God's own people.

That is exactly what happens, too. Hell is loosed on earth as the fifth and sixth angels blow their trumpets. There are visions of horrible locust-like creatures up from hell, creatures with stings like scorpions who were told to injure only people who did not have God's seal on their foreheads. Those they stung wouldn't die—as much as they wanted to—but would be tortured for five months.

The sixth trumpet blast brought four angels who would kill one-third of the people on earth through three plagues—fire, smoke, and burning sulfur coming out of the mouths of horrible horselike creatures (Revelation 9:13–19). Still, those who didn't die from these horrible plagues refused to repent and turn to God.

Between describing the seventh trumpet, John describes two witnesses for God—men who will have powers much like Moses and Elijah—but who would be killed after they were done testifying by "the beast that comes up out of the bottomless pit" (Revelation 11:7). The wicked people of the world will celebrate their deaths, but three and a half days later, they would rise from the dead.

FACT

The name or word *Antichrist* doesn't appear in the book of Revelation, but it does appear in one of the apostle John's own epistles where he writes, "Dear children, the last hour is here. You have heard that the Antichrist is coming…" (1 John 2:18).

After that, the seventh trumpet would be blown, and there would be loud voices from heaven praising God: "The world has now become the Kingdom of our Lord and of his Christ, and he will reign forever and ever" (Revelation 11:15). Also, the twenty-four elders would fall on their faces and worship God and acknowledge that the time of judgment and wrath had come (Revelation 11:16–19).

Study Questions

○ What sorts of natural events do you think will bring to pass all the things written of in the book of Revelation?

○ How do you reconcile the fact of a loving God with what is happening in the world described in Revelation?

The Arrival of the Antichrist (Revelation 12–14)

As Revelation 12 begins, John has a vision of a woman "clothed with the sun, with the moon beneath her feet, and a crown of twelve stars on her head" (Revelation 12:1). The woman was pregnant and in labor.

John also saw a large red dragon with seven heads and ten horns, with crowns on each head. He saw a war in heaven, as Michael and his angels defeated the dragon—identified as Satan, the deceiver of the whole world—and his angels and threw him out of heaven (Revelation 12:9). When the dragon realized he'd been kicked out of heaven, he pursued the woman and her male child, but she was protected from the dragon (Revelation 12:13–14).

Then John saw a beast rising up out of the sea—a beast with seven heads and ten horns and ten crowns on its horns, and on each head were blasphemous names. The beast looked like a leopard but had the feet of a bear and the mouth of a lion. The dragon, who had waited on the shore, gave the beast his own power and throne (Revelation 13:1–3).

The beast was allowed to blaspheme God and to do whatever it wanted for forty-two months, including wage war against God's people and even to conquer them. The people who were of the world—not those whose names were written in the Lamb of God's Book of Life—worshipped the beast (Revelation 13:5–8).

Then John saw a second beast, one who came up out of the earth. This beast had two horns like those of a lamb but spoke with the voice of a dragon. He had the same authority as the first beast and required all people to worship the first beast, with anyone refusing to worship being put to death.

This beast "required everyone—small and great, rich and poor, free and slave—to be given a mark on the right hand or on the forehead. And no one could buy or sell anything without that mark, which was either the name of the beast or the number representing his name. Wisdom is needed here. Let the one with understanding solve the meaning of the number of the beast, for it is the number of a man. His number is 666" (Revelation 13:16–18).

E ALERT!

The apostle Paul also makes mention of the beast—or the Antichrist—referring to him as "the man of lawlessness—the one who brings destruction" in his second epistle to the Thessalonians. This was because Paul wanted to deal with some confusion on the part of the Thessalonians about the second coming of Jesus Christ.

Things don't look at all good for believers in the world at that time, but John gives them some hope, telling them about 144,000 people who refused to take the mark of the beast but instead took God's seal (Revelation 14:1–5). Three angels arrived—the first announcing the need to fear God and give glory to Him, the second proclaiming the fall of the city of Babylon because of her immorality, the third warning all who could hear that those who worship the beast or accept his mark would face God's wrath (Revelation 14:6–12).

Then came a voice from heaven saying, "Write this down: Blessed are those who die in the Lord from now on. Yes, says the Spirit, they are blessed indeed, for they will rest from their hard work; for their good deeds follow them!" (Revelation 14:13). What followed was the deaths of the wicked people of the earth as God's judgment came down (Revelation 14:14–20) as well as the rewarding of those who refused to worship the beast or take his mark (Revelation 15:2–4).

Study Questions

○ How are the destinies of those who "die in the Lord" different from those who are wicked?

○ Why do you think those who "die in the Lord" from this time on are blessed?

The "Bowl" Judgments (Revelation 15–18)

John's vision of God's wrath and judgment continues in chapter 15, which begins, "Then I saw in heaven another marvelous event of great significance. Seven angels were holding the seven last plagues, which would bring God's wrath to completion" (Revelation 15:1). Those last plagues were "bowls of the wrath of God" (Revelation 16:1), and He commanded them to go and pour them out on the earth. These bowls of wrath are:

- terrible sores on those who received the "mark of the beast" (Revelation 16:2)
- the sea turns to blood (16:3)
- the waters turn to blood (16:4–7)
- people are scorched by the sun (16:8–9)
- darkness and pain for humanity (16:10–11)
- the Euphrates River dries up and the battle of Armageddon takes shape (16:12–16)
- the earth is terribly shaken with the worst earthquake in human history (16:17–21)

This obviously is a horrible time of suffering on earth, but it wouldn't last forever. There would be a new heaven and a new earth, but only after the final conflict between good and evil, between God and Satan.

ESSENTIAL

While there are other verses and passages of the Bible that imply a final conflict between good and evil, it is in Revelation 16:16 that we find the only mention in the Bible of Armageddon. Many other of Israel's biggest military battles have taken place at that location, which is on the plain at the foot of Mount Megiddo.

When the seventh bowl is poured out, a loud shout came saying "It is finished!" The city of Babylon was split into three sections, and the cities of many nations were reduced to piles of rubble. This was the wrath of God falling on Babylon for its sins, and it included the disappearance of every island, the leveling of every mountain, and falling hailstones weighing seventy-five pounds each. Still, people continued to curse God (Revelation 16:17–21).

Another angel appeared, announcing the fall of Babylon and that all the world leaders who had "committed adultery" with her would cry and mourn when they saw her burning. Merchants would mourn because they would no longer have Babylon as a business partner. There would be absolutely no hope for the future of the city.

Study Questions

○ What would be your response if you were in the midst of everything described in Revelation 15–18?

○ How much of what you read in Revelation do you take absolutely literally and how much do you believe is meaningful symbolism?

The Rider to the Rescue (Revelation 19–20)

Right after reporting the announcement of the destruction of Babylon, John hears what sounded like "a vast crowd in heaven shouting, 'Praise the Lord! Salvation and glory and power belong to our God. His judgments are true and just. He has punished the great prostitute who corrupted the earth with her immorality. He has avenged the murder of his servants'" (Revelation 19:1–2).

As words of praise like these continued, John saw heaven opened and a white horse whose rider was named "Faithful and True, for he judges fairly and wages a righteous war" (Revelation 19:11). His eyes were like blazing fire and he had many crowns on his head. He wore a robe dipped in blood, and he was called "the Word of God" and on his robe and thigh were written the name "King of all Kings and Lord of all Lords" (Revelation 19:11–16).

Then John saw the "beast and the kings of the world and their armies gathered together to fight against the one sitting on the horse and his army" (Revelation 19:19). In other words, they were preparing to fight against Jesus Christ himself! The beast and the false prophet were captured and thrown alive into a lake of fire. An angel then descends from heaven, binds the devil, and throws him into the "bottomless pit," where he stays with the beast and the false prophet for a period of a thousand years (Revelation 20:1–5).

At the end of the thousand years, the devil is released from the pit and allowed to deceive people once again. He even attempts to gather an army and surrounds God's people, but fire falls from heaven and destroys the army. Then the devil is thrown into a "fiery lake of burning sulfur," where he, the beast, and the false prophet would be tormented for all of eternity.

With the devil put in his eternal place, the end of this age comes as all those who had died were judged before a "great white throne," which was God's throne (Revelation 20:11–12). The dead would then be judged according to the things they had done, and those whose names were not found in the Book of Life were thrown into the lake of fire, along with death and the grave itself.

Study Questions

○ How does knowing the devil's ultimate end affect your life of faith?
○ Do you find the prophecies in the book of Revelation more frightening or more comforting? Why?

A New Heaven and New Earth (Revelation 21–22)

As horrible, disturbing, and frightening as some of John's images in the book of Revelation may seem, his description of what was ahead for those who had placed their faith in Christ will make enduring those things worth it. The prophecies in Revelation are difficult to decipher, but the description of how faithful believers will be rewarded once all those things have come to pass is fairly clear and straightforward. This, John said, is "a new heaven and a new earth, for the old heaven and the old earth had disappeared" (Revelation 21:1). Also gone was the sea, and John also saw the "new Jerusalem," coming down out of heaven like a bride beautifully adorned for her groom (Revelation 21:2). Then John heard a voice from the throne, saying, "Look, God's home is now among his people! He will live with them, and they will be his people. God himself will be with them. He will wipe every tear from their eyes, and there will be no more death or sorrow or crying or pain. All these things are gone forever" (Revelation 21:3–4).

John heard that same voice saying, "Look, I am making everything new!... Write this down, for what I tell you is trustworthy and true... It is finished! I am the Alpha and the Omega—the Beginning and the End. To all who are thirsty I will give freely from the springs of the water of life. All who are victorious will inherit all these blessings, and I will be their God, and they will be my children" (Revelation 21:5–7). Indeed, everything will be new—a new heaven and earth (Revelation 21:1), a new people (21:2–8), a new bride of Christ (21:9), a new home (21:10–21), and a new Temple (21:22).

FACT

The Bible more or less begins and ends with the Tree of Life. Back in the Garden of Eden, a fallen Adam and Eve were not permitted to eat from it or even go near it (Genesis 3:22–24), but in the New Jerusalem, everyone is allowed to eat from it (Revelation 22:13, 19).

The book of Revelation presents a pretty disturbing picture of what the end times will look like. But it also gives us the ultimate happily ever after ending, one where the devil will be handed his defeat—a defeat he's had coming for thousands and thousands of years—for all of eternity and one where those who have put their faith in Jesus Christ will find that all things truly have become new.

Study Questions
○ Which of the "new" things Jesus Christ has promised do you look forward to most?
○ Reread Revelation 21:5–8. How does the contrast in that passage change your approach to sharing your faith with others?

Appendix A

Help for Studying the Bible

Study and Devotional Bibles

The Disciple's Study Bible. Eugene, OR: Harvest House Publishers, 1984.

Life Application Study Bible. Wheaton, IL: Tyndale House Publishers, 1988.

The New Jerusalem Bible, Reader's Edition. New York: Doubleday, 1990.

The New Oxford Annotated Bible with the Apocrypha: Revised and Expanded. New York: Oxford University Press, 1994.

The NIV Quiet Time Bible. Downer's Grove, IL: Intervarsity Press, 1994.

The NIV Serendipity Bible: For Personal and Small Group Study, Revised and Expanded. Grand Rapids, MI, and Littleton, CO: Zondervan Publishing House and Serendipity House, 1988.

The One-Minute Bible: The Heart of the Bible Arranged into 366 One-Minute Readings. Kohlenberger, John R., III, ed. Bloomington, MN: Garborg's, 1992.

Ryrie Study Bible, Expanded Edition. Chicago: Moody Press, 1994.

The Thompson Chain Reference Study Bible. Nashville: Thomas Nelson Publishers, 1983.

Bible Study Series

Faithwalk Bible Studies. Wheaton, IL: Crossway Books, 2000.

Fisherman Bible Study Guides. New York: Random House, Inc., 1992.

God's Word for Today's Bible Studies. St. Louis, MO: Concordia Publishing House, 1995.

Bible Reference Books

HarperCollins Bible Dictionary. Achtemeier, Paul J., Gen. ed. San Francisco: HarperCollins Publishers, 1985.

Where to Find It in the Bible: The Ultimate A to Z Resource. Anderson, Ken. Nashville: Thomas Nelson Publishers, 1996.

The Moody Atlas of Bible Lands. Beitzel, Barry J. Chicago: Moody Press, 1985.

Roget's Thesaurus of the Bible. Day, A. Colin. New York: Harper Collins, 1992.

The New Bible Commentary. Guthrie, D., and J.A. Motyer, eds. Grand Rapids, MI: William B. Eerdmans Publishing Company, 1970.

Living by the Book. Hendricks, Howard G., and William D. Chicago: Moody Press, 1991. [inductive Bible study method]

What the Bible Is All About, Revised Edition. Mears, Henrietta C. Ventura, CA: Regal Books, 1983.

Manners and Customs of the Bible. Packer, J.I., and M.C. Tenney, eds. Nashville, TN: Thomas Nelson Publishers, 1980.

The New Strong's Exhaustive Concordance of the Bible. Strong, James. Nashville, TN: Thomas Nelson Publishers, 1995.

Unger's Bible Handbook. Unger, Merrill F. Chicago: Moody Press, 1967.

Description of the Books of the Bible

There are a grand total of sixty-six books in the Bible—thirty-nine in the Old Testament and twenty-seven in the New Testament. Here is a quick overview of each of those books.

B

The Old Testament

Genesis

The word *genesis* means "beginnings," and that makes it a fitting title for the first book of the Bible. The book of Genesis, which is commonly believed to have been written by Moses, contains the stories of the beginning of the universe, the beginning of the planet Earth, the beginning of humankind, the beginning of human civilization, the beginning of sin, the beginning of the Jewish race, and the beginning of God's plan for the salvation of all humankind.

Exodus

Also commonly accepted to have been recorded by Moses, the book of Exodus tells us the story of how Moses, despite his own misgivings about his ability to lead, obeyed God's call to lead the Hebrew people out of Egyptian slavery. It also tells the story of how God gave His people the Law of Moses, including the Ten Commandments.

Leviticus

The third book of the Bible, Leviticus, was also recorded by Moses, and it deals with the laws, regulations, and commandments concerning sacrifices to God, the priesthood, ceremonial purity, and dietary and other laws the people of Israel were to observe.

Numbers

The book of Numbers is important historically because it gives the details of the route the Israelites took out of Egypt and also their important encampments on their way to the Promised Land. Numbers includes the numbering of the Israelites, an account of the journey from Sinai to Moab, and the Jewish people's rebellion because of their fear.

Deuteronomy

This book, which was also recorded by Moses, consists of four addresses to the Israelites by Moses shortly before his death. The first address (chapters 1–4) covers the historic events during the Israelites' forty years in the wilderness. This book also contains the laws and guidelines for the Israelites' conduct in Canaan, the Promised Land. As Deuteronomy closes, Moses prepares himself for death and appoints Joshua to take his place.

Joshua

Moses, who led the people of Israel out of Egyptian captivity, has died, and in his place God has raised up Joshua as the leader who will now—forty years too late because of their own rebellion—guide the people of Israel into the Promised Land. This book covers the conquest of Canaan (chapters 1–12), the allotment of the land to the twelve tribes (13–22), and the farewell speeches from Joshua (23–24).

Judges

This book, which contains some of the greatest stories in the Bible, tells us the history of Israel from the death of Joshua to the beginning of the monarchy under Saul, Israel's first king. The book gets its name from the fact that it records the history of Israel's government under fourteen judges who ruled over the nation prior to the monarchy.

Ruth

The story of Ruth is set during the time of the judges—a time when the nation of Israel had plunged into a time of unfaithfulness to God. Ruth, on the other hand, was faithful, and she was rewarded with a new husband, Boaz, and with a place in the lineage of King David (she was his great-grandmother) and, eventually, Jesus Christ.

1 Samuel

First Samuel records the leadership transition in Israel from judges to kings. It is named for Samuel, the last judge and first prophet of Israel, and it includes the account of the monarchy of Saul and the preparation of David, who has been anointed but wasn't yet recognized as Saul's successor.

2 Samuel

The book of Second Samuel records the highlights of the reign of King David—first over the territory of Judah and later over the entire nation of Israel. It records David's ascension to the throne, his sin of adultery and murder, and the consequences of those sins for himself, his family, and his nation.

1 Kings

This book tells the story of Solomon, the son and successor of King David. It was under Solomon's leadership that Israel rose to the peak of its power and influence worldwide and the holy Temple was constructed. This book also tells the sad story of how Solomon's zeal for God faded in his later years.

2 Kings

Second Kings picks up where 1 Kings leaves off, and it tells the terrible story of a kingdom divided into two nations—Israel and Judah—and of those two nations' rebellion and their path toward captivity. Second Kings also records the ministry of the prophet Elisha, who ministered during terrible times.

1 and 2 Chronicles

These books cover the same period in the history of Israel as 1 and 2 Kings but with a different emphasis. The books of Chronicles are not just repetition of what has already been recorded. They give the reader a more spiritual look at the terrible events that led to the fall and captivity of a once great and blessed nation.

Ezra

The book of Ezra, named for an important priest by that name, tells the story of the two returns of the people of Judah from captivity in Babylon. The first of those returns was led by Zerubbabel, and it was to rebuild the temple (chapters 1–6). The second was led by Ezra, and it was to begin a spiritual awakening or revival of the people (7–10).

Nehemiah

This book, which is thought to be an autobiography of Nehemiah, can be seen as a continuation of the book of Ezra. It tells the story of the rebuilding of Jerusalem (chapters 1–7), the spiritual state of the Jewish people at that time (8–10), and other events, including the dedication of the wall around Jerusalem and the spiritual reforms carried out by Nehemiah (12–13).

Esther

The inclusion of the book of Esther in the Scriptures has been a source of debate for centuries. For one thing, God is not mentioned at all in the book, and there are only passing references to any kind of spiritual disciplines. However, if you read closely, you'll see that the hand of God in the affairs of His people is evident throughout the book.

Job

This is believed to be the earliest written book of the Bible. The story is set during the time of the patriarchs (Abraham, Isaac, Jacob, and Joseph) and tells the story of a man whose faith and devotion to God is challenged when he loses everything he has—his wealth, his family, even his health—and is left asking why.

Psalms

Written over a period of several centuries, the book of Psalms is a collection of individual writings—by several authors—that cover the full range of humanity's interactions with its Creator.

There are many themes in the Psalms, the most prominent ones being prayer, praise, and worship of God. Outside of Isaiah, the Psalms are the most quoted Old Testament writings in the New Testament.

Proverbs

The Bible tells us that King Solomon prayed for one thing, wisdom (2 Chronicles 1:10), which can be defined as the ability and knowledge it takes to live a Godly life. The book of Proverbs gives the reader some of Solomon's wisdom, covering such topics as work, pride, greed, friendship, anger, words, sex, procrastination, and many others.

Ecclesiastes

King Solomon is traditionally believed to be the author of the book of Ecclesiastes, which has as its main theme the vanity or futility of a life—even what appears to be a successful, comfortable, happy life—outside of a real relationship with God. Nothing, we learn from reading this book, can take the place of living with and for God.

Song of Solomon

Written by King Solomon, this book—also called the Song of Songs—is a love song filled with erotic imagery and metaphors. It depicts Solomon's joyful courtship of and wedding with a shepherdess named Shulamite, but metaphorically it has been seen as a picture of God's love for Israel and for Christ's church.

Isaiah

The prophet Isaiah ministered over a span of at least forty years and under the reigns of four kings of Judah. His book of prophecies records the dire warnings of coming judgment for a wayward people, but it also contains wonderful promises of coming redemption and salvation—salvation through the coming Messiah and Savior—for all humankind.

Jeremiah

This book contains the prophecies of the man who has been called "the weeping prophet," and it carries a heartbreaking message of doom and judgment on a people Jeremiah repeatedly points out have "forgotten God." Throughout his sermons and warnings, Jeremiah staunchly declares that the only hope for the people of Judah is to return to their God.

Lamentations

This book, written by Jeremiah, is a continuation of the messages of the book of Jeremiah, and it describes the horrible aftermath of the invasion of Jerusalem by the Babylonians. There is death and destruction all around, and Jeremiah is heartbroken over what has happened to this great city and to the people who lived there.

Ezekiel

The prophet Ezekiel ministered during the worst time in the history of Judah: the seventy-year period of Babylonian captivity. His prophecies can be seen as companions for those of Jeremiah, but while Jeremiah focused on death and destruction, Ezekiel focused on God's eventual restoration and salvation for his people.

Daniel

Like the book of Ezekiel, Daniel is set during the Babylonian captivity. Daniel was one of the many Jewish people who had been taken from his home to Babylon, and he was picked for government service, a position he used to speak God's prophetic message to Jews and Gentiles alike.

Hosea

The prophet Hosea, whose name means "salvation," ministered to the northern kingdom of Israel, which is enjoying a time of national prosperity but which is also in a state of spiritual decay. In order to dramatize the unfaithfulness of his people, God calls Hosea to marry an immoral and unfaithful woman named Gomer.

Joel

Sudden disaster has struck the land of Judah in the form of a black cloud of locusts, which devour every living green thing in their path. While it's not clear in this book whether the locusts were literal or a vision of things to come, the prophet Joel uses the occasion to call his countrymen to repentance.

Amos

Like Hosea, the prophet Amos ministered to Israel in a time of national prosperity and expansion. But also like Hosea, he ministered in a time of religious and spiritual decay. Amos, a farmer turned prophet, speaks out fearlessly against the sin of the people, warning them of coming judgment if they don't turn back to God.

Obadiah

The shortest book of the Old Testament, Obadiah centers on a centuries-old feud between the Israelites, the descendants of Jacob, and the Edomites, the descendants of Esau. In this book, God has pronounced judgment against Edom for its continued hostility toward Israel.

Jonah

Called by God to go and preach to the wicked people in Nineveh, the prophet Jonah refuses and instead boards a boat and heads in the opposite direction. But God never lets Jonah out of His sight and eventually brings him back to a place where he can minister as God had called him to in the first place.

Micah

The prophet Micah was a contemporary of Isaiah, and he spoke a message of reproof for the rich and influential people of Jerusalem who had been mistreating or neglecting the poorest and neediest among them. He rebukes those who would use their power for personal gain. His message was for the people to "do what is right, to love mercy, and to walk humbly with your God" (Micah 6:8).

Nahum

The Assyrian capital of Nineveh, where Jonah had preached, resulting in repentance and a stay of God's judgment, has a hundred years later turned back to evil ways and is about to feel the wrath of God. Nahum prophesies the utter destruction of the city, which will come at the hands of the Babylonians.

Habakkuk

The prophet Habakkuk ministers to the kingdom of Judah during her final moments prior to the Babylonian invasion, which God will use to mete out His wrath on His rebellious people. Although they have repeatedly been called to repentance, the people stubbornly refuse to change their ways. Habakkuk, knowing the sinfulness of his countrymen, asks God how long it can continue.

Zephaniah

Judah's political and religious history included occasional reform, the kind of reform preached by the prophet Zephaniah. His book contains the twin themes of the severity and lovingness of God, and it also speaks of God's judgment on sin and of God's restoration and salvation of the nation He loves.

Haggai

The terrible period in Jewish history known as the Babylonian captivity is past, and they have returned to their homeland and started rebuilding the temple. But sixteen years after the project is started, it has yet to be finished—all because the people have allowed their personal affairs to keep them from God's work. The book of Haggai contains fiery calls to finish the work so that God can bless His people.

Zechariah

The prophet Zechariah was a contemporary of Haggai, and he addressed the same issue: the unfinished temple. However, Zechariah is more positive in his tone, focusing on the presence of God to give the people strength to finish the task before them. He gives great encouragement to the governor Zerubbabel.

Malachi

Years after God had lovingly and graciously returned His people from Babylon to the Promised Land, they again began backsliding and falling into the same kinds of sins that led to the Babylonian captivity in the first place. Malachi directs his message of judgment to a people who had a false sense of security when it came to their relationship with God.

The New Testament

Matthew

While the message of Matthew's gospel is for everyone today, it was written especially for the Jewish people of his time, a people who had waited for centuries for the promised Messiah. Matthew, one of the twelve apostles, continually points out that Jesus was the One they had waited

for simply because he fulfilled the Old Testament prophecies—more than forty of which Matthew lists in his gospel account.

Mark

The shortest of the four Gospels, Mark portrays Jesus as a servant of his Father in heaven, as a preacher, teacher, and healer who took care of the needs of others all the way to his death on a cross. Mark himself is identified as "the son of Mary of Jerusalem" (Acts 12:12) and as "John Mark" (Acts 12:25).

Luke

The Gospel of Luke—which, along with the Acts of the Apostles, was written by the physician Luke—focuses on the perfect humanity of Jesus Christ. Luke tells his readers upfront that he wasn't one of Jesus' apostles or even an eyewitness to the earthly ministry of Christ. Luke's gospel was the only one of the four written by a Gentile, and it includes many details left out of the other accounts.

John

While Luke presents Jesus as the perfect human, or "the Son of Man," the apostle John presents him as the perfect, sinless Son of God. One of the recurring phrases in the Gospel of John is "I am," which was spoken by Jesus several times as he identified himself as the Son of God, the Messiah, and the Savior.

Acts of the Apostles

Dr. Luke, apparently an avid historian and researcher, compiled and wrote the account of how the church got its start. In this book we read of how the believers received the Holy Spirit (chapter 2), and many of them—including Peter, John, and the apostle Paul—went out into the world and preached what Jesus Christ had taught.

Romans

Paul's epistle to the Romans is considered his greatest work. The Gospels recount the life of Jesus and present his words and deeds, but the book of Romans explains the significance of his life and of his death and resurrection, namely that these events were accomplished so that all humanity—Jew and Gentile alike—could have fellowship with God.

1 Corinthians

The city of Corinth was one of the most important in Greece during Paul's day. As a port city, it was the hub of commerce and trade. But it was also a center of immorality and idolatrous religious practices. It was the influences of these things that Paul addressed as he wrote his letter to a church he had founded earlier.

2 Corinthians

Since Paul had written his first letter to the Corinthian church, it had been infiltrated by false teachers who had stirred the people against his teachings. Upon hearing about that, Paul sent an associate, Titus, to deal with the problems. Upon the return of Titus, Paul was overjoyed to hear of the Corinthians' change of heart. This letter is Paul's expression of thanksgiving to the church for its about-face.

Galatians

The Galatian church has been influenced to leave the life of faith and follow after teachings based on works of the law and the flesh. Paul was disturbed at this development and wrote this epistle in an attempt to get them to follow a gospel based on faith.

Ephesians

Paul's epistle to the Ephesians is addressed to a church that doesn't quite seem to understand what riches they have in Jesus Christ. They are called to higher living, yet they live like paupers only because they don't understand what they have in him. Chapters 1–3 of this epistle spell out for these Ephesians what they have, which is every spiritual blessing they could ever need.

Philippians

Paul's letter to the Philippians is different from his others simply because he isn't correcting any major problems within the church. Instead, he writes with great warmth and affection to these believers in Philippi, who had helped him out in his hour of need. In writing this letter, Paul spells out the central truth that it is only in Christ that believers can have real unity and joy.

Colossians

This letter has as its emphasis the works, the person, and the character of Jesus Christ. Paul wanted his readers to understand that Christ should be first and foremost in people's lives and that their lives should reflect that fact. The first two chapters of this letter give the readers the doctrine of who Jesus is, while the second two spell out what that means in how we live.

1 Thessalonians

Paul's first letter to the newly founded Thessalonian church expresses his words of praise for their faith, hope, love, and perseverance—all in the face of the severe persecution that churches faced in those days. He also encourages them to grow in their faith and in their love for one another and to continue praying, rejoicing, and giving thanks in all things.

2 Thessalonians

Since Paul's first letter to the Thessalonian church, some false teaching had made its way into the church causing these believers to falter in their faith. In writing 2 Thessalonians, Paul was attempting to rid the church of this false teaching and put them back on the right path of faith.

1 Timothy

This is a letter Paul wrote to his young protégé Timothy, a pastor at the church in Ephesus who was faced with the challenging tasks of ridding the church of false teaching, making sure public worship was conducted properly, and developing mature leadership. Paul wanted Timothy to understand that his youthfulness could be used as an asset in his ministry and that he had to be on his guard against false teaching and pursue the things a godly man should.

2 Timothy

This epistle is one of several Paul wrote from prison, and like the others it is a letter of encouragement. Again, Paul is encouraging Timothy to be on the alert for false or faulty teaching and to cling to the truth—even though there would be those who wanted to hear something other than the truth of Jesus Christ.

Titus

Titus, like Timothy, was a young pastor who faced some daunting challenges. In this case, it was setting in order the church in Crete. Paul wants him to understand the importance of making sure that the leadership in the church were the kind of men who would lead by example in the area of spiritual maturity.

Philemon

Paul's letter to Philemon, a fellow Christian, is the shortest of his epistles that appear in the Bible. In it, he is pleading the case of Onesimus, a runaway slave who had become a Christian. Paul is pleading with Philemon to take Onesimus back in the spirit of brotherly love and forgiveness.

Hebrews

The first Christians recorded in the Bible were Jewish people who had converted. Many of them struggled with the persecution by their countrymen and from the Roman authorities and were considering leaving Christianity and going back to Judaism. The writer of Hebrews (it's not certain who that was) wanted to encourage them to continue on, and he did so by showing them the superiority of Christ over any of the religious systems they knew.

James

While no one can be saved on the basis of their deeds, true faith in Christ will manifest itself in the deeds we do. That is the point the apostle James—it isn't certain who this is, but it has been generally accepted as the one referred to as "the Lord's brother" (Galatians 1:19)—was making when he wrote, "faith is dead without good deeds" (Galatians 2:26). Faith takes us through trials, repels temptation, and motivates us to obey the Word of God.

1 Peter

Jesus never told anyone that following him would be easy or that they wouldn't face opposition. In fact, he promised exactly the opposite. The apostle Peter, who followed Jesus for nearly the entirety of his earthly ministry, wanted the readers of this epistle to understand that following Jesus meant facing trials but that those who persevered through those things would receive the reward.

2 Peter

In his second epistle, Peter warns believers about false teachers who were sure to come into their midst trying to sell false and damaging teaching. He wanted them to understand that they would need to be diligent in examining their personal lives and in pursuing the kind of personal conduct God had called them to.

1 John

The apostle John, who had enjoyed close fellowship with Jesus while he was on earth and who still enjoyed close fellowship with him as he was in heaven, wanted his readers to see that God is three things: light, love, and life. And because of those things, those of us who know Jesus Christ are allowed to walk and live in those three things.

2 John

The apostle John had already said that loving one another is the equivalent of walking according to God's commandments. However, John wrote that love must also be discerning. It can't be naïve, ignorant, or open to anything and anyone. That is because there are a lot of false teachers who do not acknowledge Christ as having come in the flesh.

3 John

In this letter, the apostle John encourages Christians to have brotherly fellowship with one another. John expresses his love for a person named Gaius, then assures him of his prayers for his health and proclaims his joy over Gaius's steady walk with the Lord.

Jude

This epistle—which was likely written by Jude, the brother of James—encourages believers to fight and contend for the faith, particularly when people fall away, when false teachers appear, and when the truth of God comes under attack. In the face of such things, Christians should not be caught off guard but should be ready to contend for their faith.

Revelation

Revelation, written by the apostle John, is the book of finalities—or how things turn out for us. In this book, we see God's final plan for the redemption of humankind and the judgment of all evil unfold. This is the book of unveiling or disclosure of all things eternal.

How the Bible Came to Be

Have you ever looked at the copy of that leather-backed book on your bookshelf or nightstand and wonder how we got it? How the individual books came to be or how these particular books ended up in the Bible we have today? Was it the result of someone just randomly choosing a bunch of interesting stories for bedtime reading? Or did it happen when some committee of religious people got together and decided what to leave in and what to leave out?

In truth, very few people open their Bibles and give thought to how it came to be or how or why the sixty-six books in it are there. Most of us just open the Bible and start reading, feeling comfortable in our belief that what's in the Bible is what God wanted to be included. The way it all came about is actually a very interesting story—far more interesting than the scenarios listed above.

Becoming a Part of the Canon

The recording of the written Word of God began in around 1400 B.C. when Moses received the Ten Commandments on the stone tablets. By around 400 B.C., all of the original Hebrew manuscripts that make up the thirty-nine books of the Old Testament had been completed.

In the third century B.C. these books—as well as fourteen books of what is called the Apocrypha—were translated into Greek, the dominant language of the time. This translation was called the Septuagint. Legend held that it took seventy-two scholars seventy-two days to get the job done, but it in fact took much longer than that. This version was very popular in the Greek-speaking early church as well as with Jews in and around Palestine who no longer spoke Hebrew.

All of the original copies of the Hebrew Scriptures are long gone, but the copying was done with meticulous care and precision, ensuring that the copies were completely accurate. Traditionally, the Jews held the text of the Scriptures in such high esteem that they buried copies that

had aged to the point where they had become difficult to read.

By the end of the first century A.D.—or around seven decades after the death of Jesus Christ—all of the books included in the New Testament today—from Matthew to Acts to the epistles to Revelation—had been written. In the second century all these books as a group comprised the collection of writings that would become the New Testament. But it would not be until a few centuries later that the books in the list were canonized, meaning that they were accepted as having been divinely inspired and, therefore, included in the Bible we have today.

Why the Canon?

There were numerous reasons why the church needed to come up with a final, official list of readings for its members. First of all, the apostles and other eyewitnesses to the life, work, and words of Christ had long since died, and the members of the church wanted something in writing that would spell out for them the messages of Jesus and the apostles.

Another reason the church needed the list was that it was customary at the time for church leaders to read to the people in the congregation. At first, all of the readings done in the church were taken from the Old Testament—after all, there was nothing else to read at that time—but later the leaders also began reading to the congregation what were called the Memoirs of the Apostles. These leaders wanted to make sure they had readings that reflected the message of

God as it came through Jesus Christ himself and the apostles who continued his work on earth.

Obviously, there was a need for a list of readings to be compiled. But how was it going to be accomplished?

The Standard for Canonization

The early church fathers—those second- and third-century writers and teachers who took the place of the apostles as leaders in the church—knew they needed to figure out which of the many books and letters available from various sources belonged in their collection of accepted readings—also known as the canon.

The church fathers believed that the only requirement for inclusion in the canon was that the books and letters be inspired—specifically inspired by God—meaning that they were the words God would speak to them if He were to allow His voice to be heard in the congregations.

The obvious problem with that kind of test was figuring out how a book or letter—and there were many of them to choose from—was truly inspired by God. It didn't take too long before the early church fathers realized that they would need other tests in order to decide on the canon of Scripture.

One of those tests for canonizing a book or letter was whether it was written by an apostle or someone who was close to an apostle. So the books by the apostles Matthew, John, Peter, and Paul were included. Luke the physician, who wrote the gospel that bears his name as well as the Acts of the Apostles, was not an apostle. However, he had a very close relationship with the apostle Paul and even traveled with him during his missionary journeys. For that reason, two of his writings ended up as part of the New Testament we have today.

Gradually, over the course of centuries, the canon developed. It is believed that by about A.D.175, the canon included essentially the same books as our present day New Testament. By the year 200 the church widely accepted this list as canonical, and it was used widely in church services. Clement, the Bishop of Alexandria, recognized the books, as did many other church leaders of his time.

Still, it would be nearly 200 years before the canon of Scripture was officially recognized. In the year 397 a meeting of church leaders, called the Third Council of Carthage (modern-day Tunis)—it wasn't actually a general council but a regional council of African bishops, heavily influenced by Augustine, the Bishop of Hippo—acknowledged the twenty-seven books of the New Testament as we know them today. Most of the books had already been treated as Scripture for years, but around a half dozen books needed further discussion for final acceptance.

While the Third Council of Carthage acknowledged the twenty-seven books of the New Testament as we now have them, it wasn't until the Council of Chalcedon that the canon was officially accepted and approved by the church. Interestingly enough, there were several books included in the canon at the Third Council of

Carthage that can no longer be found in modern-day Bibles—with the exception of some Catholic Bibles. These other books—known as the Apocrypha—were included in the original King James Bible but were removed in 1885, leaving the sixty-six books we have today.

Not long after the canon was officially recognized at the third Council of Carthage and adopted at the Council of Chalcedon, another historic milestone concerning the Bible took place. On or around the year 400, the entire Bible was translated, primarily by a Christian leader named Jerome (340–420), into Latin. This version was known as the "Vulgate" which means "written in the language of the people." Since that time, the Bible has been translated into more than 500 languages and dozens of versions or translations, some of which got the translators in major hot water with the ruling religious authorities of the time.

Putting the Bible in the Hands of the People

There was a time when the government/religious authorities (they were one in the same back then) kept the general public from reading the Bible for themselves. But many of the reformers—including the ones prior to the sixteenth-century Protestant Reformation—believed that the general public needed the right and privilege of reading the Bible and even owning one.

That led to several translations of the Bible, including a hand-copied one by John Wycliffe, who in the late 1300s was the first person to produce a copy of the complete Bible in English. Many other translations followed over the next several centuries, and in around 1455, a German named Johann Gutenberg developed a printing press that revolutionized printing and allowed for easier dispersal of all printed materials, including the Bible.

In a time when we can often obtain a Bible for free, or at least buy one for a small amount of money, it's hard to imagine a time when people couldn't even afford one. But that was the situation during the Middle Ages, when a Bible cost the equivalent of one year's wages. It was Gutenberg's development of the printing press that began to change that situation.

The first book off Gutenberg's press was a Bible, and it didn't take long for the Scriptures to become available throughout Europe and in all European languages.

The All-Time Number One Bestseller

The best-known of all Bible translations is the King James Version, which was commissioned by King James I of England in 1611 and completed by a team of fifty-four of the world's finest linguists. These were incredibly well-qualified men who had an excellent grasp on the Hebrew, Aramaic, and Greek languages of the Bible. On top of that, they were all devout Christians who held the Bible in the highest esteem. Their work is still praised for its accuracy in holding to the original manuscripts, and it has become by far the world's best-selling book of all time. Since that time, there have been many translations and paraphrases of the Bible.

Here is a timeline of some of the key dates in the writing and translation of the Bible, courtesy of *www.greatsite.com* and adapted for this book. Please note that some of the dates may be approximate:

- **1400 B.C.**—the first written Word of God: the Ten Commandments delivered to Moses

- **400 B.C.**—completion of all original Hebrew manuscripts that make up the thirty-nine books of the Old Testament

- **200 B.C.**—completion of the Septuagint Greek manuscripts that contain the thirty-nine Old Testament books and fourteen Apocrypha books

- **First century A.D.**—completion of all original Greek manuscripts that make up the twenty-seven books of the New Testament

- **315**—Athanasius, the Bishop of Alexandria, identifies the twenty-seven books of the New Testament that are today recognized as the canon of Scripture

- **382**—Jerome's Latin Vulgate manuscript produced, which contains all eighty books (thirty-nine Old Testament, fourteen Apocrypha, and twenty-seven New Testament)

- **500**—Scriptures have been translated into over 500 languages

- **600**—Latin was the only language allowed for Scripture

- **995**—Anglo-Saxon translations of the New Testament produced

- **1384**—Wycliffe is the first person to produce a (hand-written) manuscript copy of the complete Bible (all eighty books)

- **1455**—Johann Gutenberg invents the printing press; books may now be mass produced instead of individually hand-written; the first book ever printed is Gutenberg's Bible in Latin

- **1516**—Erasmus produces a Greek/Latin parallel New Testament

- **1522**—Martin Luther's German New Testament

- **1526**—William Tyndale's New Testament, the first New Testament printed in the English language

- **1535**—Myles Coverdale's Bible, the first complete Bible printed in the English language (all eighty books)

- **1537**—Tyndale-Matthews Bible, the second complete Bible printed in English; done by John "Thomas Matthew" Rogers (all eighty books)

- **1539**—the Great Bible printed, the first English language Bible authorized for public use (eighty books)

- **1560**—the Geneva Bible printed, the first English language Bible to add numbered verses to each chapter (eighty books)

- **1568**—the Bishops Bible printed; the Bible which the King James revised (eighty books)

- **1609**—the Douay Old Testament is added to the Rheims New Testament (of 1582) making the first complete English Catholic Bible; translated from the Latin Vulgate (eighty books)

- **1611**—the King James Bible printed, originally with all eighty books; the Apocrypha was officially removed in 1885 leaving only sixty-six books

- **1782**—Robert Aitken's Bible, the First English language Bible (KJV) printed in America

- **1791**—Isaac Collins and Isaiah Thomas respectively produce the first family Bible and first illustrated Bible printed in America; both were King James Versions with all eighty books

- **1808**—Jane Aitken's Bible (daughter of Robert Aitken); the first Bible to be printed by a woman

- **1833**—Noah Webster's Bible; after producing his famous dictionary, Webster printed his own revision of the King James Bible

- **1841**—English Hexapla New Testament, an early textual comparison showing the Greek and six famous English translations in parallel columns

- **1846**—The Illuminated Bible; the most lavishly illustrated Bible printed in America. A King James Version, with all 80 books

- **1885**—the English Revised Version Bible, the first major English revision of the KJV

- **1901**—the American Standard Version, the first major American revision of the KJV

- **1971**—the New American Standard Bible (NASB) is published as a modern and accurate word for word English translation of the Bible

- **1973**—the New International Version (NIV) is published as a modern and accurate phrase for phrase English translation of the Bible

- **1982**—the New King James Version (NKJV) is published as a modern English version maintaining the original style of the King James Version

- **2002**—the English Standard Version (ESV) is published as a translation to bridge the gap between the accuracy of the NASB and the readability of the NIV

Index

YOU SHOULD CAREFULLY READ THE FOLLOWING TERMS AND CONDITIONS BEFORE USING THIS SOFTWARE PRODUCT. INSTALLING AND USING THIS PRODUCT INDICATES YOUR ACCEPTANCE OF THESE CONDITIONS. IF YOU DO NOT AGREE WITH THESE TERMS AND CONDITIONS, DO NOT INSTALL THE SOFTWARE AND RETURN THIS PACKAGE PROMPTLY FOR A FULL REFUND.

1. Grant of License

This software package is protected under United States copyright law and international treaty. You are hereby entitled to one copy of the enclosed software and are allowed by law to make one backup copy or to copy the contents of the disks onto a single hard disk and keep the originals as your backup or archival copy. United States copyright law prohibits you from making a copy of this software for use on any computer other than your own computer. United States copyright law also prohibits you from copying any written material included in this software package without first obtaining the permission of F+W Publications, Inc.

2. Restrictions

You, the end-user, are hereby prohibited from the following:
You may not rent or lease the Software or make copies to rent or lease for profit or for any other purpose.
You may not disassemble or reverse compile for the purposes of reverse engineering the Software.
You may not modify or adapt the Software or documentation in whole or in part, including, but not limited to, translating or creating derivative works.

3. Transfer

You may transfer the Software to another person, provided that (a) you transfer all of the Software and documentation to the same transferee; (b) you do not retain any copies; and (c) the transferee is informed of and agrees to the terms and conditions of this Agreement.

4. Termination

This Agreement and your license to use the Software can be terminated without notice if you fail to comply with any of the provisions set forth in this Agreement. Upon termination of this Agreement, you promise to destroy all copies of the software including backup or archival copies as well as any documentation associated with the Software. All disclaimers of warranties and limitation of liability set forth in this Agreement shall survive any termination of this Agreement.

5. Limited Warranty

F+W Publications, Inc. warrants that the Software will perform according to the manual and other written materials accompanying the Software for a period of 30 days from the date of receipt. F+W Publications, Inc. does not accept responsibility for any malfunctioning computer hardware or any incompatibilities with existing or new computer hardware technology.

6. Customer Remedies

F+W Publications, Inc.'s entire liability and your exclusive remedy shall be, at the option of F+W Publications, Inc., either refund of your purchase price or repair and/or replacement of Software that does not meet this Limited Warranty. Proof of purchase shall be required. This Limited Warranty will be voided if Software failure was caused by abuse, neglect, accident or misapplication. All replacement Software will be warranted based on the remainder of the warranty or the full 30 days, whichever is shorter and will be subject to the terms of the Agreement.

7. No Other Warranties

F+W PUBLICATIONS, INC., TO THE FULLEST EXTENT OF THE LAW, DISCLAIMS ALL OTHER WARRANTIES, OTHER THAN THE LIMITED WARRANTY IN PARAGRAPH 5, EITHER EXPRESS OR IMPLIED, ASSOCIATED WITH ITS SOFTWARE, INCLUDING BUT NOT LIMITED TO IMPLIED WARRANTIES OF MERCHANTABILITY AND FITNESS FOR A PARTICULAR PURPOSE, WITH REGARD TO THE SOFTWARE AND ITS ACCOMPANYING WRITTEN MATERIALS. THIS LIMITED WARRANTY GIVES YOU SPECIFIC LEGAL RIGHTS. DEPENDING UPON WHERE THIS SOFTWARE WAS PURCHASED, YOU MAY HAVE OTHER RIGHTS.

8. Limitations on Remedies

TO THE MAXIMUM EXTENT PERMITTED BY LAW, F+W PUBLICATIONS, INC. SHALL NOT BE HELD LIABLE FOR ANY DAMAGES WHATSOEVER, INCLUDING WITHOUT LIMITATION, ANY LOSS FROM PERSONAL INJURY, LOSS OF BUSINESS PROFITS, BUSINESS INTERRUPTION, BUSINESS INFORMATION OR ANY OTHER PECUNIARY LOSS ARISING OUT OF THE USE OF THIS SOFTWARE.
This applies even if F+W Publications, Inc. has been advised of the possibility of such damages. F+W Publications, Inc.'s entire liability under any provision of this agreement shall be limited to the amount actually paid by you for the Software. Because some states may not allow for this type of limitation of liability, the above limitation may not apply to you.
THE WARRANTY AND REMEDIES SET FORTH ABOVE ARE EXCLUSIVE AND IN LIEU OF ALL OTHERS, ORAL OR WRITTEN, EXPRESS OR IMPLIED. No F+W Publications, Inc. dealer, distributor, agent, or employee is authorized to make any modification or addition to the warranty.

9. General

This Agreement shall be governed by the laws of the United States of America and the Commonwealth of Massachusetts. If you have any questions concerning this Agreement, contact F+W Publications, Inc., via Adams Media at 508-427-7100. Or write to us at: Adams Media, an F+W Publications Company, 57 Littlefield Street, Avon, MA 02322.

THE EVERYTHING SERIES!

BUSINESS & PERSONAL FINANCE

Everything® Accounting Book
Everything® Budgeting Book
Everything® Business Planning Book
Everything® Coaching and Mentoring Book, 2nd Ed.
Everything® Fundraising Book
Everything® Get Out of Debt Book
Everything® Grant Writing Book
Everything® Guide to Foreclosures
Everything® Guide to Personal Finance for Single Mothers
Everything® Home-Based Business Book, 2nd Ed.
Everything® Homebuying Book, 2nd Ed.
Everything® Homeselling Book, 2nd Ed.
Everything® Improve Your Credit Book
Everything® Investing Book, 2nd Ed.
Everything® Landlording Book
Everything® Leadership Book
Everything® Managing People Book, 2nd Ed.
Everything® Negotiating Book
Everything® Online Auctions Book
Everything® Online Business Book
Everything® Personal Finance Book
Everything® Personal Finance in Your 20s and 30s Book
Everything® Project Management Book
Everything® Real Estate Investing Book
Everything® Retirement Planning Book
Everything® Robert's Rules Book, $7.95
Everything® Selling Book
Everything® Start Your Own Business Book, 2nd Ed.
Everything® Wills & Estate Planning Book

COOKING

Everything® Barbecue Cookbook
Everything® Bartender's Book, 2nd Ed., $9.95
Everything® Calorie Counting Cookbook
Everything® Cheese Book
Everything® Chinese Cookbook
Everything® Classic Recipes Book
Everything® Cocktail Parties & Drinks Book
Everything® College Cookbook
Everything® Cooking for Baby and Toddler Book
Everything® Cooking for Two Cookbook
Everything® Diabetes Cookbook
Everything® Easy Gourmet Cookbook
Everything® Fondue Cookbook
Everything® Fondue Party Book
Everything® Gluten-Free Cookbook
Everything® Glycemic Index Cookbook
Everything® Grilling Cookbook
Everything® Healthy Meals in Minutes Cookbook
Everything® Holiday Cookbook

Everything® Indian Cookbook
Everything® Italian Cookbook
Everything® Low-Carb Cookbook
Everything® Low-Cholesterol Cookbook
Everything® Low-Fat High-Flavor Cookbook
Everything® Low-Salt Cookbook
Everything® Meals for a Month Cookbook
Everything® Mediterranean Cookbook
Everything® Mexican Cookbook
Everything® No Trans Fat Cookbook
Everything® One-Pot Cookbook
Everything® Pizza Cookbook
Everything® Quick and Easy 30-Minute,
        5-Ingredient Cookbook
Everything® Quick Meals Cookbook
Everything® Slow Cooker Cookbook
Everything® Slow Cooking for a Crowd Cookbook
Everything® Soup Cookbook
Everything® Stir-Fry Cookbook
Everything® Sugar-Free Cookbook
Everything® Tapas and Small Plates Cookbook
Everything® Tex-Mex Cookbook
Everything® Thai Cookbook
Everything® Vegetarian Cookbook
Everything® Wild Game Cookbook
Everything® Wine Book, 2nd Ed.

GAMES

Everything® 15-Minute Sudoku Book, $9.95
Everything® 30-Minute Sudoku Book, $9.95
Everything® Bible Crosswords Book, $9.95
Everything® Blackjack Strategy Book
Everything® Brain Strain Book, $9.95
Everything® Bridge Book
Everything® Card Games Book
Everything® Card Tricks Book, $9.95
Everything® Casino Gambling Book, 2nd Ed.
Everything® Chess Basics Book
Everything® Craps Strategy Book
Everything® Crossword and Puzzle Book
Everything® Crossword Challenge Book
Everything® Crosswords for the Beach Book, $9.95
Everything® Cryptic Crosswords Book, $9.95
Everything® Cryptograms Book, $9.95
Everything® Easy Crosswords Book
Everything® Easy Kakuro Book, $9.95
Everything® Easy Large-Print Crosswords Book
Everything® Games Book, 2nd Ed.
Everything® Giant Sudoku Book, $9.95
Everything® Kakuro Challenge Book, $9.95
Everything® Large-Print Crossword Challenge Book
Everything® Large-Print Crosswords Book
Everything® Lateral Thinking Puzzles Book, $9.95

Everything® **Literary Crosswords Book, $9.95**
Everything® Mazes Book
Everything® Memory Booster Puzzles Book, $9.95
Everything® Movie Crosswords Book, $9.95
Everything® Music Crosswords Book, $9.95
Everything® Online Poker Book, $12.95
Everything® Pencil Puzzles Book, $9.95
Everything® Poker Strategy Book
Everything® Pool & Billiards Book
Everything® Puzzles for Commuters Book, $9.95
Everything® Sports Crosswords Book, $9.95
Everything® Test Your IQ Book, $9.95
Everything® Texas Hold 'Em Book, $9.95
Everything® Travel Crosswords Book, $9.95
Everything® TV Crosswords Book, $9.95
Everything® Word Games Challenge Book
Everything® Word Scramble Book
Everything® Word Search Book

HEALTH

Everything® Alzheimer's Book
Everything® Diabetes Book
Everything® Health Guide to Adult Bipolar Disorder
Everything® Health Guide to Arthritis
Everything® Health Guide to Controlling Anxiety
Everything® Health Guide to Fibromyalgia
Everything® Health Guide to Menopause
Everything® Health Guide to OCD
Everything® Health Guide to PMS
Everything® Health Guide to Postpartum Care
Everything® Health Guide to Thyroid Disease
Everything® Hypnosis Book
Everything® Low Cholesterol Book
Everything® Nutrition Book
Everything® Reflexology Book
Everything® Stress Management Book

HISTORY

Everything® American Government Book
Everything® American History Book, 2nd Ed.
Everything® Civil War Book
Everything® Freemasons Book
Everything® Irish History & Heritage Book
Everything® Middle East Book
Everything® World War II Book, 2nd Ed.

HOBBIES

Everything® Candlemaking Book
Everything® Cartooning Book
Everything® Coin Collecting Book
Everything® Drawing Book

Everything® Family Tree Book, 2nd Ed.
Everything® Knitting Book
Everything® Knots Book
Everything® Photography Book
Everything® Quilting Book
Everything® Sewing Book
Everything® Soapmaking Book, 2nd Ed.
Everything® Woodworking Book

HOME IMPROVEMENT

Everything® Feng Shui Book
Everything® Feng Shui Decluttering Book, $9.95
Everything® Fix-It Book
Everything® Green Living Book
Everything® Home Decorating Book
Everything® Home Storage Solutions Book
Everything® Homebuilding Book
Everything® Organize Your Home Book, 2nd Ed.

KIDS' BOOKS

All titles are $7.95
Everything® Kids' Animal Puzzle & Activity Book
Everything® Kids' Baseball Book, 4th Ed.
Everything® Kids' Bible Trivia Book
Everything® Kids' Bugs Book
Everything® Kids' Cars and Trucks Puzzle and Activity Book
Everything® Kids' Christmas Puzzle & Activity Book
Everything® Kids' Cookbook
Everything® Kids' Crazy Puzzles Book
Everything® Kids' Dinosaurs Book
Everything® Kids' Environment Book
Everything® Kids' Fairies Puzzle and Activity Book
Everything® Kids' First Spanish Puzzle and Activity Book
Everything® Kids' Gross Cookbook
Everything® Kids' Gross Hidden Pictures Book
Everything® Kids' Gross Jokes Book
Everything® Kids' Gross Mazes Book
Everything® Kids' Gross Puzzle & Activity Book
Everything® Kids' Halloween Puzzle & Activity Book
Everything® Kids' Hidden Pictures Book
Everything® Kids' Horses Book
Everything® Kids' Joke Book
Everything® Kids' Knock Knock Book
Everything® Kids' Learning Spanish Book
Everything® Kids' Magical Science Experiments Book
Everything® Kids' Math Puzzles Book
Everything® Kids' Mazes Book
Everything® Kids' Money Book
Everything® Kids' Nature Book
Everything® Kids' Pirates Puzzle and Activity Book
Everything® Kids' Presidents Book
Everything® Kids' Princess Puzzle and Activity Book
Everything® Kids' Puzzle Book
Everything® Kids' Racecars Puzzle and Activity Book
Everything® Kids' Riddles & Brain Teasers Book
Everything® Kids' Science Experiments Book
Everything® Kids' Sharks Book

Everything® Kids' Soccer Book
Everything® Kids' Spies Puzzle and Activity Book
Everything® Kids' States Book
Everything® Kids' Travel Activity Book

KIDS' STORY BOOKS

Everything® Fairy Tales Book

LANGUAGE

Everything® Conversational Japanese Book with CD, $19.95
Everything® French Grammar Book
Everything® French Phrase Book, $9.95
Everything® French Verb Book, $9.95
Everything® German Practice Book with CD, $19.95
Everything® Inglés Book
Everything® Intermediate Spanish Book with CD, $19.95
Everything® Italian Practice Book with CD, $19.95
Everything® Learning Brazilian Portuguese Book with CD, $19.95
Everything® Learning French Book with CD, 2nd Ed., $19.95
Everything® Learning German Book
Everything® Learning Italian Book
Everything® Learning Latin Book
Everything® Learning Russian Book with CD, $19.95
Everything® Learning Spanish Book with CD, 2nd Ed., $19.95
Everything® Russian Practice Book with CD, $19.95
Everything® Sign Language Book
Everything® Spanish Grammar Book
Everything® Spanish Phrase Book, $9.95
Everything® Spanish Practice Book with CD, $19.95
Everything® Spanish Verb Book, $9.95
Everything® Speaking Mandarin Chinese Book with CD, $19.95

MUSIC

Everything® Drums Book with CD, $19.95
Everything® Guitar Book with CD, 2nd Ed., $19.95
Everything® Guitar Chords Book with CD, $19.95
Everything® Home Recording Book
Everything® Music Theory Book with CD, $19.95
Everything® Reading Music Book with CD, $19.95
Everything® Rock & Blues Guitar Book with CD, $19.95
Everything® Rock and Blues Piano Book with CD, $19.95
Everything® Songwriting Book

NEW AGE

Everything® Astrology Book, 2nd Ed.
Everything® Birthday Personology Book
Everything® Dreams Book, 2nd Ed.
Everything® Love Signs Book, $9.95
Everything® Love Spells Book, $9.95
Everything® Numerology Book
Everything® Paganism Book
Everything® Palmistry Book
Everything® Psychic Book
Everything® Reiki Book
Everything® Sex Signs Book, $9.95

Everything® Spells & Charms Book, 2nd Ed.
Everything® Tarot Book, 2nd Ed.
Everything® Toltec Wisdom Book
Everything® Wicca and Witchcraft Book

PARENTING

Everything® Baby Names Book, 2nd Ed.
Everything® Baby Shower Book, 2nd Ed.
Everything® Baby's First Year Book
Everything® Birthing Book
Everything® Breastfeeding Book
Everything® Father-to-Be Book
Everything® Father's First Year Book
Everything® Get Ready for Baby Book, 2nd Ed.
Everything® Get Your Baby to Sleep Book, $9.95
Everything® Getting Pregnant Book
Everything® Guide to Pregnancy Over 35
Everything® Guide to Raising a One-Year-Old
Everything® Guide to Raising a Two-Year-Old
Everything® Guide to Raising Adolescent Boys
Everything® Guide to Raising Adolescent Girls
Everything® Homeschooling Book
Everything® Mother's First Year Book
Everything® Parent's Guide to Childhood Illnesses
Everything® Parent's Guide to Children and Divorce
Everything® Parent's Guide to Children with ADD/ADHD
Everything® Parent's Guide to Children with Asperger's Syndrome
Everything® Parent's Guide to Children with Autism
Everything® Parent's Guide to Children with Bipolar Disorder
Everything® Parent's Guide to Children with Depression
Everything® Parent's Guide to Children with Dyslexia
Everything® Parent's Guide to Children with Juvenile Diabetes
Everything® Parent's Guide to Positive Discipline
Everything® Parent's Guide to Raising a Successful Child
Everything® Parent's Guide to Raising Boys
Everything® Parent's Guide to Raising Girls
Everything® Parent's Guide to Raising Siblings
Everything® Parent's Guide to Sensory Integration Disorder
Everything® Parent's Guide to Tantrums
Everything® Parent's Guide to the Strong-Willed Child
Everything® Parenting a Teenager Book
Everything® Potty Training Book, $9.95
Everything® Pregnancy Book, 3rd Ed.
Everything® Pregnancy Fitness Book
Everything® Pregnancy Nutrition Book
Everything® Pregnancy Organizer, 2nd Ed., $16.95
Everything® Toddler Activities Book
Everything® Toddler Book
Everything® Tween Book
Everything® Twins, Triplets, and More Book

PETS

Everything® Aquarium Book
Everything® Boxer Book
Everything® Cat Book, 2nd Ed.
Everything® Chihuahua Book

Everything® Cooking for Dogs Book
Everything® Dachshund Book
Everything® Dog Book
Everything® Dog Health Book
Everything® Dog Obedience Book
Everything® Dog Owner's Organizer, $16.95
Everything® Dog Training and Tricks Book
Everything® German Shepherd Book
Everything® Golden Retriever Book
Everything® Horse Book
Everything® Horse Care Book
Everything® Horseback Riding Book
Everything® Labrador Retriever Book
Everything® Poodle Book
Everything® Pug Book
Everything® Puppy Book
Everything® Rottweiler Book
Everything® Small Dogs Book
Everything® Tropical Fish Book
Everything® Yorkshire Terrier Book

REFERENCE

Everything® American Presidents Book
Everything® Blogging Book
Everything® Build Your Vocabulary Book
Everything® Car Care Book
Everything® Classical Mythology Book
Everything® Da Vinci Book
Everything® Divorce Book
Everything® Einstein Book
Everything® Enneagram Book
Everything® Etiquette Book, 2nd Ed.
Everything® Guide to Edgar Allan Poe
Everything® Inventions and Patents Book
Everything® Mafia Book
Everything® Martin Luther King Jr. Book
Everything® Philosophy Book
Everything® Pirates Book
Everything® Psychology Book

RELIGION

Everything® Angels Book
Everything® Bible Book
Everything® Bible Study Book with CD, $19.95
Everything® Buddhism Book
Everything® Catholicism Book
Everything® Christianity Book
Everything® Gnostic Gospels Book
Everything® History of the Bible Book
Everything® Jesus Book
Everything® Jewish History & Heritage Book
Everything® Judaism Book
Everything® Kabbalah Book
Everything® Koran Book

Everything® Mary Book
Everything® Mary Magdalene Book
Everything® Prayer Book
Everything® Saints Book, 2nd Ed.
Everything® Torah Book
Everything® Understanding Islam Book
Everything® Women of the Bible Book
Everything® World's Religions Book
Everything® Zen Book

SCHOOL & CAREERS

Everything® Alternative Careers Book
Everything® Career Tests Book
Everything® College Major Test Book
Everything® College Survival Book, 2nd Ed.
Everything® Cover Letter Book, 2nd Ed.
Everything® Filmmaking Book
Everything® Get-a-Job Book, 2nd Ed.
Everything® Guide to Being a Paralegal
Everything® Guide to Being a Personal Trainer
Everything® Guide to Being a Real Estate Agent
Everything® Guide to Being a Sales Rep
Everything® Guide to Being an Event Planner
Everything® Guide to Careers in Health Care
Everything® Guide to Careers in Law Enforcement
Everything® Guide to Government Jobs
Everything® Guide to Starting and Running a Catering Business
Everything® Guide to Starting and Running a Restaurant
Everything® Job Interview Book
Everything® New Nurse Book
Everything® New Teacher Book
Everything® Paying for College Book
Everything® Practice Interview Book
Everything® Resume Book, 2nd Ed.
Everything® Study Book

SELF-HELP

Everything® Body Language Book
Everything® Dating Book, 2nd Ed.
Everything® Great Sex Book
Everything® Self-Esteem Book
Everything® Tantric Sex Book

SPORTS & FITNESS

Everything® Easy Fitness Book
Everything® Krav Maga for Fitness Book
Everything® Running Book

TRAVEL

Everything® Family Guide to Coastal Florida
Everything® Family Guide to Cruise Vacations
Everything® Family Guide to Hawaii
Everything® Family Guide to Las Vegas, 2nd Ed.
Everything® Family Guide to Mexico
Everything® Family Guide to New York City, 2nd Ed.
Everything® Family Guide to RV Travel & Campgrounds
Everything® Family Guide to the Caribbean
Everything® Family Guide to the Disneyland® Resort, California Adventure®, Universal Studios®, and the Anaheim Area, 2nd Ed.
Everything® Family Guide to the Walt Disney World Resort®, Universal Studios®, and Greater Orlando, 5th Ed.
Everything® Family Guide to Timeshares
Everything® Family Guide to Washington D.C., 2nd Ed.

WEDDINGS

Everything® Bachelorette Party Book, $9.95
Everything® Bridesmaid Book, $9.95
Everything® Destination Wedding Book
Everything® Elopement Book, $9.95
Everything® Father of the Bride Book, $9.95
Everything® Groom Book, $9.95
Everything® Mother of the Bride Book, $9.95
Everything® Outdoor Wedding Book
Everything® Wedding Book, 3rd Ed.
Everything® Wedding Checklist, $9.95
Everything® Wedding Etiquette Book, $9.95
Everything® Wedding Organizer, 2nd Ed., $16.95
Everything® Wedding Shower Book, $9.95
Everything® Wedding Vows Book, $9.95
Everything® Wedding Workout Book
Everything® Weddings on a Budget Book, 2nd Ed., $9.95

WRITING

Everything® Creative Writing Book
Everything® Get Published Book, 2nd Ed.
Everything® Grammar and Style Book
Everything® Guide to Magazine Writing
Everything® Guide to Writing a Book Proposal
Everything® Guide to Writing a Novel
Everything® Guide to Writing Children's Books
Everything® Guide to Writing Copy
Everything® Guide to Writing Graphic Novels
Everything® Guide to Writing Research Papers
Everything® Screenwriting Book
Everything® Writing Poetry Book
Everything® Writing Well Book